MIDWEST EDITION
Animal Tracks

D1304368

by Jonathan Poppele

Adventure Publications
Cambridge, Minnesota

Acknowledgements

I am deeply indebted to many people who helped bring this book about. I must begin with a special thank you to my first tracking teachers, Tom Brown Jr. and Jon Young, for igniting my love for tracking and teaching me to slow down and look closely. A warm thank you also to the many trackers who have shared their knowledge and experiences so generously through their writing. The work of Paul Rezendes, Olaus Murie, Jim Halfpenny, Louis Liebenberg, Jim Lowery, and many others have taught me and inspired me. A special thank you to Mark Elbroch, whose work as a teacher, author and advocate for tracking will doubtless last for generations to come. Thanks also to the Minnesota Zoo, the Como Zoo and the Lake Superior Zoo and to the entire staff of Wilderness Awareness School. And finally, thank you to the team who helped with the production of this book. Thank you to Julie Martinez and Bruce Wilson for their excellent illustrations; to Brett Ortler and the staff at Adventure Publications for transforming my rag-tag manuscript into this book; and to George Leoniak for his technical review and feedback.

Illustrations by Julie Martinez and Bruce Wilson
Cover and book design by Jonathan Norberg; edited by Brett Ortler
Front cover photo: Black bear by Stan Tekiela
Photo Credits: **Kim A. Cabrera:** 62 (scat), 102 (scat), 146 (scat) **Mary Clay/Dembinsky Photo Associates:** 178 (main) **Tanya Dewey:** 162 (scat) **Mark Elbroch:** 54 (scat), 78 (scat), 86 (scat), 240 (scat) **Jonah Evans:** 186 (scat) **Dwight Kuhn:** 82 (main) **Maslowski Wildlife Productions:** 78 (main), 110 (main) **Connor O'Malley:** 58 (scat) **Jonathan Poppele:** 12, 17, 22 (both), 23, 43, 118 (main), 234 (scat) **Jennifer Schlick:** 194 (scat) **Ann and Rob Simpson:** 90 (main) **Sandra Slaymaker:** 130 (scat) **James N. Stuart:** 218 (scat) **Stan Tekiela:** 35 (right two photos), 50 (scat), 54 (main), 70 (both), 74 (scat), 86 (main), 94 (both), 98 (main), 106 (scat), 110 (scat), 114 (main), 118 (scat), 122 (scat), 134 (scat), 138 (scat), 142 (scat), 150 (scat), 154 (scat), 158 (both), 166 (scat), 170 (scat), 174 (scat), 178 (scat), 182 (scat), 190 (scat), 198 (scat), 204 (scat), 208 (scat), 222 (scat), 226 (scat), 230 (scat), 244 (scat), 248 (scat), 254 (scat), 260 (scat) **www.octrackers.com:** 90 (scat)

10 9 8 7 6 5 4 3

Copyright 2012 by Jonathan Poppele
Published by Adventure Publications
820 Cleveland Street South
Cambridge, Minnesota 55008
(800) 678-7006
www.adventurepublications.net
Printed in China
ISBN: 978-1-59193-324-3

Table of Contents

Squirrels

Rabbits & Hares

Weasels

Skunks

Armadillos

About This Guide

Go for a walk in the woods, or even at a local park, and you are likely to see a tremendous variety of birds, flowering plants, and trees. Go to a lake and you may see an abundance of fish swimming in the shallows or lined up on an angler's stringer. Yet except for a few species well adapted to human development, wild mammals tend to elude us. This may lead us to think that there are few mammals around. In fact, they are quite common, but they are often inconspicuous. Unlike birds, many mammals are primarily nocturnal or crepuscular, coming out only when the light is dim. Mammals are usually shades of brown, and blend in with the ground. Mammals are generally fairly quiet, relying on scent and signs to mark territories, rather than using songs and calls. The tracks and signs they leave behind are often our only indications that they are nearby. To get to know about the mammals of your area you almost certainly must learn something about tracks. Tracking is a window into the lives of the secretive mammals that live around us.

What is Tracking?

Tracking is the study and interpretation of the tracks (footprints) and other signs left behind by animals as they go about their lives. Tracking does not necessarily mean following a string of footprints to locate the animal that made them. It means understanding the footprints, scrapes, chews, digs, and scat (animal waste) that we inevitably run across when we are out in nature. Tracking begins with identifying the animal that left the tracks and signs behind for us to see, and grows into an understanding of the intimate details of that animal's life.

Why Go Tracking?

Tracking may be the most ancient of all sciences. As a matter of survival, all of our distant ancestors learned to read animal signs. Today, tracking is a way for us to connect more deeply with nature. Tracking can help us feel that we are at home in the outdoors, and that we are part of an intimate conversation with the other animals that share our world.

Tracking is easy to learn. Seeing a set of footprints in the snow or across a sandy beach awakens our natural curiosity. Like crime scene investigators, we try to piece together what happened from clues an animal left behind. What once looked like an empty woodlot or an abandoned streambank becomes a bustling bed of animal activity—with each crisscrossing trail telling a different animal's story. Learning just a little bit about identifying tracks brings empty landscapes to life and can lead us on endless adventures.

No one ever completely masters tracking. It is possible to learn to accurately identify every tree or wildflower or bird that you see, but no one can identify every track or interpret every trail. There may be too few clues for even the best detectives to solve a particular mystery. Each mystery we solve leads us to even more mysteries. There is always more to learn, and there are always new mysteries being created.

This book will help you get out on the trail to solve some of those mysteries, and discover even more to engage your curiosity. Tracking is your invitation to a life of adventure and wonder.

Species Included in this Book

This book includes 55 entries filled with information about the tracks and signs of 96 species of mammals found in the states of Illinois, Indiana, Iowa, Kansas, Kentucky, Michigan, Minnesota, Missouri, Nebraska, North Dakota, Ohio, South Dakota and Wisconsin. While many birds, reptiles, amphibians and invertebrates leave prominent tracks and signs, including all of them in a single book is not practical.

Bats are also not included. Bats rarely leave tracks, and the tracks they do leave are usually quite faint and nondescript. In addition, a few mammal species, such as the nutria, may be found on the fringes of our region but are not common enough in our region to merit inclusion in this book.

Finally, not every species of small mammal is discussed individually in this book. While there are important ecological differences between the many species of small mammals, their tracks and signs are often too similar to distinguish in the field. In this guide, many species of small mammals have been grouped together with other similar species. For example, the four different species in the genus *Spermophilus* found in our region have all been grouped together here under the heading "Ground Squirrels." This book will help you identify the group of small mammals that could have left a particular set of tracks. Once you have identified the group to which a track belongs, you can then use the detailed range, habitat and behavioral information found in any good field guide to mammals to narrow the possibilities even further. The index on pages 343–346 includes a complete list of all 96 species of mammals covered by this guide.

Fortunately, for the true tracking enthusiast, there are now some excellent guidebooks available that focus exclusively on the tracks and signs of birds and insects, and a good field guide to mammals will provide information about bats and small mammals.

About the Illustrations

There are many ways to illustrate animal tracks. In the field, I usually make simple line-drawings that show only the outline of each pad. These crisp drawings are excellent for field notes, but don't actually look much like a track on the ground, and they capture too little detail to be of much use in a field guide. Sometimes, I will add some shading to my field drawings to show depth or soil movement. Shaded pencil drawings do a good job capturing the overall shape and the variations in depth across a track, but rarely capture the texture of a real-life footprint. Pencil drawings can easily show soft shading and crisp lines, but tracks on the ground have a distinctive look that is not captured well by either of these.

Of all the illustration styles I have seen, the stippling style we used for this book appears the most lifelike. Stippled illustrations have distinct yet porous and slightly irregular edges, just as real-life tracks do. The stippling itself resembles the texture of soil or sand, which is the stuff tracks are made of. Simply put, stippled illustrations can look a lot like footprints.

Another choice we made was to show the tracks of every species at a typical real-life size. Size is one of the first and most obvious clues that helps us narrow down the possibilities when we are trying to identify a track. By showing the tracks life-size, we have insured that what you look at in the book will be as similar as possible to what you look at on the ground. Of course, different members of the same species will often have different sized tracks, but we have tried to make these illustrations as representative as possible. For a few species in the book, the life-size illustrations did not fit on the page opposite the track descriptions. For these species, a reduced version of the illustration appears opposite the description and a full life-size illustration appears on a separate spread at the end of the species account.

I was fortunate to work on this project with two highly accomplished science, nature and wildlife illustrators, Julie Martinez and Bruce Wilson. Both Julie and Bruce are superb artists and naturalists who brought their considerable talents to the challenging task of creating these realistic track illustrations. Julie and Bruce began by creating pencil sketches of each track. I then worked closely with them to refine their sketches—sometimes going through nearly a dozen drafts—until we arrived at an illustration that captured the size, proportions, details and overall character of real-life tracks. Bruce and Julie then created a stippled version of each illustration. Sometimes, these first stippled drawings required some additional tweaking and in a few cases they had problems that literally sent us "back to the drawing board" to rework the pencil sketch. It was a time consuming process, but in the end I am extremely happy with the work of these two fine artists, and I think you will be as well.

Organization of This Book

The individual species accounts in this book are organized into groups based on similarities in track appearance and normal gaits or patterns of movements. Within each group, species are organized by track size from smallest to largest, with a few minor exceptions to keep similar looking tracks next to each other in the book. The groups themselves are organized based on the typical gaits of members of the group, with bounding animals in the beginning; loping animals and animals with lumbering or otherwise unusual walking gaits in the middle; and animals with smooth trotting or walking gaits at the end. Organized in this way, the groups also roughly follow an organization from smaller to larger. The groups also come close to following standard taxonomic divisions, but the correlations are not perfect and readers familiar with mammalian taxonomy will find a few notable differences. Here is an outline of the groups in the order they appear.

The first three groups, tiny mammals (pgs. 53–99), squirrels (pgs. 101–135) and rabbits and hares (pgs. 137–151) are all relatively small animals that typically travel using a whole-body bounding gait. With the exception of the shrews and moles included in the tiny mammal group, these three groups also align closely with standard taxonomic divisions, with the tiny mammals and squirrels falling within the order Rodentia and the rabbits and hares falling within the closely related order Lagomorpha. The next group, weasels (pgs. 153–175), average a bit larger and typically travel using whole-body loping gaits. These are followed by the skunks (pgs. 177–183), which sometimes lope, but incline more toward walking. These two groups align with the closely related families of Mustelidae and Mephitidae in the order Carnivora. Following the weasels and skunks is a slight hodgepodge of medium to large mammals loosely grouped together based on similarities in tracks, gaits and sometimes taxonomy. The nine-banded armadillo (pg. 185) sits between groups and is followed by a group of large rodents (pgs. 189–201) that tend to walk rather than bound like their smaller kin. Next is a group of flat-footed walkers (pgs. 203–215), which includes North America's lone marsupial mammal, the Virginia opossum, and two representatives of the order Carnivora—the black bear and the raccoon. The final three groups in the book are all "diagonal striders," medium to large animals that typically travel in a smooth, efficient walk or trot, and that often place their hind foot exactly on top of their front track in a "direct register." The first of these are the dogs (pgs. 217–237) and cats (pgs. 239–257), which fall into the Canidae and Filidae families in the order Carnivora. And rounding out the book are the hoofed animals (pgs. 259–287), which are all members of the order Artiodactyla.

While this order may be unfamiliar at first, I think you will find that it works very well in the field for identifying tracks. Generally, placing a track into the correct group is relatively simple, and for the times when it is not, each species account includes detailed comparisons to similar looking tracks to guide you to other likely possibilities. To help identify the group a track belongs to and to help you find the correct section of the book, we have included a Track Group Chart on pages 18–19 that lists the name, page numbers, and identifying characteristics of the members of each track group.

The right front track of a raccoon along a muddy river bank.

How to Use This Book

Like all detective work, tracking can be tricky business. Usually, we are dealing with only bits and pieces of tracks, trails and signs. This book gives you several tools to help identify prints you find. When I was learning to track, my teachers all emphasized taking a variety of perspectives on any set of tracks I was trying to identify. I was trained to look closely at individual footprints; to look around at the whole pattern of tracks and the other signs an animal may have left; and to put everything I was seeing into the context of the landscape, the habitat, and the location I was tracking in. Each perspective gives a different view of the tracks and different clues for identifying their maker. While I discuss these perspectives in order here in the introduction, the process is holistic and you will find it natural to move back and forth between the fine details and the big picture as you track.

Getting Close:
Individual Track Identification

It is natural to hone in on individual tracks when we spot them in the field. I enjoy getting down on my hands and knees and studying the details of a print. Sometimes I get so captivated by a print that I will spend hours squatting over it as I measure it, draw it, photograph it, and study it. Looked at close-up, every track contains a miniature landscape waiting to be explored.

When looking at individual prints, it is useful to identify both the front and hind tracks of the animal if you can. Once you know which foot made the print you are looking at, there are four steps that can help identify the track:

1. Study the overall shape of the track

2. Count the number of toes

3. Look for claws

4. Measure the size of the track

STEP 1. STUDY THE OVERALL SHAPE OF THE TRACK

Look at the general shape of the track. Is it circular, oval or lopsided? Is it wider at the front or wider at the back? Are the toes roughly symmetrically spaced or asymmetrical? Oftentimes, individual toes and palm pads are not clear and we must rely primarily on the overall shape of a track to guide us in identification.

STEP 2. COUNT THE NUMBER OF TOES

Count the toes. Be careful as you do this—there are a lot of things that can confound this seemingly simple task. One or more toes may not register clearly, or toes may be set far off to the side and appear to belong to a separate track. One track may be set imperfectly on top of another, giving the appearance of an extra toe. I once puzzled for several days over a photo I had of a 5-toed track in the snow before realizing that it was both the front and rear prints of a 4-toed cat, slightly offset from each other. If you can, find a couple of prints from the same foot to verify your count. If you count a different number of toes in the two prints, go back and check again.

STEP 3. LOOK FOR CLAWS

Look to see if claws are present. Some animals, like dogs and skunks, nearly always show claw marks. Other animals, such as cats, almost never do. The presence or absence of claws can frequently help you narrow your choices. At the same time, don't let claws rule out otherwise logical candidates. I have seen many cat tracks that showed prominent claw marks, and some dog tracks that appeared to be missing claws. Claws are great clues, but are not always diagnostic.

STEP 4. MEASURE THE SIZE OF THE TRACK

Measure the track's length and width. While animal foot sizes can vary tremendously within a species, track size will help you narrow down your possibilities. Once you identify the animal that made the prints, track size will help you determine how large the individual, as foot size is generally closely correlated with body size within a given species.

With the information you get following these four steps, you can use the Track Group Chart on pages 18–19 and the Quick Reference Size Chart on pages 20–21 to narrow down the possibilities.

Notes About Measuring Tracks

Obtaining accurate measurements can be tricky. An animal's toes spread differently on different surfaces and when moving at different speeds. Momentum can distort the length of the track, soft ground, sand and snow can alter size, and uneven ground can skew shape. Careful measuring technique and attention to detail can minimize these problems and offer you useful clues for identifying the animal you are tracking. To get good measurements, look for clear tracks relatively free from distortion. If you can, measure several tracks to get an average. Even when I am not taking field notes, I like to measure tracks I find. Measuring tracks not only gives me a more objective sense of the size of a track, it also forces me to look closely at exactly what is the track and what is not. It is not rare for me to spot details I missed at first glance when I am trying to decide exactly where my measurement should begin or end.

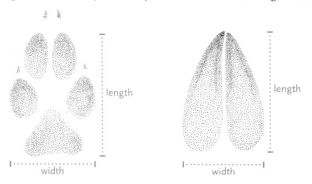

WHAT TO MEASURE

Measure tracks along their longest and widest points. Be sure to measure both the front and the hind tracks. Just as human hands and feet vary in size by person, track size ranges widely within most species. This book provides a typical size range for each track. These ranges are somewhat generous and cover the vast majority of adults within each species, as well as some juveniles and sub-adults.

Generally, I measure track length from the rear edge of the rearmost palm or heel pad to the front edge of the foremost toe pad. With very few exceptions, I do not include claws, or the dewclaws on hoofed animals, in my basic measurements of the tracks, and the measurements in this book do not include claws except where noted otherwise. I measure track width across the widest part of the foot, including all of the toes, but not including the claws.

TRACK FLOOR VS. TRACK COMPRESSION

A major challenge when measuring tracks is the distortion of the apparent size of tracks made on soft surfaces. A track compression is the total surface area pressed down by an animal's foot. The track floor is only the area of the ground that supported the animal's weight. Depending on the surface, the track compression may be much larger than the track floor.

Imagine standing barefoot on a solid surface, like the deck of a swimming pool. The bottom of your foot flattens slightly, supporting your weight and creating a solid connection with the ground. When you step away, you leave behind wet footprints. Each print has a clear, well-defined outline that exactly matches the weight-bearing portions of your foot. Here, the track compression and the track floor are exactly the same size, making measurements easy.

Now imagine standing on a soft surface, like the wet sand at your favorite beach. The bottom of your foot still flattens slightly, supporting your weight, but now your feet sink into the spreading sand. When you step away, you leave behind a large impression—much larger than the wet footprint you left on the pool deck. In this case, the track compression is much larger than the track floor, making measurements more difficult. But it is still possible to make accurate measurements because the track floor will be almost exactly the same size as your wet footprint on the pool deck.

While the size of compression will vary tremendously with changes in substrate (soil type), the size of the track floor will show little variation. When measuring tracks, measure the track floor, not the whole compression. Look for the place in the track compression where the gently curving track floor meets the steep-sloping side wall of the track. Determining where the track floor ends and the side wall of the track begins is a matter of judgment. With practice, however, you will find yourself making consistent and highly accurate measurements.

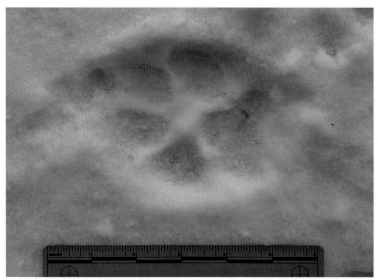

This wolf track in snow illustrates the difference between the track compression and the track floor. The compression measures 5⅛" long by 3⅝" wide. The track floor (the darkest part of the track) is less than three-quarters that size, measuring just 3⅜" long by 2¾" wide.

TRACK GROUP CHART

Track Group	STEP 1: Overall Shape	STEP 2: Number of Toes	STEP 3: Claws Show?
TINY MAMMALS	Tracks are generally well under 1".	4 or 5 (front) 5 (hind)	Yes
SQUIRRELS	Triangular palm pad and long toes. Front foot often shows 2 heel pads.	4 (front) 5 (hind)	Yes
RABBITS	Egg shaped. Pads usually indistinct because of thick fur on the sole.	4 (front) 4 (hind)	Yes, may be obscure
WEASELS	Toes usually form an arc above a chevron-shaped palm pad.	5 (front) 5 (hind)	Yes
SKUNKS	Compact, with stubby toes that rarely splay.	5 (front) 5 (hind)	Yes
ARMADILLO	Unique bird-like tracks. Outer toes often do not register.	4 [2] (front) 5 [3] (hind)	No
LARGE RODENTS	Each of the members of this group is distinctive.	4 (front) 5 (hind)	Yes
FLAT-FOOTED WALKERS	Tracks of members of this group often resemble human hand or foot prints.	5 (front) 5 (hind)	Yes
DOGS	Oval. Large triangular palm pad. Claws usually show.	4 (front) 4 (hind)	Yes
CATS	Round. Very large triangular palm pad. Retractable claws rarely show.	4 (front) 4 (hind)	No
HOOFED MAMMALS	Distinctive cloven hoof prints. Often heart shaped.	2 (front) 2 (hind)	Dewclaws

Typical Gaits	Group Members	Pages
Bound or walk/trot	Shrews, moles, mice, rats, gophers	53–99
Bound or trot	Ground squirrels, chipmunks, tree squirrels, prairie dogs, marmots	101–135
Bound	Rabbits & hares	137–151
Lope	Weasels, mink, marten, fisher, otter, badger	153–175
Irregular lopes & walks	Striped skunk, spotted skunk	177–183
Lope or walk	Nine-banded armadillo	185–187
Walk	Porcupine, muskrat, beaver	189–201
Walk	Opossum, raccoon, bear	203–215
Trot	Foxes, coyote, wolf	217–237
Walk	Bobcat, lynx, cougar	239–257
Walk	Pronghorn, deer, elk, moose, bison	259–287

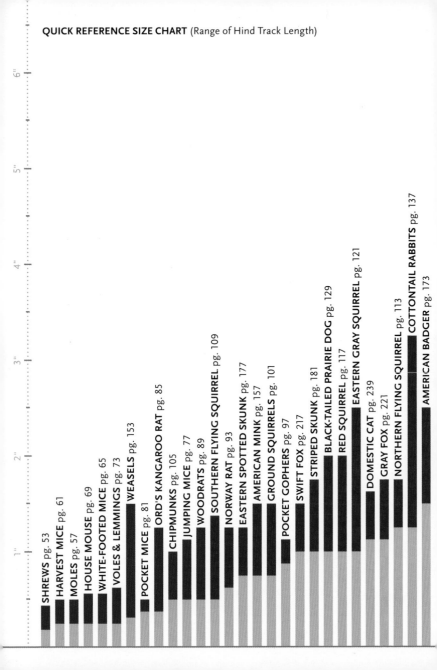

QUICK REFERENCE SIZE CHART (Range of Hind Track Length)

SHREWS pg. 53

HARVEST MICE pg. 61

MOLES pg. 57

HOUSE MOUSE pg. 69

WHITE-FOOTED MICE pg. 65

VOLES & LEMMINGS pg. 73

WEASELS pg. 153

POCKET MICE pg. 81

ORD'S KANGAROO RAT pg. 85

CHIPMUNKS pg. 105

JUMPING MICE pg. 77

WOODRATS pg. 89

SOUTHERN FLYING SQUIRREL pg. 109

NORWAY RAT pg. 93

EASTERN SPOTTED SKUNK pg. 177

AMERICAN MINK pg. 157

GROUND SQUIRRELS pg. 101

POCKET GOPHERS pg. 97

SWIFT FOX pg. 217

STRIPED SKUNK pg. 181

BLACK-TAILED PRAIRIE DOG pg. 129

RED SQUIRREL pg. 117

EASTERN GRAY SQUIRREL pg. 121

DOMESTIC CAT pg. 239

GRAY FOX pg. 221

NORTHERN FLYING SQUIRREL pg. 113

COTTONTAIL RABBITS pg. 137

AMERICAN BADGER pg. 173

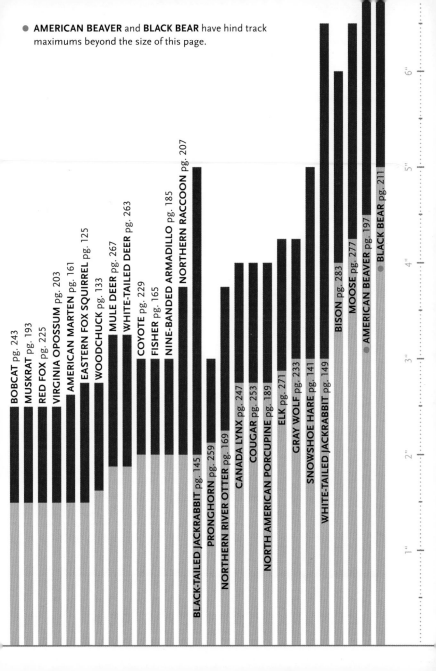

● **AMERICAN BEAVER** and **BLACK BEAR** have hind track maximums beyond the size of this page.

BOBCAT pg. 243
MUSKRAT pg. 193
RED FOX pg. 225
VIRGINIA OPOSSUM pg. 203
AMERICAN MARTEN pg. 161
EASTERN FOX SQUIRREL pg. 125
WOODCHUCK pg. 133
MULE DEER pg. 267
WHITE-TAILED DEER pg. 263
COYOTE pg. 229
FISHER pg. 165
NINE-BANDED ARMADILLO pg. 185
NORTHERN RACCOON pg. 207
BLACK-TAILED JACKRABBIT pg. 145
PRONGHORN pg. 259
NORTHERN RIVER OTTER pg. 169
CANADA LYNX pg. 247
COUGAR pg. 253
NORTH AMERICAN PORCUPINE pg. 189
ELK pg. 271
GRAY WOLF pg. 233
SNOWSHOE HARE pg. 141
WHITE-TAILED JACKRABBIT pg. 149
BISON pg. 283
MOOSE pg. 277
● AMERICAN BEAVER pg. 197
● BLACK BEAR pg. 211

1"
2"
3"
4"
5"
6"

Looking Around: Gaits & Other Signs

Raccoon walking up the shore of a river.

While individual tracks are captivating, they usually represent only a fraction of a second in the life of an animal. Standing up and looking around gives us a broader perspective on the movement and activity of the animal that made the track. Looking around we can study the animal's gait—the way in which it moves its body while traveling—and see other signs of the animal's presence.

An animal's gait determines the pattern of the footprints it leaves on the ground. Looking at a string of tracks, we can see if an animal was walking, like a deer, loping, like an otter, or bounding, like a squirrel.

Gaits

This section focuses on understanding the basics of gaits—the body mechanics of animal movement and the patterns of footprints each type

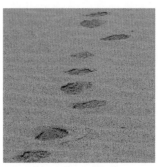

Coyote lopes along a beach.

of movement leaves behind. Nearly all wild mammals in the Midwest region are quadrupedal, meaning that they almost always walk on all four feet. Four legged movement is more complicated than the two legged movement used by us bipeds. Understanding the diversity of gaits used by quadrupeds requires careful thought and some special terminology that goes beyond our familiar "walking" and "running." The following pages are an introduction to the ways in which Midwestern mammals move and will give you a place to start in interpreting gaits. The purpose of understanding gaits and the patterns of tracks they leave behind is to interpret how an animal was moving when it passed by. With some practice and a dose of imagination, you will find that it is possible to use your mind's eye to see an animal making its tracks in front of you.

A tracker role-playing an animal to understand its gait.

One of the best ways to develop this skill is to simply watch animals making tracks. Most trackers I know love to watch wildlife films, and go to the zoo just to see how animals move. There is a small municipal zoo right on my commuting route that I often visited while I was writing this book. Where it is possible, you can learn even more about gaits when you can watch the animal move then immediately go look at the tracks it created. A nearby beach where people walk or play with their dogs can be perfect for this. And to fully experience how an animal moves to create a particular pattern of tracks, try making it yourself. Get down on all fours and figure out how to move your own body to reproduce a particular pattern of tracks. Or watch an animal and practice copying its movement. This kind of whole-body engagement speeds up the learning process and is a whole lot of fun. When I go out in the field with other trackers, we usually end up on the ground at some point, trying to reproduce a track pattern that we've run across. The San Bushmen of the Kalahari Desert, widely known for their exceptional skill as trackers, are also famous for role-playing the animals they are tracking.

When I wrote this section of the book, I began by drafting an outline based on course notes and my academic study of animal movement. Then I headed down to the Minnesota Zoo for a few days of up-close animal watching. I spent hours sitting in front of the coyote pen, the bobcat cage, the otter exhibit, and the bear enclosure. I watched moose walk, wolverines lope and wolves trot. I watched how their legs and bodies moved and where their feet landed on the ground. I imagined how it would feel to move my own body in the same way. When no one was watching, I would get down on all fours and copy the animal I was observing. After a couple full days of watching and copying the animals at the zoo, I sat down in the cafeteria with my outline and began to fill in the text.

A NOTE ON TERMINOLOGY

The terms used to describe different forms of animal movement are not completely universal. While I use widely adopted terms in this book, different authors and tracking teachers may use different terms for the same gait, or use the same term in different ways. Part of the difficulty is the animals themselves, who insist on displaying a broad range of movement that defies simple categorization. As a result, words such as "lope," "gallop" and "bound," while clearly defined in this section, may only loosely apply in the field and may not align perfectly with the descriptions in some other books on tracking. What is important in the end, however, is our ability to understand how an animal moved when it made a set of tracks. The discussion on gait categorization that follows is designed to help you as you develop that ability for yourself.

IDENTIFYING & CATEGORIZING GAITS

Four-legged animal gaits can be broadly divided into two categories: stepping gaits and whole-body gaits. In stepping gaits, movement comes primarily from the legs, and the body stays relatively still. These gaits have steady rhythm, like two-legged walking and running do for people, and produce a string of evenly spaced pairs of tracks.

In whole-body gaits, the body flexes and extends, and the movement is created by the body and legs working together. These gaits have a syncopated rhythm, like a child "galloping" on a hobbyhorse, and produce distinct groups of four tracks.

MEASURING GAITS

Accurate measurements of track patterns can help to pin down a gait and aid us in identifying an animal. It can also provide clues about the animal's activity, its speed of travel, and even its mood. There are a number of measurements that are particularly helpful to make:

Stride: I call the distance from one hind track to the next hind track on the same side of the body the stride. This is the distance one foot moves in one cycle of steps. To get an accurate measurement, be sure to measure to the same part of each track. For some animals, it is easiest to measure from the back edge of the heel on one track to the back edge of the heel on the next. For other animals, it is easier to measure from the front edge of the toe on one track to the front of the toe on the next. Just look for the clearest edge on the tracks you are measuring. Note: Some other authors use the word "stride" to refer to the distance from one hind track to the next hind track on the opposite side of the body. In this book, that measurement is called a step. A stride is identified here as the distance between two tracks made by the same foot, because that measurement applies to all gait patterns, while a step is only a meaningful measurement for stepping gaits.

Trail Width: The distance between the outer edge of the tracks on one side of the trail and the outer edge of the tracks on the other side of the trail is called the trail width. To measure trail width, identify a section of trail where the animal is walking straight. Next, stretch a string or place a straight edge along the outside edge of two or more consecutive tracks on one side of the trail. Measure the distance between your string and the outside edge of a track on the opposite side of the trail.

A wolf direct register trotting gait showing stride, step and trail width.

Stride and trail width are closely associated with an animal's speed of travel. In general, as an animal speeds up, its stride will increase and its trail width will decrease.

Group Length: Used to measure whole-body gaits, group length is the distance between the back edge of the rearmost track in the group to the front edge of the foremost track in the group.

Intergroup Distance: The distance between the front edge of the foremost track in a group and the rear edge of the rearmost track in the next group is the intergroup distance. The group length plus the intergroup distance is equal to the animal's stride.

A woodchuck bounding gait showing group length, intergroup distance, stride and trail width.

These parameters also help us to understand the diversity of stepping and whole-body gait patterns.

STEPPING GAITS

Stepping gaits result from an animal keeping its body relatively still and moving its legs in an even rhythm. The result is a continuous line of tracks with each front-hind pair spaced evenly apart.

Stepping gaits are distinguished from each other by the way the animal coordinates its legs. When each leg moves independently, the result is a walk. When legs diagonally opposite each other move together, the result is a trot. Each gait can produce a range of track patterns, depending on the speed the animal is moving.

Walking

Walking is a slow, stable and energy efficient form of movement. When walking, an animal moves each leg independently and always has at least one foot on the ground. Walking is the most common gait for beavers, bears, raccoons and members of the deer family and the cat family. While rare for some mammals, such as weasels and rabbits, all mammals will slow to a walk at least some of the time.

When walking, an animal will move each foot in turn, stepping with the hind, then with the front foot on one side, followed by the hind then the front foot on the other side. Many animals walk by lifting their front foot just as the hind foot is about to touch down. The hind foot then lands on top of the track made by the front foot, creating a diagonal track pattern similar that made by two-legged animals. This pattern is known as a direct register walk.

A white-tailed deer showing a direct register walk.

Note that in a direct register walk, each compression is actually made of two tracks—with the hind track superimposed on top of the front track. A walking animal may also place its hind foot down behind or in front of the front track. These gaits are called understep or overstep walks, respectively. A few animals, such as bison, commonly use an understep walk, while several species, including black bears, cougars and pronghorn regularly use an overstep walk. For species that typically walk in a direct register, an understep walk is generally an indication that the animal is moving slowly, while an overstep walk means that the animal has sped up.

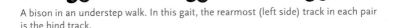

A bison in an understep walk. In this gait, the rearmost (left side) track in each pair is the hind track.

A black bear in an overstep walk. In this gait, the rearmost (left side) track in each pair is the front track.

An extreme variation of the understep walk is the gait used by predators when they are stalking. In this gait, the animal will move only one foot at a time, usually pausing in between each step.

Raccoon Walk

Raccoons typically walk with an extreme overstep that places their hind foot right beside the opposite front foot. Although the body mechanics of this gait are nearly the same as for the more common diagonal walk, the resulting trail pattern shows side-by-side pairs of tracks.

A raccoon showing its distinctive walking pattern. Each pair of tracks is a hind print next to a front print.

As with a diagonal walk, raccoons may show an extended or shortened version of their gait, based on their speed.

A raccoon in an extended version of its typical walk. Here, the hind tracks register slightly in front of the front tracks in each pair.

Trotting

Trots are faster than walks and result from a different coordination of leg movement. In a walk, each foot moves independently, and the animal never loses contact with the ground. In a trot, the two legs diagonally opposite each other move at the same time and there is a split second in which the animal has all four feet off the ground. The difference between walking and trotting in a four-legged animal is analogous to the difference between walking and jogging in people. Trots are the most common gait for members of the dog family, as well as some voles and shrews. The slight bounce created while trotting can be easily seen in any canine, including domestic dogs.

A coyote displaying a precise direct register trot.

While walks and trots can produce similar looking alternate track patterns, trots can usually be easily distinguished by their longer stride and narrower trail.

Trotting requires more energy than walking, but results in faster movement, and trotting can be quite efficient for its speed. Many animals will move in a trot at least some of the time. Animals that typically walk will often speed up to a trot when they need to cover ground more quickly. House cats, for example, typically trot when they are coming to get dinner.

As with walking, it is very common for a trotting animal to place its hind foot down on top of its front track. This is called a direct register trot.

Many animals will also speed up into an overstep trot, where each rear foot moves past the front foot on the same side before landing. Overstep trots require a change in posture for the animal to allow the rear foot to clear the front foot. There are two basic ways that mammals do this. The first is by spreading the rear legs out, so they pass to the outside of the front legs. This is called a straddle trot, and is a common gait for elk.

An elk shows a straddle trot. The front tracks land in a nearly straight line with the hind tracks falling out to the sides.

Another overstep trot, common in canines, is the side trot. Here, the animal turns its body at a slight angle to its line of travel, allowing the hind feet to pass to the side of the front feet. This gait is easily observed in domestic dogs, and produces two lines of nearly paired tracks. All of the hind tracks appear on one side of the trail, and all of the front tracks appear on the other. Generally, the hind track appears a bit in front of the font track.

A red fox in a side trot. The front and hind tracks lie along separate rows with each hind track slightly in front of the corresponding front track.

Bipedal Stepping Gaits

There is only one mammal in the Midwest that regularly uses bipedal stepping gaits, and that is the familiar and ubiquitous *Homo sapiens*. Given our species' distinctive behavior, especially the habit of wearing shoes, you are unlikely to confuse a trail left by a person with one left by another mammal in our region. However, many birds travel on the ground using bipedal stepping gaits, and under some tracking conditions, these trails can resemble those left by mammals, so it is useful to be familiar with these gaits. Fortunately, being bipeds ourselves, understanding bipedal stepping gaits comes very naturally to us.

Like the stepping gaits of four-legged animals, bipedal stepping gaits can be divided into two categories, in this case walking and running. The gait is a walk if the animal always has at least one foot on the ground while stepping and a run if there is a moment mid-stride when both of the animal's feet are off of the ground. Jogging, even jogging very slowly, is a form of running based on this definition. The primary difference in the trail pattern left by these two gaits is that running gaits tend to have a longer stride and a narrower trail width than walking gaits. Both walking and running produce a zigzagging string of evenly spaced tracks that looks similar to the direct register walking and trotting patterns left by quadrupeds. The difference, however, is that each compression is only a single track.

WHOLE-BODY GAITS

Whole-body gaits are produced by an animal flexing and extending its body, and using its body and legs together to produce locomotion. They have a cycling, rather than continuous, rhythm and produce groups of four tracks clustered together, rather than the continuous string of regularly spaced pairs of tracks produced by stepping gaits.

Whole-body gaits can be broadly divided into two categories: those where each foot lands independently, called lopes and gallops, and those where the hind feet land together, called hops and bounds. These two groups can be further divided into gaits where the hind feet land behind or even with the front feet (lopes and hops), and gaits where the hind feet land in front of the front feet (gallops and bounds). Whole-body gaits can be very fast, and all quadrupedal mammals will use whole-body gaits at least some of the time when speed is required. For some animals, including most squirrels, rabbits and weasels, whole-body gaits are the norm, even when moving slowly.

Loping and Galloping

In both lopes and gallops, each foot moves independently as the animal flexes and extends its body. Lopes and gallops are distinguished based on how many times in each flexion-extension cycle the animal has all four feet off the ground. A gait is considered to be a lope when there is a single moment in each movement cycle when the animal is airborne, with all four feet off the ground. A gait is considered to be a gallop when there are two separate moments in each movement cycle when the animal has all four feet off the ground. Unfortunately for us as trackers, this definition does not always serve us in the field. While it is sometimes obvious that an animal is airborne, researchers often need to resort to the use of high-speed cameras and slow-motion video of a live animal to determine conclusively whether a gait is a lope or a gallop. For this reason, I follow many other trackers in using a pragmatic, though not technically precise, definition of a lope. When tracking, we can consider a gait to be a lope if the animal places at least one of its hind feet down behind or even with its foremost front foot.

A striped skunk loping. The order of the footfalls in each group is left front, left hind, right front, right hind.

A prairie dog in a lope. Here, the order of the footfalls in each group is right front, right hind, left front, left hind.

Loping can be an easy, gentle gait. Some animals such as weasels lope most of the time, covering large distances. Gallops, on the other hand, are almost always all-out sprints, usually maintained for only a few seconds when speed is of the essence, such as when chasing prey or being chased by a predator. We can consider a gait to be a gallop when both of the animal's hind feet land in front of both front feet.

A gray wolf galloping trail. The order of the footfalls in each group is left front, right front, right hind, left hind. Note that there may be a large gap between the two groups.

Weasel 2x2 and 3x4 Lope

There are two loping gaits that are common among members of the weasel family that bear special attention—the 2x2 lope and the 3x4 lope. In a 2x2 lope, both of the animal's hind feet land exactly in the tracks made by the front feet, leaving a pair of compressions. Each compression is, in fact, both a front and a hind track, and each group contains all four tracks, registering in just two spots. The 2x2 lope is commonly used by the smaller members of the weasel family and many animals use a variation of this gait in deep snow.

A mink displays a 2x2 lope. While this looks similar to a canine side trot or a raccoon 2x2 walk, each compression is made from 2 overlapping prints.

In a 3x4 lope, one of the animal's hind feet sometimes lands in the track made by one of the front feet producing what looks like a group of three, rather than four, prints. This gait is also common among members of the weasel family.

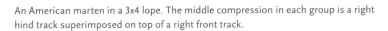

An American marten in a 3x4 lope. The middle compression in each group is a right hind track superimposed on top of a right front track.

The 3x4 lope can be an irregular gait, with groups of 3 and groups of 4 tracks intermixed with no obvious pattern.

A river otter displays an irregular 3x4 lope. Despite the irregular foot placement, the order of the tracks in each group is some version of front, hind, front, hind.

Hopping and Bounding

Hopping and bounding are similar to loping and galloping except that the animal's hind feet move forward together and strike the ground at nearly the same time. Hops and bounds are distinguished in exactly the same way as lopes and gallops. A gait is a hop when there is one airborne phase each cycle and a bound if there are two airborne phases each cycle. Just as with lopes and bounds, however, this is difficult to determine in the field and I use a pragmatic definition when interpreting tracks patterns. Four our purposes, a gait is considered a hop when the hind feet land behind or even with the front feet and a bound when the hind feet land in front of the front feet. Rabbits and many rodents hop or bound most of the time, even when traveling slowly. Hoppers and bounders typically move by pushing off primarily with their hind legs. Their hind legs are usually larger and stronger than their front legs, and often their hind tracks will be noticeably larger than their front tracks.

A meadow vole showing a hop. In each group, the front tracks land ahead of the hind tracks.

When bounding, an animal's hind feet will straddle its front feet, passing to the outsides. This causes the hind tracks to register wider than the front tracks and produces a distinctive pattern, which is common to rabbits and squirrels.

A gray squirrel bounding. Note that the front tracks appear side by side behind the hind tracks in each group.

Animals that spend a large portion of their time in trees, such as gray squirrels, tend to place their front feet side by side when they bound. Animals that do not climb, such as rabbits and ground squirrels, tend to place one foot in front of the other when they bound.

An eastern cottontail bounding. Here, the front tracks land one in front of the other behind the hind tracks.

Bipedal Whole-body Gaits

There is one mammal found in our Midwestern region that regularly travels using bipedal whole-body gaits, and that is the Ord's kangaroo rat. Like their Australian namesakes, kangaroo rats typically bound on their hind legs, leaving a distinctive trail of side-by-side pairs of hind tracks. Since the hind feet move together, and the body flexes and extends with each leap, this gait is considered a bound. Unlike a quadrupedal bound, a bounding biped lands on its hind feet, rather than its front. Because of this, bipeds that travel in a bound have large tails that act as a counterbalance to provide stability and rhythm in the gait. You may notice that while it is easy for us as humans to jump up and down, jumping forward with both feet together is not a smooth or natural gait. This is partly because we lack a counterbalancing tail. In addition to the Ord's kangaroo rat, many songbirds move on the ground using a bipedal hop—but you are unlikely to confuse a kangaroo rat's trail with that of a songbird.

A kangaroo rat bounding. Note that each group is comprised of only the two hind tracks.

At high speeds, Ord's kangaroo rats also sometimes break into a bipedal gallop, in which the hind feet touch down in quick succession rather than at the same time. This gait is similar to a child "galloping" on a hobby horse.

A kangaroo rat galloping. Here, the hind feet land with one slightly in front of the other rather than side by side.

Signs

Signs are any clues left behind by an animal other than its footprints. Signs can include scat (animal droppings), digs, chews, nests and much more. Each individual species or group account in this book includes a description of the scat, plus information about other common signs. These signs offer important clues for identifying tracks, and can also reveal the presence of an animal when there are no tracks visible at all.

SCAT

Scat, or fecal droppings, can provide important clues for identifying an animal. An animal's droppings give us information about its diet—helping us to distinguish carnivores from herbivores from omnivores.

The size, shape, and content of a scat is sometimes enough to identify the species that left it behind, and often enough to narrow down the possibilities.

DENS, NESTS, BURROWS AND OTHER SHELTERS

Many animals dig burrows or build nests. The size and form of these shelters gives us information about the architect. When burrowing, some animals, such as ground squirrels, throw loose soil out of the opening, creating a fan of dirt in front of the entrance. Other animals, such as chipmunks, carry the excavated soil away, leavening a clean hole with no disturbed earth nearby. Different animals also leave different-shaped burrow entrances. Badger burrows are wide and squat, while swift fox burrow may have a keyhole shape. Nests can sometimes be identified by size, shape and the materials used to make them. And some animals' shelters, such as the beaver's lodge, are instantly recognizable.

OTHER SIGNS

In addition to scat and shelters, animals may leave a variety of distinctive signs. Bears leave large claw marks in trees, red squirrels leave behind piles of discarded pine cone remains, and red fox urine has a distinctive odor that many trackers find unmistakable. Each species or group account in this book contains information about distinctive signs left behind by the animal.

Putting it in Context: Trails, Habitat & Range

I'm often a better tracker after I stop looking at the tracks themselves. While it is easy to get focused in on individual footprints, my tracking teaches always emphasized putting everything I was seeing in context by looking at trails, habitat and range. Sometimes I would do this by drawing freehand maps of the trails, terrain and features of the areas I tracked. At other times, I would use a GPS unit and handheld computer loaded with CyberTracker software to plot what I saw in the field, then come back and view my data on topographical maps.

Taking a "bird's-eye" perspective helps us to make connections that we can easily miss when our focus is on the individual tracks. I learned a great lesson in the power of this perspective a few years ago when I gave a presentation on wolf tracking to a group of Environmental Studies majors at a local university. None of the students had ever been tracking and most had little or no knowledge about wolves. After a 10 minute introduction to wolf ecology and behavior, I showed the students a map from a tracking expedition in which our team had used CyberTracker to plot our data in the field. The first map showed all of our data about elk, the wolves' primary food in that area; coyotes, which tend to steer clear of wolves; and human traffic, which the wolves tend to avoid. The map covered some 300 square miles of rugged wilderness. I asked the students where they would go to look for wolf sign. Seeing the big picture, the students quickly identified the exact locations where we found the most wolf activity. When we put everything in context, even a little bit of knowledge can go a long way.

Even while you are still out in the field, as you examine a track or analyze a gait, it's helpful to take a step back and look at the context: the animal's trail, habitat and range. The trail is the path the animal travels across the land. When you look at a trail, ask yourself if the animal moved straight across the land, like a coyote, or zigzagged between bushes and trees, like a weasel. Look to see if tracks begin or end at a tree, like those of a squirrel, or at the edge of a stream, like those of an otter. Trails provide important clues for identifying tracks and also give you a window into the animal's behavior. Each species or group account in the book gives you information about the animal's behavior that will help you interpret trails.

Another factor to consider is the preferred habitat of each species. Our region is broadly divided into three major biomes: grasslands, eastern broadleaf forests and northern boreal forests. Within and across these major biomes, there are wetlands, lakes and riverways, developed lands and transitional areas. Each species account includes a section describing the preferred habitat of the animal.

 Finally, consider the normal range of an animal. This book includes small range maps showing the typical, known range for each species. While range maps are useful, they are an imperfect source of information. Mammals are well equipped with feet and many have a habit of wandering far away from the areas where they are "supposed" to be. It is not uncommon to find a lone individual hundreds of miles outside of its known range. Moose from northern Minnesota sometimes wander as far south as Iowa and cougars from the western Dakotas sometimes show up in Wisconsin. In addition, range maps will often include many places that are completely unsuitable to a particular species. River otters, muskrats and beavers, for example, have extensive ranges, but are usually only found near open bodies of water. For this reason, it is important to use range maps, habitat information and interpretation of trails together. Taken together, these contextual clues will often provide the key to identifying a mysterious group of tracks.

Frequently Asked Questions:

What is a track?

A track is a footprint left behind by an animal. As an imprint of the animal's foot, it shows both the structure of the foot and how the foot moved as it bore the animal's weight. Because tracks are made on a variety of surfaces, and the same animal can move its feet in a variety of ways, there is a great deal of diversity in the appearance of tracks—even those left by the same animal.

What is a sign?

A sign is any indication left behind of an animal's presence and activity, besides footprints. Signs include scat, hair, burrows, nests, scent posts, body prints, chewed vegetation, carcasses and more. Any clue about an animal's past activity can be considered a sign.

What is tracking?

Tracking is the art of interpreting the tracks and other signs left behind by animals to answer questions about the natural world. These questions may be simple, such as "who walked through the snow in front of my house before I got up today?" or quite involved, such as "what caused this rabbit to suddenly stop feeding and dart into those bushes?" Tracking includes the skills of identification (who made these tracks?), interpretation (what was the animal doing?), aging (when did the animal pass?), and trailing (where is the animal now?). This guide focuses on identification, which is fundamental to all of tracking.

Is it hard to identify animal tracks?

No. With a little practice, you will find that it is quite easy to identify the clear tracks of many species with confidence. Most of the tracks you will encounter in the field will not be clear prints, however, and will be faint or partial prints. These take more practice to identify with confidence.

Is it always possible to identify what made a track?

No. Even the best trackers can't always make a correct identification. In fact, most footprints by themselves are too faint, too worn or too distorted to allow for positive identification. Using all of the available clues, an experienced tracker will often be able to identify an animal from surprisingly subtle tracks and signs. But often there are simply not enough clues to give positive identification. Plus, mammals are highly adaptable and creative creatures and can often surprise us. Part of the joy of tracking is that no matter how good we get, we will never run out of mysteries.

What is the best place to look for tracks?

Tracks can be found nearly anywhere. While it is easy to think that we need to get deep into the woods to find mammals, I have tracked deer, foxes and skunks through urban backyards; mink, otters, beavers and coyotes along urban waterways; and cougars across suburban parklands. Tracks are easiest to see in sand, mud or dust. Rivers, streams and lakeshores are great places to find tracks, but so are some dirt roads, sand traps on golf courses, and dusty corners of city lots and construction sites. Surfaces that naturally get washed or blown clean and smooth each day create a "blank slate" for fresh tracks. It is great to learn the places near your house that record lots of tracks. And of course, fresh snow is a tracker's delight!

Isn't tracking just for hunters?

No. Tracking is for anyone interested in learning more about the natural world around them.

Is it possible to preserve tracks I find?

Yes. There are three ways to preserve tracks: photographing, drawing, and casting. See the Field Notes & Preserving Tracks section (pg. 41) for information about each of these techniques.

Do animals always leave tracks?

Yes, but most of the tracks they leave behind are too subtle for us to see. Only under exceptional conditions do animals leave tracks that we can easily study.

If it is so hard to find clear footprints, how do trackers follow a trail?

Trackers use a large number of clues from the environment to follow a trail, including partial footprints, bits of hair, disturbed vegetation, and a sophisticated knowledge of the habits of the animal being followed.

For an excellent treatise on following animal trails in the field, check out *Practical Tracking: A Guide to Following Footprints and Finding Animals* by Mark Elbroch, Louis Liebenberg and Adriaan Louw.

Do I need any special equipment to track?

No. All you need are your own two eyes and a curiosity about the natural world around you. If you want to record your observations, you will want to carry a small notepad, a pencil, a ruler and a tape measure. For more detailed records or longer excursions, you might want a camera, a map and compass or GPS (both to navigate and to record the location of your observations), and materials to make plaster casts. And of course, remember to bring this book!

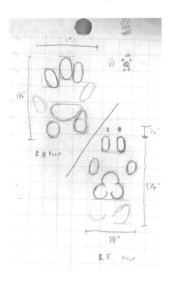

Field Notes & Preserving Tracks

When we find something exciting or beautiful in nature, it is natural to want to take home a reminder of what we have seen. Tracks lend themselves well to making permanent records; unlike the animals that made them, tracks do not run away! Taking field notes is a great way to increase your tracking skills. Making notes about each perspective of tracking—the individual footprint, the track groups and signs, and the trails, habitat and range—will help you quickly learn and grow as a naturalist. Oftentimes, I have found tracks that I could not identify in the field, but was able to pin down later from the information in my notes. Field notes can also provide evidence for things you discover. Trackers often find evidence of animals outside of their known ranges and habitats. Your findings may be of great interest to local wildlife professionals—but you will need excellent records to demonstrate your findings.

I always carry a small notepad and a mechanical pencil with me in the field. Like many trackers, I prefer pencils to pens because they don't freeze, you can erase mistakes, they work in the rain and don't run if the paper gets wet. Of course, you can buy special waterproof paper and "write anywhere" pens developed for NASA's space missions. But if you don't have a NASA-like budget, the low-tech solution may be the best.

There are many systems for taking detailed notes, but the important thing is just to make a record. In time, you may develop your own system. That said, it is a good idea to at least include the following:

- The date, time, and location of your observations.

- Notes, measurements, and images about each perspective of tracking:
  - the individual footprints
  - the track groups and other signs
  - the trails, habitat and landscape

There are three basic ways to create images of the tracks you find: photographing, drawing and casting.

Photographing Tracks

Photographing tracks used to be a challenging affair, mastered by only a few specialists. Digital cameras have revolutionized photography and made it much easier for amateurs to take good quality pictures of tracks. Here are a few tips to keep in mind as you photograph tracks:

- **Shoot in the Shade:** Dappled sun is difficult to expose properly and shadows can distort the shape of the track.

- **Get Close:** Your track or track group should fill your frame. Use the macro setting, if your camera has one, to get good close-up focus.

This experienced tracker uses his body to shade the track, gets close to his subject, includes a ruler for scale and shoots straight down.

- **Include a Scale:** Put something in the picture that will allow you to judge the size of the track. I always carry a neutral color forensics ruler when I am in the field, but any kind of ruler or common, everyday item can work. Try to use objects of known size that have a straight edge. This book can make a fine scale.

- **Shoot Straight Down:** Shooting at even a slight angle can severely distort the shape and apparent size of the track.

- **Shoot at Different Exposures:** Many built-in light meters are fooled by sand, snow and mud. Fortunately, most cameras allow you to easily adjust the exposure. Different surfaces will respond best to different exposures. It is a good idea to shoot several pictures, "bracketing" the exposure. Try using the camera's automatic setting, then experiment with adjusting the exposure up and down by one or even two stops.

- **Take Lots of Pictures:** Film is cheap, and electrons are even cheaper. Especially if you are shooting digital, take lots of pictures using lots of different settings, then pick out the best ones to keep.

- **Take Pictures of the Trail and the Surroundings:** Remember the three scales of tracking. Your photographic record will be more useful as well as more interesting if you include pictures of the animal's trail and the landscape that it was passing through.

- **Take Notes:** In the field, we often think we will remember where and how we took a picture. Yet we often forget important details. It is a good idea to record where and when you took a picture, as well as information about the surrounding area, for context.

For more information about photographing tracks, especially using film cameras, I recommend *The Keeping Track Guide to Photographing Animal Tracks and Signs* as a reference, available from Keeping Track, Inc.

Drawing Tracks

Drawing tracks is not only a good way to record what you see in the field, it is also one of the best ways to learn to identify tracks. Many times, I have been able to positively identify a track only after I started drawing it. The close observation required to make a sketch focuses my awareness and helps me see details I might otherwise overlook. I had this experience recently when I spotted a clear canine track in a small patch of sand as I was walking across my local park. Many people walk their dogs in this park, and I assumed I was looking at the print of a small house dog. As I drew the track, however, I was pulled out of my assumptions and into the details of the track I was looking at. By the time I was done drawing, I realized that it was not the track of a house dog at all, but the hind print of a red fox. It was a nice reminder to me about how much wildlife there is here in the middle of the city. It was also a nice reminder to be more careful about my initial assumptions and to always look closely with an open mind.

Drawing tracks does not require special skill or artistic talent, just a bit of patience and an interest in details. When drawing tracks, it is a good idea to first measure the track, then transfer those measurements to your notebook or sketch pad. This makes it much easier to get proportions and scales correct when you begin drawing.

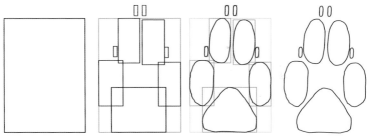

By carefully copying the measurements of each pad in the track to a sketch pad, it is possible to make highly accurate illustrations.

I usually take this process one step further, placing two rulers down along the side and bottom of the track, then transferring a detailed grid outlining each toe, pad and claw to my notebook before I sketch in the curves. It is possible to take a long time with this, and, meticulously done, this technique produces highly accurate and consistent drawings. It can also be done quite quickly, however, and does a lot to improve your eye as a tracker.

Casting Tracks

Plaster casts are a traditional way to preserve tracks in the field. Casts allow us and others to experience a "real life" track even years after the original print was made. Making casts is easy to do, though it may take many tries before you get consistently good results. Here is the basic procedure:

- Mix 2 parts plaster to 1 part water by volume. Adjust the proportions to produce a pancake batter- or milkshake-like consistency.

- Put a small retaining wall around the track. You can use a paper or plastic hoop for this, or build a small wall out of soil. The wall should be 1/4" to 1/2" taller than the track.

- Gently pour the plaster onto the track, filling your retainer.

- Wait 20–40 minutes for the plaster to cure.

- Carefully remove the cast from the ground and wrap it in paper.

- When the track is thoroughly cured—typically the next day—carefully clean it to remove excess dirt or sand. Do not scrub or polish the cast. You will damage delicate features and the shiny white plaster will just hide details.

A simple casting kit that you can carry in the field will include:

- Two pounds of dry plaster (about enough for 4 medium-sized tracks), stored in a large bag.

- A large paper or plastic beverage cup for mixing plaster.

- Stirring sticks.

- A bottle of water, in case there is no water available near the track.

Nearly any type of plaster will work, except for drywall compound, which doesn't dry hard. You can buy plaster at hobby shops or drugstores, but it is cheaper at lumberyards and hardware stores.

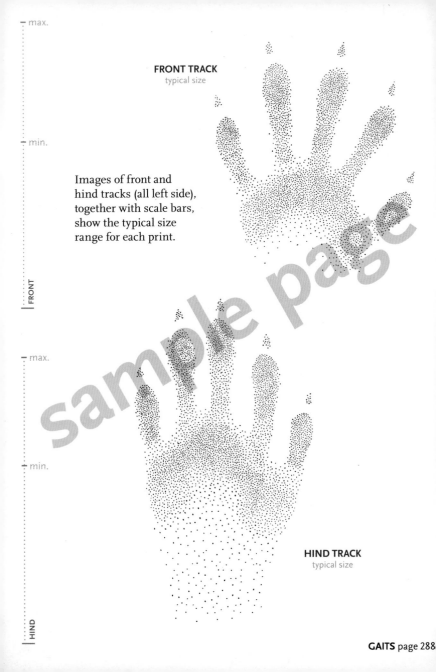

FRONT TRACK
typical size

Images of front and
hind tracks (all left side),
together with scale bars,
show the typical size
range for each print.

FRONT

max.

min.

HIND TRACK
typical size

HIND

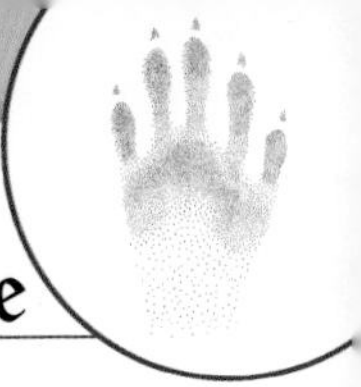

Species (or group) common name

Scientific name

A brief introduction to this species or group.

FRONT TRACK

A detailed description of the front footprint, including typical measurements, as it typically appears under excellent tracking conditions—such as in dust, fine mud or a thin layer of fresh snow. Most tracks will not show the level of detail included in these descriptions.

HIND TRACK

A detailed description of the hind footprint, also including typical measurements.

GAITS

A short description of the most common gaits used by the species or group. For additional information about gaits, see the gait section on page 288.

QUICK ID TIPS:
• Key points to help you identify this species' or group's tracks.

AN ILLUSTRATION OF A GAIT PATTERN FOR THE SPECIES OR GROUP

HABITAT:
The environments where the species or group is usually found. This may include information about vegetation cover, proximity to water, or tolerance for human development.

OTHER SIGNS:
Notes about scat and other signs, such as nests, burrows, and feeding sign, commonly left by members of this species or group.

ACTIVITY:
The times of year and times of day you can expect members of this species to be most active.

SIMILAR SPECIES:
Information about other species or groups that leave similar tracks, and tips for distinguishing them.

NOTES:
Detailed notes about the species or group that may be of particular interest to trackers.

AN ILLUSTRATION OF A GAIT PATTERN FOR THE SPECIES OR GROUP

HIND TRACK
typical size

FRONT TRACK
typical size

FRONT max. 5/16"
min. 3/16"

HIND max. 7/16"
min. 3/16"

Shrews

Sorex, Blarina and *Cryptotis* spp.

Shrews are the smallest Midwestern mammals and leave tiny, delicate tracks that are only visible under ideal conditions. In fine dust or light snow, however, it can be obvious that these insect hunters are quite common in our region.

FRONT TRACK

LENGTH: 3/16"–5/16", **AVERAGING:** 1/4"; **WIDTH:** 3/16"–5/16", **AVERAGING:** 1/4"

Five tiny toes with claws. The middle toe is longest and points directly forward; other toes point farther to the sides, creating an arc. Palm pads form an arc behind the toes. Two small heel pads may register. The front and hind tracks are similar in size.

HIND TRACK

LENGTH: 3/16"–7/16", **AVERAGING:** 1/4"; **WIDTH:** 3/16"–5/16", **AVERAGING:** 1/4"

Five tiny toes with claws. The three middle toes are nearly the same length and usually point forward together. Palm pads form an arc behind the toes. Two small heel pads may register. Similar in size to front tracks, hind tracks measure about 1/4" across, but are more likely to be a bit longer than they are wide.

GAITS

Smaller shrews typically travel in a bound; these trails resemble white-footed mouse trails in miniature, though the track group is usually more compact, with the hind feet registering closer to the front. Larger shrews more commonly trot, leaving a vole-like trail. Most shrew species bound in deeper snow. Shrews also tunnel under snow; tunnels are under 1" in diameter and may be dime-sized in diameter.

QUICK ID TIPS:
- Five long toes on each tiny foot
- Track sizes range from mouse-sized down to the smallest of all mammal tracks
- Small shrews tend to bound; larger shrews tend to trot

BOUND (SMALL SHREWS)

HABITAT:
Most species prefer moist habitats with a debris layer on the ground, but may be found nearly anywhere with cover and with invertebrates for food.

OTHER SIGNS:
Scat: Shrews drop scat at random along travel routes and near their burrows. The structure of the scat varies with diet, and ranges from formless to tiny capsules, depending on how many hard-bodied insects the shrew has eaten. Scat typically measures under ½" and is often less than ¼" in length.

Burrows: Shrew burrows can be tiny and may be confused with a hole created by a large earthworm. Long-tailed shrew burrow entrances are usually ¾", but can be much smaller—sometimes hardly more than pencil-width. Short-tailed shrew burrows are somewhat larger, typically 1" across.

ACTIVITY:
Active year-round, though some species become torpid in extremely cold weather. Primarily nocturnal, but may be active any time of day or night.

SIMILAR SPECIES:
Mice (pgs. 61–83) have four toes on their front feet and five toes on their

hind feet. Pocket mice (pg. 81) have four toes visible on each foot and often overlap their front feet while bounding. Least Weasels (pg. 153) have different gait patterns, typically traveling in a 2x2 lope. Moles (pg. 57) have much larger claws and their toe and palm pads rarely register. All other tracks are much larger.

NOTES:

The shrew family includes the smallest mammals in the Midwest. Members of this diminutive group are renowned for their voracious appetites and high-strung personalities. The smallest shrews seem to approach the lower size limit for a warm-blooded animal and need to feed almost constantly to maintain a consistent body temperature. In captivity, shrews have been observed eating two times their own body weight in food each day and may starve to death if left without food for as little as four hours. In the wild, some shrews enter into torpor (inactivity) when not feeding. Bundles of nervous energy, with a heart rate close to 1,000 beats per minute, shrews aggressively defend nests against intruders of all sizes, and agitated shrews have been known to literally scare themselves to death.

There are two main groups of shrews in our region: the tiny long-tailed shrews, which may weigh as little as 2 grams, and the somewhat larger short-tailed shrews, which are about the size of mice. The long-tailed shrews leave the tiniest tracks of any mammal, sometimes measuring less than $1/4$" across.

Shrews eat mostly worms, larvae, adult insects and other invertebrates. Shrews are not the dedicated diggers that moles are, but often go underground, readily hunting in mole tunnels. They also forage on the surface, following vole trails and digging through leaf litter.

Shrews seem to be common and abundant in most areas, but are generally elusive, and population estimates for most species are inconclusive. Frequently killed by predators, shrews make up a large fraction of the contents of owl pellets in many areas. Curiously, many mammalian carnivores often kill shrews and then discard them uneaten, perhaps because of a musky odor the shrews produce.

Shrews are so light that their tracks will not show on many surfaces. Their tiny tracks are easiest to find in snow, but also appear in fine mud or in dust under logs and other woody debris.

TROT (LARGE SHREWS)

FRONT TRACK
typical size

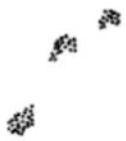

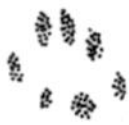

HIND TRACK
typical size

max. ⅝"

min. ⅜"

FRONT

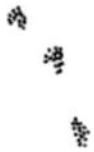

max. ½"

min. ¼"

HIND

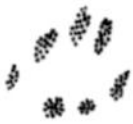

Moles

Condylura, Parascalops and *Scalopus* spp.

Moles are the Midwest's most fossorial (underground) mammal and produce unusual tracks that are rarely seen in the field. The prominent signs of these powerful diggers, however, are often conspicuous.

FRONT TRACK

LENGTH: $3/8$"–$5/8$", AVERAGING: $1/2$"; WIDTH: $3/8$"–$5/8$" AVERAGING: $1/2$"

Five toes with large, prominent claws. Feet are rotated sharply outward—an adaptation for digging straight ahead. When walking on the surface, only 3 of their 5 toes show and usually only the claws register. Because of the unusual structure and movement of the front foot, it is usually impossible to use standard conventions for measuring the track.

HIND TRACK

LENGTH: $1/4$"–$1/2$", AVERAGING: $3/8$"; WIDTH: $1/4$"–$1/2$", AVERAGING: $3/8$"

Five toes with large, prominent claws. Often only claws register. Occasionally toes show as well, but the palm and heel usually do not. As with the front track, it can be difficult to follow standard measuring guidelines, particularly when only claws register.

GAITS

Moles travel aboveground in a kind of modified walk in which the body is flexed from side to side. This helps them take longer steps with their short legs, which are specialized for digging rather than walking. This kind of walk is unusual in mammals but common among some other long-bodied, short-legged animals, such as lizards and salamanders.

QUICK ID TIPS:
- Usually only claw marks show in tracks
- Typically three claw marks show in each front track, five in hind tracks
- Runways and molehills are the most common signs

WALK

HABITAT:

Fields or woods with soft soils. Avoids heavy clay and gravelly or rocky soils. Most species avoid wet soils as well, but the star-nosed mole prefers these.

OTHER SIGNS:

Scat: Moles usually deposit scat underground, but will sometimes form latrines next to burrow entrances underneath a log or similar cover. Scat shows varying amounts of structure depending on diet. When well formed, scat is cord-like, twisted and measures about ⅛" in diameter and ½"–1" in length.

Molehills: As moles dig underground, they push excavated soil up to the surface, where it may form a small mound. These molehills are not burrow entrances, as moles do not generally leave their tunnel systems.

Runways: Moles sometimes travel by tunneling just beneath the surface, pushing up a line of soil as they do. These runways mark temporary travel routes; the permanent network of tunnels is much deeper underground.

Burrow: Burrow entrances are usually found under cover and measure about 1"–1½" in diameter.

ACTIVITY: Active year-round and at all times of the day and night.

SIMILAR SPECIES:

Tracks are unlikely to be confused with those of any other mammal, but can resemble the trails of some large insects. Digging signs may be confused with those of pocket gophers. Pocket gophers (pg. 97) push soil out of their burrows at an angle, creating a fan shape with a plugged entrance at the base of the fan. Soil castings created by pocket gophers sit on top of undisturbed ground; mole runways mark subterranean tunnels.

NOTES:

Moles are highly adapted for fossorial (burrowing) life. They have tiny eyes, no external ears, and velvety fur that can flow in either direction, allowing them to back up in their tunnels with ease. Their spade-like front feet are turned outwards to facilitate digging straight ahead and sport long, scoop-shaped claws. The robust claws and unusual posture of the front feet mean that this five-toed animal often leaves front tracks that show nothing but three deep claw marks.

Although they spend most of their lives underground, moles venture to the surface to forage in the debris layer and gather nesting materials. A few species venture aboveground frequently. The star-nosed mole, found in the eastern parts of our region, regularly forages in leaf litter, and spends a great deal of time hunting in water. Mole tracks are not exceptionally rare, but are small and easily missed. Since the tracks often do not show any toes or palm pads, they may be confused with the tracks of a large insect, or may be overlooked entirely. Mole runways and molehills are easy to spot.

Moles primarily eat worms, larvae, adult insects and other invertebrates that they encounter in their subterranean tunnels. Moles are closely related to shrews and were once classified in the scientific order Insectivora, together with hedgehogs. Recent research has shown that they are not closely related to other insectivores, and shrews and moles have instead been placed in the order Soricomorpha.

Moles are solitary, with adults of most species associating only to mate. They mate only once each year, producing a single litter of 2–6 young. This low reproductive rate is possible because the mole's subterranean life keeps it relatively safe from predation.

FRONT TRACK
typical size

max. ⅜"
min. ¼"
FRONT

max. ½"
min. ¼"
HIND

Harvest Mice

Reithrodontomys spp.

Harvest mice are the smallest rodents in our region and rarely leave clear tracks. More often, it is their apple-shaped nests of woven grasses that give away their presence.

FRONT TRACK

LENGTH: $^{1}/_{4}$"–$^{3}/_{8}$", AVERAGING: $^{5}/_{16}$"; WIDTH: $^{1}/_{4}$"–$^{5}/_{16}$", AVERAGING: $^{1}/_{4}$"

Four toes with tiny claws often showing. The inner- and outermost toes point to the sides; the middle toes may point forward or may splay, so all four toes form an even arc around the palm. Toe pads are slightly bulbous and occasionally connect to the palm in the track, but often appear as separate round dots. Three palm pads form a rounded pyramid behind toes. Two small heel pads may also register. Smaller than hind track, but may splay more, leaving a similarly sized print.

HIND TRACK

LENGTH: $^{1}/_{4}$"–$^{1}/_{2}$", AVERAGING: $^{3}/_{8}$"; WIDTH: $^{3}/_{16}$"–$^{5}/_{16}$", AVERAGING: $^{1}/_{4}$"

Five toes with tiny claws often showing. The middle three toes point forward; the inner- and outermost toes usually point farther to the sides. The innermost toe is longer, set farther back on the foot than in other mice species, and usually points farther to the side than the outermost toe. This is a key feature for distinguishing harvest mouse tracks. Toe pads are slightly bulbous and sometimes connect to the palm. Four palm pads register reliably. Two small heel pads sometimes register as well.

GAITS

Bounds when traveling. Like the white-footed mouse, its trail looks like that of a miniature tree squirrel. Slows to a walk when foraging. In snow, front and hind prints may blur together and tail drag may show.

QUICK ID TIPS:

- Typical mouse track: inner and outer toes extend to the sides; four bulbous toes on the front foot and five on the hind
- Innermost toe on the hind foot is longer and set farther back than in other mice
- Like that of many mice, the trail looks like that of a miniature tree squirrel

WALK

HABITAT:

Most species prefer open, grassy and brushy areas, including prairies, grasslands, cultivated and fallow fields, brier patches and forest clearings.

OTHER SIGNS:

Scat: Like many other mice, harvest mice leave tiny, irregularly shaped scat wherever they travel. The twisted, wrinkled droppings accumulate on runs and at feeding sites and usually measure ¹/₁₆" or less in diameter, and less than ¹/₄" in length. Largely indistinguishable from white-footed mouse scat.

Nests: Harvest mice, along with white-footed mice, build delicate nests of woven grasses and other plant fibers. The nests are spherical, 3"–5" in diameter, and have a small, round opening on the side. They are constructed in the branches of shrubs and trees, as well as in tall grasses. Harvest mice sometimes add a roof to an old bird nest.

ACTIVITY:

Active year-round. May hole up in nest during inclement weather. Nocturnal.

SIMILAR SPECIES:

Few other tracks are as small. Shrews (pg. 53) have five toes on each foot. White-footed mouse (pg. 65) tracks and vole (pg. 73) tracks are generally larger, and the innermost toe on the hind foot is set farther forward, roughly even with the outermost toe. Pocket mouse (pg. 81) tracks exhibit only four fully developed toes on the hind foot and show more size difference between the front and hind feet.

NOTES:

A wide-ranging, highly adaptable group of mice, harvest mice are similar in appearance, habits and behavior to white-footed mice, but are smaller in size. All members of the genus are tiny, and the group includes the smallest rodent in our region, the Western Harvest Mouse, which grows to only $2^{5}/_{8}$" long and weighs just $^{3}/_{8}$ oz. As they are tiny and nocturnal, harvest mice are rarely seen, even where they are common.

Clear tracks are also rare, as these mice are too light to leave an impression on any but the softest substrates. The clearest evidence of the presence of the harvest mouse is its globular nest, which it may build in vegetation, on the ground, or in a shallow underground burrow. Adults often maintain more than one nest, and may use one strictly as a latrine. Most nests are quite small, about the size of a baseball, but harvest mice sometimes nest communally and build larger structures to accommodate as many as half a dozen individuals. They also sometimes build small feeding platforms of sticks and leaves. Nests make good starting points for searching for other signs, including scat and well-worn trails. Harvest mice use vole runways, but they will also create their own runs and trails over time.

Like other small rodents, harvest mice generally follow the same travel routes, staying close to cover and moving directly between nesting and feeding sites. They eat mostly the seeds and flowers of various grasses and herbs, supplemented with leaves, larvae and adult insects. Adept climbers, they may forage, nest and feed at all levels of vegetation. Though most species prefer grassy habitats, they readily scale shrubs and trees and may leave signs of their presence high off the ground.

BOUND

HIND TRACK
typical size

FRONT TRACK
typical size

— max. ½"
....
min. ¼"
FRONT

— max. ⁹/₁₆"
....
min. ¼"
HIND

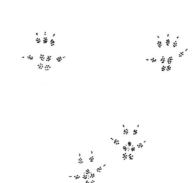

GAITS page 291

White-footed Mice
Peromyscus spp.

White-footed mice are the most abundant mammals in most of our region. Once you learn their trails and signs, you'll see them nearly everywhere.

FRONT TRACK

LENGTH: $1/4"-1/2"$, AVERAGING: $3/8"$; WIDTH: $5/16"-1/2"$, AVERAGING: $3/8"$

Four toes with tiny claws often showing. The inner- and outermost toes point to the sides. The middle toes may point forward or may splay so that all four form an even arc around the palm. Toe pads are slightly bulbous, occasionally connected to the palm in the track, sometimes appearing as separate round dots. Three palm pads form a rounded pyramid shape behind the toes. Two small heel pads may register. The foot also has a vestigial thumb that sometimes registers as a tiny dot next to the innermost heel pad. Smaller than the hind track, but sometimes splays more, leaving a similarly sized print.

HIND TRACK

LENGTH: $1/4"-9/16"$, AVERAGING: $7/16"$; WIDTH: $5/16"-1/2"$, AVERAGING: $3/8"$

Five toes with tiny claws often showing. The inner- and outermost toes point to the sides. The middle three toes point forward. The innermost toe is smallest and set farther back on the foot. Toe pads are slightly bulbous and sometimes connect to the palm in the track. Four palm pads reliably register and two small heel pads sometimes register as well.

GAITS

Usually bounds, leaving a trail pattern that looks like that of a tiny tree squirrel. Sometimes walks when foraging. A few species are also known to lope. Often travels on top of deep snow.

QUICK ID TIPS:
- Quintessential mouse track: inner and outer toes extend to the side; four bulbous toes on the front foot and five on the hind
- Trail looks like a that of a tree squirrel trail in miniature
- The most common tiny tracks in most habitats

WALK

HABITAT:

At least 1 species of white-footed mouse is found in nearly every habitat in North America. It is often the most common mammal in a given habitat.

OTHER SIGNS:

Scat: White-footed mice leave tiny, irregularly shaped scat wherever they roam. Droppings tend to accumulate along well-used trails and at feeding sites. Scat has a wrinkled appearance and typically measures $^1/_{16}$" or less in diameter and less than $^1/_4$" in length.

Feeding Sign: Look for the remains of chewed nuts and seeds underneath rocks and logs. Squirrels and birds typically leave feeding remains on top of exposed surfaces.

Nests: White-footed mice build small, spherical nests of woven grasses and other plant fibers in trees, shrubs and sometimes in tall grass. They also build nests in rock crevices, under logs, in abandoned rodent burrows, or in woodrat stick houses. Nests measure 3"–6" in diameter with a small, round opening on the side.

ACTIVITY:

Active year-round, but may hole up during bad weather. Nocturnal.

SIMILAR SPECIES:

Harvest mice (pg. 61) typically leave smaller tracks and trails and the in-nermost toe on their hind foot has a distinctive shape and is set farther back in the track. Voles (pg. 73) usually trot, sometimes hop, and rarely leave a regular bounding trail. Jumping mice (pg. 77) have much longer toes and leave a more irregular bounding trail pattern. Chipmunks (pg. 105), woodrats (pg. 89) and Norway rats (pg. 93) leave much larger tracks and trails. Shrews (pg. 53) have five toes on each foot and larger shrews commonly trot.

NOTES:

White-footed mice, also called deer mice, are the most abundant mammals in North America. Highly adaptable, they are found in nearly every habitat on the continent. Altogether, there are 15 species of white-footed mice rec-ognized in the continental U.S, four of which regularly occur in our region.

Although white-footed mice are nocturnal and generally inconspicuous, their sign is easy to find, due in large part to their robust populations. While they tend to stay near cover, they venture widely and form well-traveled runs between nesting and feeding sites. They are also more likely than other tiny mammals to travel across the top of deep snow. In most parts of our region, the majority of tiny mammal tracks are left behind by white-footed mice.

White-footed mice are excellent climbers and many species are semi-arboreal. They often forage, feed and build nests at every level of vegeta-tion, from herbaceous ground cover to the tops of the tallest trees. They will also venture underground, using burrows and tunnels excavated by other small mammals. Most species are capable swimmers as well.

White-footed mice are highly omnivorous, eating a wide variety of seeds, berries, nuts, green vegetation, insects, arthropods and fungi. They cache large amounts of food for the winter, storing it in natural cavities, such as tree cavities, hollow logs or rock crevices, but also in bird nests, abandoned burrows and buildings.

As they are so common, white-footed mice are a dietary mainstay for many small predators and medium-sized predators. They are an important food source for weasels, foxes, bobcats, hawks, owls and many snakes, and are also preyed on by larger carnivores, such as coyotes and even wolves.

FRONT TRACK
typical size

HIND TRACK
typical size

max. ½"

min. ¼"

FRONT

max. ⁹/₁₆"

min. ¼"

HIND

House Mouse
Mus musculus

As their name suggests, house mice are most often found in and around buildings and are common residents of basements, storage closets, compost piles and gardens, as well as barns and grain fields.

FRONT TRACK
LENGTH: $1/4"-1/2"$, **AVERAGING:** $3/8"$; **WIDTH:** $5/16"-1/2"$, **AVERAGING:** $3/8"$

Four toes with tiny claws often showing. The inner- and outermost toes point to the sides. The middle toes may point forward, or may splay so all four form an even arc around the palm. Toe pads are slightly bulbous and may connect to the palm, but often appear as separate round dots. Three palm pads form a rounded pyramid behind the toes. Two small heel pads may register. Front feet are smaller than hind feet, but front may splay more, so front and hind tracks can have similar dimensions.

HIND TRACK
LENGTH: $1/4"-9/16"$, **AVERAGING:** $7/16"$; **WIDTH:** $5/16"-1/2"$, **AVERAGING:** $3/8"$

Five toes with tiny claws often showing. The inner- and outermost toes point to the sides while the middle three toes point forward. The inner-most toe is the smallest and set farther back. Toe pads are slightly bulbous and sometimes connect to the palm in the track. Four palm pads reliably register and two small heel pads sometimes register as well.

GAITS
Typically travels in a walk or a trot ("scurries"), which are quite difficult to differentiate. May speed up to a bound when threatened or exposed.

QUICK ID TIPS:
- Quintessential mouse track: inner and outer toes extend to the side; four bulbous toes on the front foot and five on the hind
- Closely associated with people; almost always found in or near buildings
- Usually walks or trots

WALK/TROT

HABITAT:

Anywhere people reside. Closely associated with urban and rural human development. Found in agricultural areas, particularly grain fields, and in and around buildings.

OTHER SIGNS:

Scat: Deposit scat at random wherever they go. Droppings tend to accumulate on runs and where mice feed. Scat is somewhat irregular, with a wrinkled appearance and usually measures $1/16$" or less in diameter, and less than $1/4$" in length. Scat alone is usually indistinguishable from white-footed mouse droppings.

Damage: In buildings, house mice gnaw through walls, make holes in insulation, chew on wires, and nibble through food containers. Usually, there are droppings nearby any other mouse signs.

Nests: Like many other mice, house mice build small, globular nests. In a building, these nests tend to be made of refined or synthetic materials, rather than grass. Nests may be located in walls, building foundations, storage boxes, or even dresser drawers.

ACTIVITY:

Active year-round. Often enters buildings in cold weather. Nocturnal.

SIMILAR SPECIES:

Other mice and voles (pg. 61–83) are more likely to be found away from human development and less likely to be found in buildings, especially those in suburban and urban areas. White-footed mice (pg. 65) bound more regularly and typically leave somewhat larger tracks. Harvest mice (pg. 61) bound more regularly and the innermost toe on their hind foot is set noticeably farther back. Shrews (pg. 53) have five toes on their front feet.

NOTES:

The familiar house mouse is highly adapted to life among people. A native of Asia, this highly migratory species has been introduced worldwide and is now found nearly everywhere people reside. As the common name suggests, house mice live primarily in and around human structures and are rarely found in woodlands. They are especially common in grain fields and in buildings in rural, suburban and urban areas.

In cultivated fields, house mice may have a beneficial effect as they may eat more insects and weed seeds than grain. In buildings, however, house mice can be quite destructive. They are well known for raiding food stores. The word "mouse," in fact, comes from the Sanskrit word *musha*, meaning "thief." House mice also chew on anything and everything, putting holes in furniture, clothing, books and walls. They have even been known to cause house fires by chewing the insulation off wires. Yet the house mouse is also the source of the white laboratory mouse, which has led to immeasurable advances in science and medicine. For all the damage the house mouse does, we owe a great deal to this diminutive "thief."

House mice are primarily terrestrial, but are capable climbers. They build individual nests, but are otherwise quite social. They live in loose colonies that share feeding areas, travel routes, escape holes and latrines. Their communal habits and close association with people may be the best clues for distinguishing house mouse tracks and signs, which are otherwise quite similar to those of white-footed mice.

HIND TRACK
typical size

FRONT TRACK
typical size

max. ½"
FRONT min. ¼"

max. ⅝"
HIND min. ¼"

Voles & Lemmings

Celethrionomys, Discrostonyx,
Microtus and Synaptomys spp.

Voles are common nearly everywhere there is fresh vegetation. Though small, most species leave distinctive trails by tunneling under leaf litter or cutting runways in tall grass.

FRONT TRACK
LENGTH: 1/4"–1/2", AVERAGING: 3/8"; WIDTH: 1/4"–1/2", AVERAGING: 3/8"

Four slender toes with tiny claws sometimes showing. The inner- and outermost toes point to the sides. Middle toes may point forward, or may splay so all four toes radiate from the palm. Toe pads are less bulbous than in most mouse tracks and often connect to the palm. Three palm pads form a rounded pyramid behind the toes. Two small heel pads may register. Front feet are smaller than hind feet, but front may splay more, so front and hind tracks can have similar dimensions.

HIND TRACK
LENGTH: 1/4"–5/8", AVERAGING: 3/8"; WIDTH: 1/4"–1/2", AVERAGING: 3/8"

Five slender toes with tiny claws sometimes showing. The inner- and outermost toes point to the sides while the middle three toes point forward. The innermost toe is slightly smaller than others and set farthest back. Toe pads are less bulbous than in most mouse tracks and often connected to palm. Four palm pads are usually visible in the track. Two small heel pads may register.

GAITS
Usually travels in a direct register trot. Speeds up to a hop or lope when exposed. Sometimes walks, especially in thick cover. Rarely

QUICK ID TIPS:
- Mouse-like track: four toes on the front foot and five on the hind with the inner and outer toes extending to the sides
- Voles and lemmings typically trot, sometimes hop, but rarely bound
- Among the most common small mammal tracks in vegetated habitats

TROT

bounds. Tracks are common in light snow, but when snow is deep, voles generally tunnel under it.

HABITAT:

Found in nearly every habitat, except for arid deserts. Most species prefer open areas with thick grass or herbaceous plant growth.

OTHER SIGNS:

Scat: Drops some scat at random along travel routs, but also forms latrines. Scat has a seed-like appearance and is usually ⅛" or less in diameter and about ¼" in length.

Runways: Many species of voles form well-traveled networks of runways in tall grass. These tunnel-like runways are often hidden below a layer of lush growth. Runways measure 1"–2½" across and may be obvious in fresh-mowed grass or after the spring thaw. Under the snow, vole runways may fill with dirt and grass clippings, leaving behind a casting similar to those made by pocket gophers.

Nests: Voles typically build nests in thick cover or in underground hollows. Sometimes they also construct nests under deep snowpack, which may be exposed in the spring. Nests are fully enclosed, made of grasses, and measure about 3"–5" in diameter.

ACTIVITY:

Active year-round. Voles are active underneath the snowpack through the winter. Chiefly nocturnal, with bouts of activity both day and night.

SIMILAR SPECIES:

Shrew (pg. 53) front tracks show five toes and the palm pads typically form an arc, not a pyramid. White-footed mice (pg. 65) and harvest mice (pg. 61) usually bound, leaving a pattern like a miniature squirrel trail.

NOTES:

Voles and lemmings are among the most common mammals across much of the Midwest. In most areas, at least one species of vole or lemming is quite common. Voles are perhaps best known for their dramatic population cycles. Most species are highly prolific, capable of producing a litter or more of pups each month. When food is abundant, populations can explode. The swollen population then quickly depletes the available food resources, forcing huge numbers of animals to disperse in search of food and causing the local population to crash. Some species go through boom-and-bust cycles every year. Many species, however, follow 3–4 year cycles of population growth and decline.

Most voles are terrestrial and some are semi-fossorial, digging elaborate burrows and spending much of their time underground. Most voles do not climb, though a few venture into low shrubs. Voles generally stay under the cover of long grass or underneath the leaf litter when traveling, forming well-worn runs. For some species, such as the meadow vole, runs in the grass are very common and the most obvious sign of the animal. In winter, voles travel underneath the snow creating the same kinds of runways.

Voles eat mostly green vegetation, supplemented with roots, tubers and subterranean fungi, and spend a great deal of time foraging both day and night. When green vegetation is sparse, voles may gnaw on the inner bark of trees, sometimes girdling and killing them. Voles are a mainstay in the diet of many predators, including weasels, foxes, bobcats, coyotes, snakes, hawks and owls. Where predators rely heavily on voles for food, their populations often end up following the boom-and-bust cycles of their prey.

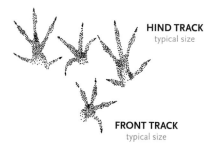

max. ⅝"

min. ⅜"

FRONT

max. 1⅛"

min. ½"

HIND

HIND TRACK
typical size

FRONT TRACK
typical size

Jumping Mice

Napaeozapus and *Zapus* spp.

Jumping mice are not closely related to the other mice in our region and their tracks are quite distinctive. They are also deep hibernators and do not leave tracks in the snow—limiting our chances to find clear prints.

FRONT TRACK
LENGTH: 3/8"–5/8", **AVERAGING:** 1/2"; **WIDTH:** 3/8"–5/8", **AVERAGING:** 1/2"

Four long, slender toes with tiny claws sometimes showing. Toes usually splay widely, with the inner- and outermost toes pointing straight to the sides or curving backwards. The slim toes don't have distinct pads and usually connect to the palm in the track. Three palm pads form a rounded pyramid at the base of toes; two heel pads may also register.

HIND TRACK
LENGTH: 1/2"–1 1/8", **AVERAGING:** 3/4"; **WIDTH:** 3/8"–3/4", **AVERAGING:** 1/2"

Five long, slender toes with claws usually showing. The middle three toes are quite long and usually spread in a narrow fan. The inner- and outermost toes are smaller, set farther back on the foot, and point farther to the sides. The innermost toe is smallest and set farthest back. Toes usually connect to palm. Palm pads are often fused together and usually indistinct. Palm is narrower and longer than in other mice. Larger than the front track.

GAITS
Bounds almost exclusively, leaving more irregular groups of four tracks than white-footed mice. Usually takes short strides of 4"–10", but capable of leaping more than 3' and perhaps as much as 10'. Not seen in snow.

QUICK ID TIPS:
- Extremely long, slender toes
- Claws on hind foot are often more pronounced than in other mice
- Middle toes on hind foot are much longer than inner and outer toes

BOUND

HABITAT:
  Damp fields, marshes, thickets, woodlands, especially riparian areas.

OTHER SIGNS:
  Scat: Scat is tiny, irregular in size and shape, and not likely to be distinguishable from that of other small mammals. It is typically ⅛" or less in diameter and may range from ¹/₁₆" to ½" in length.

  Feeding Sign: Jumping mice often clip grass and herbaceous plant stems into short lengths when feeding. These 1"–2" long clippings may accumulate in small piles.

  Nests: Jumping mice build globular nests on the ground or in a shallow underground burrow. These nests are similar to those made by other mice, and measure about 3"–6" in diameter.

ACTIVITY:
  In cold climates, jumping mice hibernate for as much as half the year and are not active from mid-fall until mid-spring. Primarily nocturnal, but sometimes active during the day.

SIMILAR SPECIES:
  Other small mammal tracks have shorter, straighter toes that don't usu-

ally connect clearly to the palm. Voles (pg. 73) are smaller and usually trot. Harvest mice and white-footed mice (pgs. 61–67) usually leave more regular bounding patterns resembling miniature squirrel trails. Pocket mice (pg. 81) often overlap their front feet when bounding. Partial jumping mouse tracks may resemble songbird tracks.

NOTES:

As the name suggests, the jumping mouse is a remarkable jumper. While it usually travels in short bounds, it is capable of leaps of 6'–8'. When startled, a jumping mouse usually takes several long, frog-like jumps, then ducks into cover, remaining motionless.

The jumping mouse has a body specialized for making powerful leaps. In addition to its large, long hind feet and powerful legs, it is adorned with an extremely long tail, which is often 1½ times the length of the rest of its body and acts as a stabilizer in the air. A jumping mouse missing part of its tail still can leap, but may tumble uncontrollably and crash-land.

Jumping mice are not closely related to other North American mice, and unlike other mice in our region, they are deep hibernators. In the northern parts of their range, jumping mice hibernate for up to half the year. They do not store food for the winter, but instead rely on fat reserves built up in the weeks before entering hibernation. A jumping mouse may add 25–50 percent of its body weight in fat in just two weeks in preparation for winter. Still, this is little reserve for these tiny mammals and about two-thirds of the population don't survive hibernation, either starving to death or by being eaten while they sleep. Some individuals avoid hibernation by moving into human homes for the winter and return outdoors in the spring. Either way, jumping mice do not make tracks outdoors in the colder months of the year.

Jumping mice are good swimmers and capable divers. They readily take to water and may dive into the water to flee. Jumping mice are omnivorous, eating seeds, berries, insects and fungi. As jumping mice recover from hibernation, insects are an important part of their spring diet. The subterranean fungus *Endogone* also makes up a substantial fraction of the diet of many jumping mice. It is likely that this fungus actually depends on jumping mice to complete its life cycle. Jumping mice not only disperse the fungi's spores, but there is evidence that the spores require exposure to the mouse's digestive system to germinate.

HIND TRACK
typical size

FRONT TRACK
typical size

max. ³/₈"
FRONT min. ¹/₄"

max. ¹/₂"
HIND min. ³/₈"

Pocket Mice

Chaetodipus and *Perognathus* spp.

Pocket mice are small, light and nocturnal, and they spend much of their time underground. However, their preference for sandy soils makes it more likely they will leave visible prints as they move about at night.

FRONT TRACK

LENGTH: $1/4"-3/8"$, **AVERAGING:** $5/16"$; **WIDTH:** $1/4"-3/8"$, **AVERAGING:** $5/16"$

Four long toes with prominent claws. Their inner- and outermost toes point out to the sides. There is a tiny, vestigial thumb that occasionally shows as well. The palm is heavily furred and often indistinct, though 3 palm pads may be visible, forming an arc behind the toes. The heel does not usually register. Front feet are smaller than hind feet, but front may splay more, so front and hind tracks can have similar dimensions.

HIND TRACK

LENGTH: $3/8"-1/2"$, **AVERAGING:** $7/16"$; **WIDTH:** $1/4"-1/2"$, **AVERAGING:** $3/8"$

Five long toes with prominent claws. The innermost toe is much smaller than others, set farther back on the foot, and often does not register clearly, giving the track a four-toed appearance. The three middle toes have similar proportions and point forward. The outermost toe may be somewhat smaller, and commonly points to the side. The palm is heavily furred and usually indistinct. The heel, which is naked in some species and partially furred in others, sometimes registers.

GAITS

Usually bounds, often overlapping its front feet. Other tiny mammals usually place their front feet side by side or one in front of the other. When a pocket mouse moves slowly, its tail may drag.

QUICK ID TIPS:
- Front feet often overlap while bounding
- Hind feet show only four distinct toes
- Palms are furred and pads are often indistinct

HABITAT:
Varies somewhat by species. Most species prefer arid regions with sandy soil and sparse vegetation, especially sand plains and sand dunes. Also found in dry grasslands, deserts, scrubland and dry open woodlands, and in areas with gravelly or rocky soil.

OTHER SIGNS:
Scat: Scat is dry and hard with a seed-like appearance. It is usually less than ¼" long and can be found near the entrances to burrows. Indistinguishable from white-footed mouse scat.

Burrows: Pocket mouse burrows are often difficult to find. Burrow openings are small, usually 1" in diameter or less, and are generally located under a plant. The burrows are similar to those of pocket gophers, but smaller. They commonly have a small mound of sand or fine soil to the side, and the entrance is often plugged from the inside.

Dust Baths: Like kangaroo rats, many species of pocket mice scoop out small, shallow depressions in the sand for dust bathing. You may find these depressions near active burrows.

ACTIVITY:

Some species are active year-round, while others become torpid in winter and do not venture aboveground in cold weather. All species are nocturnal and rarely aboveground during the day.

SIMILAR SPECIES:

Other small bounding mammals rarely overlap their front feet while bounding and have five similarly sized toes on the hind foot.

NOTES:

Pocket mice are not closely related to other mice, but are instead members of the Heteromyidae family, together with kangaroo rats and kangaroo mice. All the members of this family are unique to North America, highly adapted to arid climates, and live a nocturnal, burrowing life.

Pocket mice spend their days underground, protected from the hot, cold, and dry conditions that characterize the desert habitats where they reside. They dig large burrows with multiple chambers, which they use for sleeping, nesting and caching food. Masters of water conservation, they plug their burrows to keep moisture in, produce highly concentrated urine and dry scat, and are able to get all the water they need from digesting and metabolizing the seeds that make up the majority of their diet.

Pocket mice get their name from their large, external cheek pouches, which they use to carry seeds and other materials back to their burrows to store. Though they eat some food in the field, they cache most of the seeds underground. Stored in the damp burrow, the seeds absorb moisture from the soil, providing an additional scant source of water. Pocket mice supplement their diet of seeds with green vegetation, subterranean fungi, and insects. They also drink when open water is available.

Pocket mice are preyed on by rattlesnakes, owls, badgers, skunks, foxes, weasels and coyotes.

max. ¹/₂"

FRONT

min. ¹/₄"

FRONT TRACK
typical size

max. 1¹/₄"

min. ³/₈"

HIND

HIND TRACK
typical size

Ord's Kangaroo Rat
Dipodomys ordii

The Ord's kangaroo rat is a nocturnal creature of the arid plains. Its trails are quite distinctive as it is the only mammal in the Midwest (besides humans) that travels in a bipedal gait, leaving only hind tracks.

FRONT TRACK
LENGTH: 1/4"–1/2", **AVERAGING:** 3/8"; **WIDTH:** 1/4"–3/8", **AVERAGING:** 5/16"

Five toes—unusual for a rodent—each with prominent claws. The inner- and outermost toes are smaller and set farther back. The innermost toe is smallest and may fail to register. The palm has a single, triangular pad. Two heel pads sometimes register. The front tracks only register when the animal is moving slowly, and are much smaller than the hind tracks.

HIND TRACK
LENGTH: 3/8"–1¼", **AVERAGING:** N/A ; **WIDTH:** 3/8"–3/4", **AVERAGING:** 5/8"

Four toes with claws sometimes showing. The outermost toe is set farther back in the track. A tiny fifth toe high on the foot occasionally registers as a small dot. Other toes are deep and prominent. Toes may be held tightly together or may splay widely. Palm and heel are heavily furred and usually indistinct. The heel often registers when the animal is moving slowly, rarely when traveling fast. Significantly larger than the front track.

GAITS
Travels in a distinctive bipedal bound shared by all kangaroo rats and kangaroo mice. At high speeds, one foot may land in front of the other creating a bipedal gallop. The stride varies greatly with speed, reaching 8' when the animal is fleeing. Sometimes bounds on all four feet when foraging.

QUICK ID TIPS:
- Travels in a distinctive bipedal bound
- Hind tracks are much larger than front tracks
- Hind track shows four clear toes and an indistinct heel

HABITAT:
Dry grasslands, sagebrush and scrublands with fine sandy soil or sand dunes.

OTHER SIGNS:
Scat: Small, oval pellets have very low moisture content, helping kangaroo rats conserve as much water as possible. Scat is often deposited underground, but may be left near burrows or foraging sites. Scat may be brown or green and measure $1/8$" or less in diameter and up to $1/2$" long.

Burrows: Burrow entrances measure about 3" and are often slightly taller than wide. They are usually dug into the side of a small bank or a sand dune and have a small mound of dirt outside the entrance; entrances are usually plugged, but the plug is often too deep inside the burrow to see.

Dust Baths: Kangaroo rats scoop out small, shallow depressions in the sand for dust bathing; depressions are often found near active burrows.

ACTIVITY:
Active year-round, but typically holes up and may become torpid in cold weather or when snow accumulates. Nocturnal. Most active on cloudy or moonless nights.

SIMILAR SPECIES:

Distinctive tracks and trails are only likely to be confused with those of other kangaroo rats or kangaroo mice, and no other representatives of these groups are reliably found in the Midwest. No other mammals this size travel in a bipedal hop or exhibit such a size discrepancy between their front and hind tracks.

NOTES:

The Ord's kangaroo rat is the most common and widespread of all the kangaroo rats, and the only species reliably found in the Midwest. Kangaroo rats get their name from their distinctive bipedal hop, which resembles that of their Australian namesake. When moving with any speed, they hop on their hind feet with their forefeet and tail held aloft, leaving a distinctive trail that is not likely to be confused with that of any other animal. Kangaroo rats belong to the family Heteromyidae, which includes pocket mice and kangaroo mice. Unique to North America, the entire Heteromyidae family is highly adapted to arid environments, and is not closely related to other rats or mice. Ord's kangaroo rats are semi-fossorial, spending much of their lives underground. While their large hind feet are well suited for hopping, their small front feet are well adapted for digging. They excavate large underground burrows with multiple chambers for sleeping, nesting and food storage.

Ord's kangaroo rats eat mostly seeds, supplementing their diet with green vegetation, subterranean fungi and insects. They come out at night to forage, rarely straying more than 40' from their burrows. Though they eat when foraging, they carry most seeds back to their burrows in their large, external cheek pouches and cache them to eat later. Stored underground, these seeds absorb moisture from the damp burrow walls and provide the kangaroo rat with a modest source of water in the desert. Like members of the Heteromyidae family, Ord's kangaroo rats are so well adapted to desert life that they do not need to drink liquid water and get all the water they need from metabolizing seeds. To conserve water, they plug their burrows to keep moisture in, stay underground whenever the sun is up, and produce highly concentrated urine and bone-dry scat.

Ord's kangaroo rats are preyed on by rattlesnakes, owls, badgers, skunks, foxes, weasels and coyotes.

HIND TRACK
typical size

max. ⅞"

min. ⅜"

FRONT

max. 1¼"

min. ½"

HIND

FRONT TRACK
typical size

Woodrats
Neotoma spp.

Found in the southern and western edges of our region, woodrats' bulbous toes give their tracks a distinctive look. But it is their large houses of sticks and debris that usually give away their presence.

FRONT TRACK
LENGTH: ³/₈"–⁷/₈", AVERAGING: ⁵/₈"; WIDTH: ³/₈"–³/₄", AVERAGING: ¹/₂"

Four round, plump toes with tiny claws occasionally showing. The middle toes point forward. The inner- and outermost toes point to the sides. There is a tiny vestigial thumb set far back on the inside of the foot that may register as a dot in the track. The toe pads do not connect to the palm in the track. Three palm pads are fused together into a rounded pyramid shape behind the toes. There are two small heel pads that sometimes register as well.

HIND TRACK
LENGTH: ¹/₂"–1¹/₄", AVERAGING: ³/₄"; WIDTH: ¹/₂"–⁷/₈", AVERAGING: ⁵/₈"

Five round, plump toes, with tiny claws occasionally showing. The middle three toes point forward together while the inner- and outermost toes point farther to the sides. The innermost toe is smallest and set farther back on the foot. Unlike the front foot, the toes sometimes connect to the palm pad in the track. Large palm pads are fused together in an irregular shape behind the toes. There is an additional tiny palm pad and two tiny heel pads that may register as well. Larger than the front track.

GAITS
Usually travels in a walk in or near cover, but often bounds when in the open. Generally bounds with its front feet set one in front of the other.

QUICK ID TIPS:
- More bulbous toe pads than other small rodents
- Front toe pads do not connect to the palm pad in the track
- Builds large nests of sticks and twigs, often adorned with trinkets

WALK

HABITAT:

Various species of woodrats occupy a wide range of habitats, including woods, swamps, rocky outcroppings and deserts. They are least likely to live in marshes or grasslands.

OTHER SIGNS:

Scat: Woodrats deposit scat all around their nests and along travel routes. The droppings are capsule-shaped pellets ranging from ¼"–½" long and a little over ⅛" in diameter. Woodrats also deposit a soft, formless scat that they appear to use to scent-mark travel routes. This tar-like excrement can build up in large quantities over time.

Houses: Most woodrats construct large houses of sticks and other local debris. Houses grow year after year, and may reach over 5' in diameter and more than 4' in height, and have a jumbled, disorderly appearance. Houses are typically built at the base of a tree or between rock slabs, but are also built on high branches, inside buildings and in a variety of other locations. They are often elaborate structures containing numerous cavities for nesting, food storage and defecation. Some woodrats do not build elaborate houses, but instead nest in burrows or natural rock crevices. Sometimes, the entrances to these nests are protected by piles of sticks and debris and are similar to a house, but without any internal structure.

Runs: Woodrats maintain travel routes that radiate from their nests to foraging areas; routes also connect foraging areas. These trails measure 3"–4" wide, make use of existing cover and are usually kept free of debris.

ACTIVITY:

Most species are active year-round, but may hole up during bad weather. Nocturnal, but may be active before dark on overcast evenings.

SIMILAR SPECIES:

Norway rats (pg. 93) have more slender toes, and less robust palm pads. Chipmunks (pg. 105) usually bound, placing their front feet side by side, and have longer, more slender toes. Ground squirrels (pg. 101) have long, prominent front claws and longer toes that angle inward on the front foot, and do not show heel pads in the hind track. Mouse and vole tracks (pgs. 61–83) are smaller.

NOTES:

Woodrats, also known as packrats, are best known for their large houses of accumulated debris decorated with odd objects. Woodrats seem to have an innate building instinct, similar to that of a beaver. Members of most species are continually building, maintaining or expanding their large stick houses. Each woodrat may manage several houses, and large houses may represent the work of many generations of short-lived woodrats. In addition to sticks and other plant debris, many woodrats adorn their houses with odd artifacts, including bones, pieces of scat, tin cans, coins, spent shotgun shells, and nearly anything else that catches the woodrat's fancy. Many species seem to have a particular fondness for shiny objects and quickly drop anything they are carrying to pick up something with an attractive glint. Woodrats have even been known to haul off shiny new small mammal traps set out by researchers to collect rodents.

Primarily herbivores, woodrats eat mostly green plants, supplemented with nuts, seeds, fungi and occasional animal matter. They cache large amounts of food, both in their burrows or stick houses and in large piles in the open.

Woodrats are competent climbers, readily scale shrubs and trees to forage, and sometimes build nests in trees. Capable diggers, many species excavate sizable burrows. Burrows may supplement a stick house, be used in place of one, or serve as a "starter home" as a stick house is built.

BOUND

max. ³/₄"

min. ¹/₂"

FRONT

HIND TRACK
typical size

FRONT TRACK
typical size

max. 1¹/₄"

min. ⁵/₈"

HIND

Norway Rat
Rattus norvegicus

Like its smaller cousin, the house mouse, the Norway rat is closely associated with human habitation. A serious pest animal, its tracks and signs are common near unmaintained buildings, sewer systems and garbage dumps.

FRONT TRACK
LENGTH: 1/2"–3/4", **AVERAGING:** 5/8"; **WIDTH:** 1/2"–3/4", **AVERAGING:** 5/8"

Four long toes with tiny claws occasionally showing. Two middle toes point forward, while the inner- and outermost toes point to the sides. The toes usually connect to the palm in the track. Four palm pads are arranged in a tetrahedron shape behind the toes. Two small heel pads sometimes register. The overall shape of the track is mouse-like but larger.

HIND TRACK
LENGTH: 5/8"–1 1/4", **AVERAGING:** 7/8"; **WIDTH:** 5/8"–1", **AVERAGING:** 3/4"

Five long toes with tiny claws occasionally showing. The three middle toes register close together and point forward. The inner- and outermost toes are shorter, set farther back, and point to the sides. Toes usually connect to the palm in the track. Three palm pads form an arc behind the toes. Two heel pads may also register. Overall shape of the track is mouse-like. Larger than front tracks.

GAITS
Typically travels in a walk or a trot. May speed up to a bound when crossing open areas. Usually bounds in deep snow, leaving an obvious tail drag.

QUICK ID TIPS:
- Tracks have a mouse-like appearance, but are much larger
- Middle toes pointing forward and outer toes pointing to the sides
- Four long, slender toes on the front foot and five on the hind

WALK

HABITAT:

Closely associated with human development. Found in urban, suburban and rural areas, usually around dwellings and other man-made structures. In agricultural areas, may move into cultivated fields in the summer.

OTHER SIGNS:

Scat: The size, color and consistency of Norway rat droppings vary with its wide-ranging diet, but can be unsettlingly similar in appearance to a blackened piece of rice or other grain. The pellets typically measure $1/8"$–$1/4"$ in diameter and $1/4"$–$1"$ long. Scat is dropped randomly along travel routes, near nests, or where the rats spend time feeding.

Holes: Norway rats make use of all manner of crevices, passageways and holes in walls and other structures. When used by Norway rats, these openings typically have dirty smudges around them. Norway rats sometimes also dig burrows, which are usually connected to buildings. Entrances to these burrows typically measure 2"–3" in diameter.

ACTIVITY:

Active year-round. Primarily nocturnal, but may be active at any time.

SIMILAR SPECIES:

Red squirrels (pg. 117) and chipmunks (pg. 105) show less size difference between the front and hind tracks, have more robust palm pads, and usually bound with their front feet closer together. Mouse tracks (pgs. 61–83) and trails are much smaller.

NOTES:

This is the well-known rat of urban centers. Closely associated with people, they are common in our largest cities, as well as in suburban and agricultural areas. The Norway rat does not come from Norway, but is likely native to Central Asia and came to Europe between the sixteenth and eighteenth centuries. It was introduced to North America during the Revolutionary War on ships carrying food supplies for British troops. Since then, it has spread across the continent.

Norway rats are colonial animals and live in groups consisting of a male, several females and their young. They are prolific, year-round breeders and populations can grow very quickly when food is abundant. Females give birth to 2–20 young and can have a new litter every month under ideal conditions. Colonies live in large, elaborate networks of chambers and travel routes that are a mixture of the cavities in and around human structures and their own excavated burrows and tunnels. Though primarily terrestrial, Norway rats are capable climbers, good swimmers, and prefer damp habitats, such as sewer systems. Their trails nearly always begin and end at a hole, drain, crevice or some other burrow entrance.

Norway rats are considered the most serious pest animal in our region. They can spread disease, foul food stores and damage buildings. They have been known to start fires by gnawing on matches or through electrical wiring, and have triggered flooding by burrowing through dams. At the same time, this species is also the source of the white lab rat, which has contributed greatly to the advance of modern medicine.

BOUND

FRONT TRACK
typical size

— max. 1¼"

— min. ¾"

FRONT

— max. 1⅛"

— min. ⅞"

HIND

HIND TRACK
typical size

Pocket Gophers

Geomys and *Thomomys* spp.

Pocket gophers are the most fossorial (subterranean) rodents in the Midwest. They rarely venture far aboveground, making their tracks rare. The signs of their extensive digging, however, are often conspicuous.

FRONT TRACK

LENGTH: 3/4"–1 1/4", **AVERAGING:** 1"; **WIDTH:** 3/8"–7/8", **AVERAGING:** 5/8"

Five toes with extremely long, prominent claws. The middle toe and claw are the longest. The inner- and outermost toes are set farther back. The innermost toe is greatly reduced and set farthest back, but has a large claw that often shows in tracks. Track has three palm pads arranged in a pyramid shape; two heel pads sometimes register. The long claws may add another 1/2" or more to the track length.

HIND TRACK

LENGTH: 7/8"–1 1/8", **AVERAGING:** 1"; **WIDTH:** 3/8"–7/8", **AVERAGING:** 5/8"

Five toes with claws. The inner- and outermost toes are set farther back and point to the sides. The middle three toes point forward and register closely together. Palm and heel pads are fused together, with several small, distinct pads often visible. The heel sometimes registers. Similar in size to the front track.

GAITS

Walks or trots ("scurries") almost exclusively. Pocket gophers can walk and trot equally well forward and backward. Since these "scurrying" gaits keep the spine level, they are ideally suited to life in underground tunnels.

QUICK ID TIPS:
- Five toes on each foot
- Long, prominent claws on the front foot
- Walks or trots almost exclusively

WALK/TROT

HABITAT:
Usually found in sandy or deep loam soils in prairies, meadows, brushland, agricultural fields, disturbed forests and on roadsides.

OTHER SIGNS:
Scat: Usually deposited in underground latrines. In winter, latrines are also created underneath the snowpack; these can sometimes be found in spring after snowmelt, or in soil castings. The typical form of the scat is a smooth, oval pellet with rounded ends measuring about $1/4"$–$1/2"$ in length.

Burrows: Pocket gophers excavate large, elaborate burrow systems, then push out excavated earth and plug the entrance, resulting in a fan-shaped mound of dirt with a plugged hole at the base of the fan. Entrances may be difficult to spot. The burrow tunnels slope down from the entrance, in the opposite direction of the dirt mound.

Soil Castings: In winter, pocket gophers tunnel under snow to forage and gather nesting material. In the process, they deposit soil excavated from their burrow network. When the snow melts, the cords of excavated soil are exposed, showing where the animal traveled the previous winter. Castings measure about 2" in diameter and look like a jumble of thick rope.

ACTIVITY:

Active year-round, though they often retreat to deeper sections of their burrows in winter. May be active at any time of the day or night.

SIMILAR SPECIES:

Most other small rodents have four toes on their front feet, and commonly travel in a bound. Moles (pg. 57) push dirt out of vertical tunnels, forming symmetrical mounds around the excavation. Mole runways are created when soil is pushed up from under the surface. By contrast, pocket gopher soil castings are made of excavated soil on top of undisturbed ground.

NOTES:

Pocket gophers are among the most fossorial (subterranean) mammals in North America. They excavate large, elaborate systems of tunnels and chambers where they spend the majority of their lives. They occasionally come to the surface, especially in the spring, to gather nesting material, and it is possible to find pocket gopher tracks. Most often, however, it is signs of the pocket gophers' digging that we see. These signs are similar to those of moles, which are not closely related.

Pocket gophers have long claws, powerful front legs and small eyes and ears. Their lips close behind their incisors, allowing them to use their front teeth to dig and gnaw without getting dirt in their mouth. Like moles, their short velvety fur allows them to move in tunnels with ease.

Pocket gophers are herbivores and eat a variety of roots, tubers and green plants, usually without leaving their tunnels. They may cut off green plants and drag them underground or eat the roots, killing the aboveground portions. They can do damage to crops and gardens, but also turn, aerate and fertilize the soil, and some native plants depend on pocket gophers for survival.

Each pocket gopher maintains its own burrow system and burrows do not generally overlap. Young begin digging tunnels at a few weeks of age and can excavate their own burrow by two months of age. Burrow systems are usually excavated within a foot of the surface and include deeper nesting, food cache and latrine chambers and a shallower network of tunnels for foraging. The name pocket gopher comes from the large external cheek pouches that this animal uses to carry food and other materials.

WALK/TROT

HIND TRACK
typical size

max. 1³/₈"

min. ³/₄"

FRONT

max. 1¹/₂"

min. ³/₄"

HIND

FRONT TRACK
typical size

RANGE

Ground Squirrels

Ictidomys, Poliocitellus, Urocitellus,
Xerospermophilus spp.

Ground squirrels are diurnal and are often seen in the summertime standing bolt upright at the edge of a lawn or a road. Deep hibernators active for only a few months each year, they do not leave tracks in the snow.

FRONT TRACK
LENGTH: ³/₄"–1³/₈", AVERAGING: ⁷/₈"; WIDTH: ³/₈"–1", AVERAGING: ³/₄"

Four toes with long, prominent claws. Palm has three pads in a pyramid shape behind the toes. Two heel pads often register. Tracks are much less symmetrical than those of tree squirrels or chipmunks. All four toes point slightly inward, with middle toes parallel to each other, and inner and outer toes set somewhat wider and farther back. There is little to no fur between the pads and the toes, making pads quite distinct.

HIND TRACK
LENGTH: ³/₄"–1¹/₂", AVERAGING: 1¹/₈"; WIDTH: ⁵/₈"–1³/₈", AVERAGING: 1"

Five toes with claws usually showing. Palm has four pads that sometimes fuse into an arc. The heel may register, especially in deeper substrate; in summer, it has no fur and two small heel pads may show, but may be less distinct in winter. The middle three toes point straight ahead; inner and outer toes point to the sides. There is little to no fur between pads and toes; pads are quite distinct. Similar in size to front foot.

GAITS
Travels in a bound. May walk while foraging. Typically bounds with one front foot in front of the other, though occasionally front feet land side by side.

QUICK ID TIPS:
- Recognizably squirrel-like tracks with prominent claws on the front feet
- Usually bounds, placing one front foot ahead of the other
- Trails typically begin and end at a burrow entrance or rock crevice

WALK

HABITAT:
Varies by species. Grasslands, shortgrass prairies, fields and roadsides.

OTHER SIGNS:
Scat: The basic form of the scat is a pellet, pointed on one end and flat on the other. Pellets are typically ⅛"–¼" in diameter and ¼"–¾" long. Supple browse can lead to softer, twisted scat with two tapered ends, or scat that is clumped together. Often found around the entrances to their burrows.

Burrows: Entrances to most ground squirrel burrows are marked by conspicuous dirt mounds. Entrances usually measure 2"–4" in diameter. Conspicuous trails may radiate from a burrow location. Burrows are extensive, and may be 15'–20' long with many passages and chambers. Most passages are only 1'–2' underground, but the hibernation chamber is often much deeper.

ACTIVITY:
Most species have prolonged periods of dormancy and all hibernate in winter. In northern climates, hibernation may last 6 months or more. In hot, dry climates, many species also estivate (become dormant) through much of summer. All species are diurnal and may be active at any time of day.

SIMILAR SPECIES:

Prairie dogs (pg. 129) walk much more often and their tracks are larger. Chipmunks and tree squirrels have more symmetrical front feet with shorter claws, and usually place their front feet side by side when bounding. Chipmunk tracks (pg. 105) are usually smaller. Gray and fox squirrel tracks (pgs. 121–127) are usually larger.

NOTES:

There are four species of ground squirrel in our region and all share many similar characteristics. Ground squirrels are terrestrial and semi-fossorial, spending a significant part of their lives underground. All species in our region hibernate through winter. They spend late summer and early fall putting on a heavy later of fat before retreating to their burrow for much of the year. In fact, some individuals may be active for only a few months each year.

Ground squirrels eat mostly seeds and green vegetation and supplement their diet with insects, berries and some carrion. While they rely on fat to sustain them through the winter, they may hoard seeds in their burrows to eat when they come out of hibernation.

Different species of ground squirrels have different social habits. Thirteen-lined ground squirrels tend to be colonial, while Richardson's, Franklin's and spotted ground squirrels tend to be solitary. All, however, are quite defensive of their burrows. Burrows may be in close proximity to one another, but males fiercely defend their burrow and the area immediately around it from other males. Males regularly fight for females in the spring after emerging from hibernation and are often injured. As they are diurnal, ground squirrels are often seen. They have a habit of standing upright to survey their surroundings, a behavior that has earned them the nickname "picket pins."

Their daytime activity also makes them highly susceptible to predation. When they detect danger, ground squirrels dart down their burrows, which they always remain nearby. They often stay just inside the entrance, retreating deeper underground if the threat remains. They are preyed on by snakes, weasels and hawks, and badgers, which may dig them up while they are hibernating. Many are also killed by domestic cats and dogs.

max. ⁷/₈"

min. ¹/₂"

FRONT

max. 1"

min. ¹/₂"

HIND

FRONT TRACK
typical size

Chipmunks

Tamias striatus and *Tamias minimus*

These attractive members of the squirrel family are often seen foraging in the summer. They hibernate in the winter, but may venture out into the snow on warmer days.

FRONT TRACK

LENGTH: $1/2"–7/8"$, **AVERAGING:** $3/4"$; **WIDTH:** $3/8"–3/4"$, **AVERAGING:** $5/8"$

Four toes with small but prominent claws. The palm has three distinct pads, forming a pyramid behind the toes. Two heel pads often register, especially in deeper substrate. Middle toes point straight ahead; inner and outer toes point to the sides. A tiny vestigial thumb sometimes registers. There is little to no fur between the pads and toes, making pads quite distinct. Least chipmunk tracks are about 25 percent smaller than eastern chipmunk tracks.

HIND TRACK

LENGTH: $1/2"–1"$, **AVERAGING:** $3/4"$; **WIDTH:** $1/2"–7/8"$, **AVERAGING:** $3/4"$

Five toes with small claws usually showing. Palm has four pads that form an arc behind the toes. The furry heel sometimes registers. The middle three toes point straight ahead, while inner and outer toes point to the sides. The space between the pads and the toes shows little or no fur, making the pads quite distinct. Similar in size to the front track.

GAITS

Bounds almost exclusively, leaving a distinctive squirrel pattern. Front feet register side by side or with one foot slightly in front of the other. Hind feet usually register in front of, and outside, the front feet. Occasionally hops. Usually bounds in deep snow, leaving a single body print.

> **QUICK ID TIPS:**
> - Typical squirrel track with 4 long toes on the front foot and 5 on the hind
> - Distinctive squirrel pattern: front tracks often side by side with hind tracks wider apart and ahead of the front
> - Smaller than most other squirrel tracks

BOUND

HABITAT:

Least: Pastures, open coniferous forests, rocky cliffs, sagebrush scrubland.
Eastern: Deciduous forests, brushy forest edges, brushland, suburbs.

OTHER SIGNS:

Scat: Variable scat is difficult to distinguish from other small mammal scat. The basic form is a pellet ⅛" or less across and ⅛"–¼" long. Pellets may clump or string together and are often deposited on top of perches in the chipmunk's range.

Burrows: Entrances to chipmunk burrows measure 1½"–2" in diameter and are usually discrete, without any food scraps, scat or mounds of dirt nearby. The tunnel typically begins on flat ground and goes straight down for about 6" before leveling off into a series of tunnels and chambers. Most other small mammal burrows have an angled entrance with some debris nearby. Burrows may be elaborate, with up to 100' of tunnels.

Feeding Sign: Chipmunks often feed on an elevated perch in their territory. Look for bits of chaff on logs, stumps or rocks.

Digs: Chipmunks often make small, circular digs on the forest floor, particularly in pine needles. Red squirrels and skunks make similar digs.

ACTIVITY:

Hibernates through the winter, rousing periodically to feed and occasionally leaving its burrow on warm winter days. Diurnal. Most active in the early morning and late afternoon.

SIMILAR SPECIES:

With the exception of the southern flying squirrel, tree squirrel tracks (pgs. 113–127) are larger. Southern flying squirrels (pg. 109) have much more fur in the negative space between the toes and palm pads, the palm pads of their hind feet are fused into a tight crescent, and they often hop, instead of bound, placing the hind feet behind the front. Ground squirrel tracks (pg. 101) are generally larger and have longer claws. Mouse tracks (pgs. 61–83) are smaller. Norway rats (pg. 93) usually place one front foot far in front of the other when bounding and their front and hind tracks are less similar in size.

NOTES:

Chipmunks are small, primarily terrestrial members of the squirrel family. Frequent visitors to picnic tables and bird feeders, their tracks and trails are similar to those of tree squirrels, but smaller. Unlike their tree-dwelling cousins, they are semi-fossorial, digging burrows and spending much time underground. Their trails may end at the base of a shrub, but more often lead to a rock crevice or burrow.

Chipmunks may be best known for their large, fur-lined cheek pouches, which they use for gathering food. Chipmunks do not hibernate as deeply as ground squirrels. Instead of storing body fat to last them through winter, they amass large food stores and wake from hibernation every couple of weeks to feed before returning to sleep. Though they generally remain in their burrows all winter, they may emerge on warm days to forage.

More omnivorous than many squirrels, chipmunks supplement their diet of nuts and seeds with fungi, green plants, fruits, berries, insects and even carrion. While primarily ground dwellers, they are excellent climbers and readily venture into trees. When nuts are in season, they may make continuous trips from tree to burrow, hoarding a bushel of nuts over a few days. As they are small, chipmunks are vulnerable to predation from long-tailed weasels, hawks, bobcats, foxes and snakes. When startled, they give a distinctive "chip!" call as they retreat to cover. This is where they get their common name.

max. ³/₄"

min. ³/₈"

FRONT

max. 1³/₈"

min. ½"

HIND

FRONT TRACK
typical size

HIND TRACK
typical size

Southern Flying Squirrel
Glaucomys volans

Southern flying squirrels are the smallest tree squirrel species in the Midwest. They are also nocturnal and highly arboreal. When they do come to the ground, their distinctive hopping gait often gives away their trails.

FRONT TRACK
LENGTH: $3/8''$–$3/4''$, **AVERAGING:** $1/2''$; **WIDTH:** $3/8''$–$3/4''$, **AVERAGING:** $1/2''$

Four toes with small claws sometimes showing. Palm has three pads that sometimes fuse into a pyramid shape behind toes. Two small heel pads sometimes register. Middle toes point straight ahead; inner and outer toes point to the sides. The space between the pads and toes has much more fur than in other squirrels; pads appear smaller and less distinct.

HIND TRACK
LENGTH: $1/2''$–$1\,3/8''$, **AVERAGING:** $1''$; **WIDTH:** $3/8''$–$7/8''$, **AVERAGING:** $5/8''$

Five toes with small claws sometimes showing. Palm pads are fused together into a narrow crescent behind the toes. The heel is covered with fur, doesn't have pads, and sometimes registers in deeper substrate. The middle three toes point straight ahead; inner and outer toes point to the sides. The space between the pads and toes has much more fur than in other squirrels; pads appear smaller and less distinct. Slightly larger than the front track.

GAITS
Normally hops, rather than bounds, creating an unusual variation on the typical squirrel pattern. Front feet typically land side by side with hind feet landing behind them. The tracks are sometimes confused with those of a bounding chipmunk traveling in the opposite direction.

QUICK ID TIPS:
- Typical squirrel track with 4 long toes on the front foot and 5 on the hind
- Generally hops, rather than bounds, placing its hind feet behind its front
- Feet are heavily furred

HOP

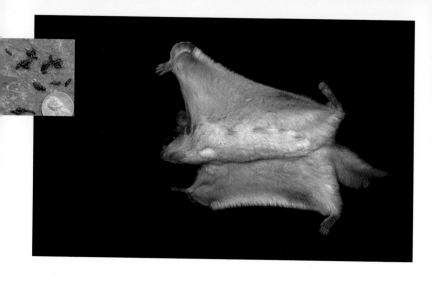

HABITAT:

Hardwood forests, especially oak-hickory and maple-beech.

OTHER SIGNS:

Scat: Scat is usually deposited in the tree cavities. Accumulated scat, often mixed with flecks of decaying wood from the tree, may flow out of one of these cavities and build up on the ground. The basic form of the scat is a tiny, oval pellet ⅛" or less in diameter and up to ¼" long.

Sitzmark: Occasionally, flying squirrels glide to the ground, leaving a body print where they land. These "sitzmarks" are a clear indication of a flying squirrel trail. However, flying squirrels usually glide from tree to tree and climb down to the ground; most flying squirrel trails don't show sitzmarks.

Feeding: Look for hickory nuts with a smooth opening on the smaller end. Red squirrels make a rough opening, larger squirrels crush the nut, while mice make 2–3 openings.

ACTIVITY:

Active year-round. May become torpid during cold winter weather. Nocturnal and rarely seen, even where common. Most active for a few hours after sunset and before dawn.

SIMILAR SPECIES:

Northern flying squirrels (pg. 113) hop much less often, leave a wider trail (typically 3" or more), and spread their front feet wider apart, leaving a "boxy" bound pattern. Chipmunks (pg. 105) bound almost exclusively, have much less fur between their toes and palm pads, and show four distinct palm pads on the hind feet. Other tree squirrels (pgs. 117–127) are much larger.

NOTES:

Flying squirrels don't actually fly, but glide from tree to tree on folds of skin stretched between their legs that act as a cross between a parachute and a glider wing. Using the tail as a rudder, they are quite agile and can make sharp turns as well as a four-point landing on a tree trunk. They are completely nocturnal and primarily arboreal.

Many people assume that flying squirrels commonly glide to the ground, but that's rarely true; instead, they usually climb down, with gliding reserved for travel between trees. Gliding to the ground leaves a telltale sitzmark (body imprint), but the absence of one in a trail is no reason to rule out a flying squirrel.

Southern flying squirrels are generally solitary in summer, but den communally in winter. In summer, they may build leaf nests, which are similar to those made by gray and fox squirrels but only 8" or so in diameter. Winter nests are often shared by groups of 3–8 animals, and groups as large as 50 have been recorded. Nests are most commonly made in an old woodpecker hole with a $1^{1}/_{2}$"–2" opening located 8'–20' up in a dead hardwood tree that is still standing. In addition to nesting, southern flying squirrels also use woodpecker holes and other tree cavities to cache food, and as latrines.

Southern flying squirrels are the most carnivorous of the tree squirrels. Their diet includes not only nuts, acorns, seeds, berries, fungi and lichens, but also birds, nestlings, eggs, insects and carrion. They will also gnaw on maple trees to drink the sap. Like other tree squirrels, they cache nuts in the fall to feed on through the winter. Nuts are usually cached in tree cavities, but some are also buried.

HOP

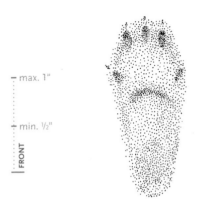

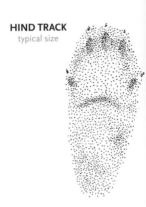

HIND TRACK
typical size

- max. 1"

- min. ½"

FRONT

- max. 1¾"

- min. 1¼"

HIND

FRONT TRACK
typical size

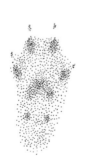

Northern Flying Squirrel
Glaucomys sabrinus

Nocturnal and highly arboreal, northern flying squirrels are rarely seen, even where they are common. Though they often avoid the ground completely, the trails they do make are usually distinctive.

FRONT TRACK
LENGTH: 1/2"–1", AVERAGING: 3/4"; WIDTH: 1/2"–3/4", AVERAGING: 5/8"

Four toes with small claws sometimes showing. Palm has three pads that sometimes fuse into a pyramid behind the toes. Two small heel pads sometimes register. Middle toes point straight ahead; inner and outer toes point to the sides. The space between the pads and toes has much more fur than in other squirrels, making the pads appear smaller and less distinct.

HIND TRACK
LENGTH: 1 1/4"–1 3/4", AVERAGING: 1 1/2"; WIDTH: 5/8"–7/8", AVERAGING: 3/4"

Five toes with small claws sometimes showing. Palm pads are fused together into a narrow crescent behind the toes. The heel sometimes registers, particularly in deeper substrate. It is covered with fur and does not have any pads. The middle three toes point straight ahead, while inner and outer toes point to the sides. The space between the pads and the toes has much more fur than in other squirrels. Larger than the front track.

GAITS
Usually bounds with its front feet wide apart, leaving a distinctively "boxy" variation on the typical squirrel pattern. Trails occasionally include some modified hops and short bounds, but less often than southern flying squirrels.

QUICK ID TIPS:
- Typical squirrel track with 4 long toes on the front foot and 5 on the hind
- Places its front feet wide apart, creating a "boxy" bounding pattern
- Palm pads on the hind feet are fused together into a narrow crescent

HABITAT:
Primarily coniferous forests. Also found in mixed woods and hardwood forests, especially those with abundant snags and woodpecker holes.

OTHER SIGNS:
Scat: Scat is deposited in tree cavities. Accumulated scat, often mixed with flecks of decaying wood, may flow out of these cavities and build up on the ground. The basic form of the scat is a tiny, oval pellet less than ¼" in diameter and ⅛"–⅜" long. Similar to southern flying squirrel scat.

Sitzmark: Occasionally glides to the ground, leaving a body print or "sitzmark." These are a clear indication of flying squirrels but most trails don't have them, as flying squirrels climb to the ground more often than glide.

Feeding Sign: Like other squirrels, flying squirrels leave gnawed shells and pine cone remains behind, but don't create large middens like red squirrels. In hardwood or mixed forests, look for acorns or hickory nuts with a single, smooth hole gnawed through one end. Red squirrels typically make a ragged opening; mice usually make 2–3 openings. Larger tree squirrels usually break nut shells into pieces.

ACTIVITY:

Active year-round. Nocturnal and rarely seen, even where quite common. Most active for a few hours after sunset and again before dawn.

SIMILAR SPECIES:

Other squirrels place their front feet closer together when they bound. Southern flying squirrels (pg. 109) usually hop rather than bound and leave a narrower trail, typically under 3". Chipmunks (pg. 105) and red squirrels (pg. 117) have much less fur between their toes and palm pads and show four distinct palm pads on their hind feet; chipmunks also have smaller tracks and leave a smaller trail. Ground squirrels (pg. 101) have longer claws, less fur between their toes and palm pads, and show four distinct palm pads on their hind feet.

NOTES:

The only nocturnal tree squirrels, flying squirrels are quite common in some areas, but rarely seen. They are primarily arboreal, even more than other tree squirrels, and often avoid the ground entirely by gliding from tree to tree. Northern flying squirrels do not truly fly, but glide on folds of skin stretched between their legs, which act as a cross between a parachute and a glider wing. They are quite agile in the air, able to make sharp turns and to pull up for four-point landings on tree trunks. They commonly glide as far as 65' between trees and have been recorded gliding as far as 300' on a downhill slope.

Northern flying squirrels eat nuts, seeds, insects and large quantities of lichens and fungi. While they mostly stay in the trees, they will also forage on the ground. Sometimes they glide to the ground, but more often they climb. Solitary foragers, they are often communal nesters, especially in the winter. They usually nest in tree cavities, particularly old woodpecker holes but also build leaf nests and build roofs on abandoned bird nests. As many as 15 squirrels may share a single nest.

Southern flying squirrels are smaller than northern flying squirrels, but more aggressive. Where ranges overlap, the smaller southern squirrel tends to displace its larger cousin. Where this happens, southern flying squirrels are more likely to be found in hardwood and mixed-forest stands, while northerns are likely to live only in pure conifer stands.

max. 1¼"

min. ⅞"

FRONT

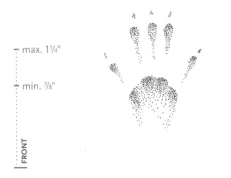

HIND TRACK
typical size

max. 2"

min. 1"

HIND

FRONT TRACK
typical size

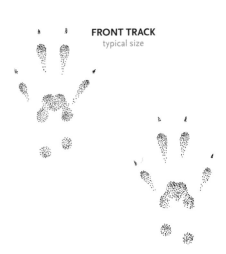

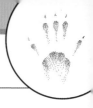

Red Squirrel

Tamiasciurus hodsonicus

Red squirrels are sentinels of the forest—raising an alarm when unknown visitors pass by. Though you usually know when red squirrels are around, it's still a pleasure to find their tracks and sign.

FRONT TRACK

LENGTH: $7/8$"–$1 1/4$", AVERAGING: $1 1/8$"; WIDTH: $1/2$"–1", AVERAGING: $3/4$"

Four toes with small claws usually showing. Palm has three pads that some-times fuse into a pyramid. Two heel pads often register, especially in deeper substrate. Middle toes point straight ahead; inner and outer toes point to the sides. The space between the pads and the toes shows little or no fur, making the pads quite distinct.

HIND TRACK

LENGTH: 1"–2", AVERAGING: $1 1/2$"; WIDTH: $3/4$"–$1 1/4$", AVERAGING: 1"

Five toes with small claws usually showing. Palm has four pads that sometimes fuse into an arc. The heel may register, especially in deeper substrate; it is covered with fur and does not have any pads. The middle three toes point straight ahead; the inner and outer toes point to the sides. The space between the pads and the toes shows little or no fur, making the pads quite distinct. Slightly larger than the front track.

GAITS

Almost always bounds, leaving a distinctive squirrel trail pattern. Front feet usually register one slightly in front of the other. When they register side by side, there is a bit of space between them. Hind feet usually register in front of and outside the front feet. In deep snow, hind feet may land in the same holes as the front feet, and

QUICK ID TIPS:

- Distinctive squirrel trail pattern: front tracks often side by side with hind tracks wider apart and ahead of the front
- Typical squirrel track with 4 long toes on the front foot and 5 on the hind
- Trails begin and end at the base of a tree

BOUND ⟩⟩⟩⟩⟩⟩⟩⟩⟩⟩⟩⟩⟩⟩⟩⟩⟩⟩⟩⟩⟩

their feet often drag on the outside of the trail, leaving an H-shaped imprint. May also tunnel in deep snow.

HABITAT:

Especially common in coniferous forests. Also found in mixed forests, hardwood forests, parkland, orchards and tree plantations, and hedgerows.

OTHER SIGNS:

Scat: Frequently used to mark prominent locations along well-used trails, both on the ground and in trees. The typical form is a small, smooth pellet about 1/8"–1/4" in diameter and 1/4"–3/8" long that is difficult to distinguish from other squirrels' scat. In winter, fresh scat often "dissolves" on snow, leaving a small, brown patch.

Feeding Sign: Red squirrels commonly feed at a prominent perch in their territory. This may be a tree branch, or an elevated rock, stump or log. Large quantities of food remnants collect at these locations. In conifer forests, these "middens" consist almost entirely of pine cone remnants. In hardwood or mixed forests, look for acorns or hickory nuts with a single, ragged hole gnawed through one end. Flying squirrels typically make a smooth opening and mice usually make 2 or 3 openings. Larger tree squirrels usually break such shells into pieces.

Digs: Red squirrels frequently dig small holes in the ground. These holes are difficult to distinguish from digs made by other animals.

Nests: Red squirrels may build tree nests, especially in conifers. Nests are usually made of grass and shredded bark and lined with fur and feathers.

ACTIVITY:
Active year-round. May hole up during inclement weather. Diurnal.

SIMILAR SPECIES:
Gray and fox squirrel tracks (pgs. 121–127) are usually larger with a wider trail. Their hind feet are bald and have two small heel pads. Their front feet have larger, more bulbous pads and appear more robust, even when they are similar in size. Flying squirrels have fused palm pads on the hind track, forming a narrower, smoother arc, and their feet are much furrier. Northern flying squirrels (pg. 113) usually place their front feet wider apart when bounding, leaving a boxier trail. Southern flying squirrels (pg. 109) are smaller, and hop, rather than bound, leaving a pattern with the front feet in front of the hind. Chipmunk (pg. 105) tracks are smaller.

NOTES:
Conspicuous and noisy forest dwellers, red squirrels are highly territorial and known for their habit of energetically scolding intruders. They defend their territories vigorously against other red squirrels, sharing their homes only for mating and raising young. Primarily arboreal, they nest in tree cavities, but also use fallen trees, leaf nests, and sometimes underground burrows. Red squirrels primarily feed on pine nuts, caching large quantities for winter. They cut green cones in fall and bury them in damp earth or hoard them in tree cavities, logs or root tangles. They typically feed perched on a particular branch, rock, stump or log near their cache. Over time, large middens (piles of food remains) build up at these sites. Red squirrels supplement their diet with nuts, seeds, berries, fungi, birds eggs and nestlings. They are known to eat *Amanita* mushrooms, which are deadly to humans, and cache them on exposed tree branches. They have even been observed making maple syrup by gnawing through the bark of sugar maples to create a trickle of sap, then returning to feed when most of the water has evaporated.

BOUND

max. 1⁵/₈"

min. 1"

FRONT

FRONT TRACK
typical size

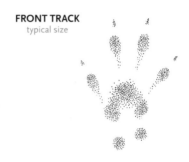

max. 2½"

min. 1"

HIND

HIND TRACK
typical size

RANGE

Eastern Gray Squirrel
Sciurus carolinensis

This is a familiar tree squirrel, common in parks and backyards and well known for its ability to raid bird feeders. Their trail pattern is easily recognizable and is a common sight throughout their range.

FRONT TRACK
LENGTH: 1"–1⅝", **AVERAGING:** 1¼"; **WIDTH:** ½"–1¼", **AVERAGING:** ¾"

Four toes with small claws usually showing. Palm has three pads that sometimes fuse into a pyramid. Two heel pads often register, especially in deeper substrate. Middle toes point straight ahead, while inner and outer toes point to the sides. There is little to no fur between the pads and the toes, making the pads quite distinct.

HIND TRACK
LENGTH: 1"–2½", **AVERAGING:** 1½"; **WIDTH:** ⅞"–1½", **AVERAGING:** 1⅛"

Five toes with small claws usually showing. Palm has four pads that sometimes fuse into an arc. Heel may register, especially in deeper substrate. In summer, the heel is not furred and two small heel pads may show; in winter, it may be less distinct. The middle three toes point straight ahead; inner and outer toes point to the sides. There is little to no fur between the pads and the toes, making the pads quite distinct. Slightly larger than the front track.

GAITS
Generally travels in a bound, but occasionally slows to a walk. Bound leaves a distinctive squirrel trail pattern. Front feet register side by side with a bit of space between them, or one slightly in front of the other. Hind feet register in front of and to the outside of front feet. In deep snow, hind may

---

QUICK ID TIPS:
- Distinctive squirrel trail pattern: front tracks often side by side; hind tracks are wider apart and ahead of the front tracks
- Typical squirrel track with 4 long toes on the front foot and 5 on the hind
- Trails begin and end at the base of a tree

BOUND

land in the same holes as the front feet, and often drag on the outside of the trail, creating an H-shaped imprint.

HABITAT:

Hardwood and mixed forests with nut-bearing trees, especially oak-hickory. Also common in parks, suburbs and cities with scattered large trees.

OTHER SIGNS:

Scat: Deposited at random and may be seen anywhere along travel routes. Scat is typically a small, smooth pellet about 1/8"–1/4" in diameter and 1/4"–3/8" long; it is difficult to distinguish from scat of other squirrels. In winter, fresh scat often "dissolves" on snow, leaving a small, brown patch.

Feeding Signs: Look for the gnawed shells of acorns, hickory nuts, walnuts, beechnuts or pecans littering the ground. Gray squirrels also feed on corn, often eating only the germ end of the kernels, leaving the rest. Fox squirrels, by contrast, eat the whole kernel when they feed on corn.

Digs: Gray squirrels leave behind small, shallow holes in snow or earth where they retrieved cached nuts during winter and spring.

Nests: Gray squirrels build large nests of leaves woven together with small branches. Nests are about 12" in diameter, quite sturdy, nearly weatherproof and often difficult to see in summer but obvious in winter. Most squirrels use more than one shelter; some may be shared. In summer, they also build looser, open leaf platforms that are less durable and provide less protection.

ACTIVITY:
Active year-round. Diurnal. Most active in the morning and evening.

SIMILAR SPECIES:
Fox squirrel tracks (pg. 125) are usually larger but similar and may not be distinguishable; use range, habitat and behavioral clues to identify prints. Red squirrel tracks (pg. 117) are generally smaller with a smaller trail, but sizes overlap. The front track usually appears more delicate, with smaller, less bulbous pads, and the hind track shows a fully furred heel with no heel pads. Cottontail rabbits (pg. 137) usually make a longer track pattern with the front feet placed one in front of the other; when the front feet are side by side, they generally touch.

NOTES:
Common and widespread, the eastern gray squirrel has adapted extremely well to human development and is found even in large cities. Primarily arboreal, they spend the majority of their lives in trees, but come to the ground frequently to forage and are most active on the ground in fall when caching nuts, and in winter when retrieving caches.

Gray squirrels rely on cached nuts to sustain them through winter. In fall, gray squirrels cache individual nuts in shallow depressions. They retrieve the nuts in winter by smell, rather than memory, and may recover nuts buried by others as often as their own. While most nuts are recovered, enough viable seeds remain to be an important source of new tree plantings.

In addition to nuts, gray squirrels eat buds, flowers, bark, and occasionally insects, bird eggs or nestlings, and tend to feed on one food at a time, rotating seasonally. Frequent visitors to bird feeders, they can work around nearly any form of "squirrel proofing." Though generally solitary, gray squirrels often congregate at good feeding locations and may den communally in winter. They den in trees year-round, using tree cavities or leaf nests. In winter, squirrels in the northern parts of our region may use only tree cavities.

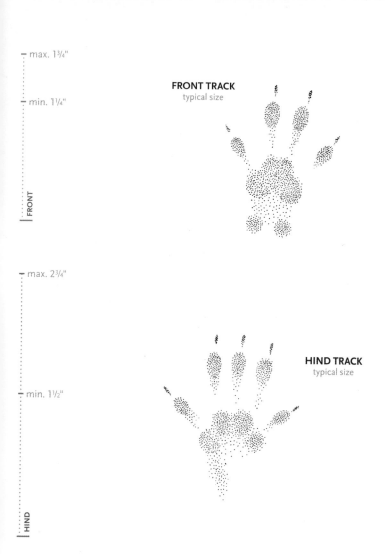

max. 1¾"

min. 1¼"

FRONT

FRONT TRACK
typical size

max. 2¾"

HIND TRACK
typical size

min. 1½"

HIND

Eastern Fox Squirrel
Sciurus niger

This large tree squirrel is expanding its range in the Midwest, sometimes displacing the smaller, but otherwise similar, gray squirrel. However, they remain much less common in cities than gray squirrels.

FRONT TRACK
LENGTH: 1¼"–1¾", **AVERAGING:** 1½"; **WIDTH:** ¾"–1½", **AVERAGING:** 1"

Four toes with small claws usually showing. Palm has three pads that sometimes fuse into a chevron. Two heel pads often register in deep substrate. Middle toes point ahead; inner and outer toes point to sides. There is little to no fur between pads and toes, making the pads distinct.

HIND TRACK
LENGTH: 1½"–2¾", **AVERAGING:** 1¾"; **WIDTH:** 1"–1¾", **AVERAGING:** 1¼"

Five toes with small claws usually showing. Palm has four pads that sometimes fuse into an arc. The heel may register in deeper substrate. In summer, heel is not furred and two small heel pads may show; in winter, heel may be less distinct. The middle three toes point ahead; inner and outer toes point to the sides. There is little to no fur between pads and toes, making the pads distinct. Slightly larger than the front foot.

GAITS
Usually bounds, leaving a distinctive tree squirrel pattern. Front feet generally register side by side with a bit of space between them. Hind feet register in front of and to the outsides of the front feet. Sometimes walks while foraging. In deep snow, may create a single body print with the feet dragging on the outside of the trail, creating an "H"-shaped imprint.

QUICK ID TIPS:
- Distinctive squirrel trail pattern: front tracks often side by side with hind tracks wider apart and ahead of the front tracks
- Typical squirrel track with 4 long toes on the front foot and 5 on the hind
- Trails begin and end at the base of a tree

BOUND

HABITAT:

Open hardwood forests, especially oak-hickory. Found in suburbs with large trees; avoids woods with a closed canopy or dense underbrush.

OTHER SIGNS:

Scat: Scat is deposited at random and may be seen anywhere along travel routes. Typical form is a small, smooth pellet about $1/8"$–$1/4"$ in diameter and $1/4"$–$3/8"$ long, and difficult to distinguish from that of other squirrels. In winter, fresh scat often "dissolves" on snow, leaving a small, brown patch.

Feeding Signs: Look for the gnawed shells of acorns, hickory nuts, walnuts, beechnuts or pecans littering the ground. Fox squirrels also feed on corn, leaving behind only the cob and scattered debris; gray squirrels, by contrast, often eat only the germ end of the kernels.

Digs: In winter and spring, fox squirrels dig up cached nuts, leaving behind small, shallow holes in the snow or earth.

Nests: Fox squirrels build large nests of leaves woven together with small branches. Difficult to see in the summer as they blend into the canopy, they are quite obvious in winter. Nests typically measure about 12" in diameter, are quite sturdy and nearly weatherproof.

ACTIVITY:

Active year-round. Diurnal. Most active in morning and late afternoon.

SIMILAR SPECIES:

Gray squirrel tracks (pg. 121) range somewhat smaller, but are very similar and may not be distinguishable. Use range, habitat and behavioral clues to help identify prints. Red squirrel tracks (pg. 117) are generally smaller with a smaller trail, but may overlap in size. The front track usually looks more delicate, with smaller, less bulbous pads. Hind track shows a fully furred heel with no heel pads. Cottontail rabbits (pg. 137) usually make a longer track pattern, with their front feet placed one in front of the other. When they do place their front feet side by side, they generally touch.

NOTES:

The fox squirrel is slightly larger than the gray squirrel, but the tracks and sign of these close relatives are nearly identical. Like gray squirrels, fox squirrels have adapted well to human habitation, though they haven't adapted to cities as well as their smaller cousins. In natural environments, fox squirrels prefer open woods or savannah with little ground cover and some space between trees, while gray squirrels frequent denser woods with a closed canopy and heavier underbrush. Not surprisingly, fox squirrels spend more time on the ground and tend to wander farther from trees than gray squirrels do.

Fox squirrels feed mainly on nuts, especially acorns and hickory nuts, supplementing their diet with seeds, fruits, buds and fungi. They cache nuts in the fall to last through the winter. Nuts are usually buried individually, but sometimes large caches of nuts are stored in tree cavities.

Fox squirrels often den in tree cavities, especially in winter, and they also build leaf nests, which are similar to those made by gray squirrels. Fox squirrels typically use between 3 and 6 leaf nests, in addition to tree cavity dens. Each nest may be used by several different animals, though usually at different times. Like gray squirrels, fox squirrels are solitary animals; their apparent collective feeding behavior is a response to concentrated food sources, such as a nut tree in season.

BOUND

max. 1½"

min. 1"

FRONT

max. 2"

min. 1"

HIND

FRONT TRACK
typical size

HIND TRACK
typical size

Black-tailed Prairie Dog
Cynomys ludovicianus

Once ubiquitous across the Great Plains, prairie dog "towns" are now quite rare. Wherever these large burrowing squirrels still reside, their expansive communal burrows are unmistakable.

FRONT TRACK
LENGTH: 1"–1½", **AVERAGING:** 1¼"; **WIDTH:** ⅞"–1⅜", **AVERAGING:** 1⅛"

Four toes with long, prominent claws. Three palm pads form a pyramid behind the toes. Two heel pads sometimes register. Toes angle inward and track has a distinct asymmetry. The outer toe is set farthest back on the foot. There is little fur between the pads, making them quite distinct.

HIND TRACK
LENGTH: 1"–2", **AVERAGING:** 1½"; **WIDTH:** ⅞"–1⅜", **AVERAGING:** 1⅛"

Five toes with claws. Palm has four pads that form an arc behind toes. Heel is covered with fur and sometimes registers. The middle three toes point slightly inward; inner and outer toes point farther to the sides. The space between the pads and toes shows little or no fur, making pads distinct. Similar in size to front foot.

GAITS
Walks most of the time with the hind track usually covering or partially covering the front track. May lope when covering open ground and bound when fleeing. Drags its feet when walking in snow.

QUICK ID TIPS:
- Asymmetrical, but distinctly squirrel-like track
- Lives in enormous "towns" made up of prominent burrows
- Trails reliably begin and end at a burrow entrance

WALK

HABITAT:
Shortgrass prairies and well-grazed grasslands.

OTHER SIGNS:
Scat: Basic form of the scat is a pellet, about $\frac{1}{4}"-\frac{1}{2}"$ in diameter and $\frac{1}{2}"-2"$ long. Softer scat may clump or string together, sometimes forming long chains. Scat are dropped near burrow entrances and accumulate throughout towns.

Towns: Prairie dogs live in unmistakable collections of colonial burrows called "towns." Some burrow entrances are flush to the ground, but others have a large mound of excavated dirt around them and look like tiny volcanoes. In the Midwest, these "rim crater" burrows are unique to black-tailed prairie dogs. Burrow entrances typically measure 4"–6" across.

ACTIVITY:
Active year-round, but may hole up in its burrow for a few days during inclement weather. Primarily diurnal. Most active in the morning and evening during hot weather. Active all day during cooler weather.

SIMILAR SPECIES:
Ground squirrels (pg. 101) typically bound when traveling, walking only

when foraging, and their tracks are smaller. Larger tree squirrels (pgs. 121–127) also bound and have more symmetrical tracks with shorter, slimmer claws.

NOTES:

The signs of this highly communal squirrel are unmistakable. Prairie dogs live in large colonial burrow systems called "towns" that may contain several thousand individuals and cover more than 100 acres. Each town is divided into wards and each ward is further divided into coteries, or family groups. Coteries are made up of a male, one to four females, and pups and yearlings. Members of a ward collectively care for burrow systems, groom each other, and "kiss" one another in greeting, touching noses, then incisors, together.

Prairie dogs are semi-fossorial, spending much of their lives underground, and rarely stray far from their burrows, which provide protection from the elements and predators. For added safety, they clear the area around their burrows of vegetation for an unobstructed view of the surroundings. Highly vocal, they have a well-developed system of alarms to warn each other of danger.

Prairie dogs almost exclusively eat the roots and leaves of green plants, especially grasses, which they can consume in great quantities. Though they don't hibernate, they put on large stores of fat in the fall to sustain them through the lean winter. Their voracious appetite for grass and their habit of clearing away vegetation has put them at odds with ranchers. Prairie dog populations spiked in the 1800s after extermination of the bison. As competition with cattle grew, prairie dogs became the targets of extermination campaigns; populations declined more than 90 percent, nearly leading to the extinction of their traditional predator, the black-footed ferret. Today, black-tailed prairie dogs are quite rare, inhabiting only about 2 percent of their historic range.

Some ranchers still poison prairie dogs, but most protect prairie dog towns, recognizing that moderate populations enhance rangeland. With the ferret all but gone, the prairie dog's primary predators are now coyotes, bobcats, eagles, hawks, snakes and badgers.

max. 2½"

min. 1⅝"

FRONT

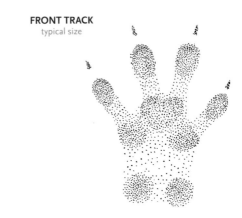

FRONT TRACK
typical size

max. 2¾"

min. 1⅝"

HIND

HIND TRACK
typical size

Woodchuck
Marmota monax

Woodchucks are the largest member of the squirrel family in the Midwest. Their sizable burrows often give away their presence, and it is also common to see this diurnal rodent sunning itself on warm days.

FRONT TRACK
LENGTH: 1⅝"–2½", **AVERAGING:** 2"; **WIDTH:** 1⅛"–1⅞", **AVERAGING:** 1½"

Four toes with prominent claws usually showing. Distinctive squirrel shape; the two middle toes point forward and the inner and outer toes point to the sides. The inner toe is farther forward on the foot than the outer toe, and all the toes angle slightly inward. Palm pads are distinct, showing two closely spaced leading lobes and two widely spaced trailing lobes. Two heel pads often register.

HIND TRACK
LENGTH: 1⅝"–2¾", **AVERAGING:** 2¼"; **WIDTH:** 1¼"–1⅞", **AVERAGING:** 1½"

Five toes with claws usually showing. Three middle toes point forward and inner and outer toes point farther to the sides. Palm pads are usually distinct and form a broad arc close to the toes. Trailing edge of palm pads may be indistinct. Heel occasionally registers, showing two heel pads. Similar in size to the front track.

GAITS

Walks most of the time with the hind track next to or partially covering the front track. May trot or lope across open ground and may bound when fleeing. Trots look like the walking pattern, but with a longer stride and slightly narrower trail. Bounding pattern is similar to a raccoon's.

QUICK ID TIPS:
- Largest squirrel-like track in our region
- 4 long toes on front feet, 5 on hind, with outside toes set farther back and pointing to the sides while middle toes point forward
- Front tracks are asymmetrical and have prominent claws

WALK

HABITAT:
Prefers open, dry, sloping ground. Found in fields, meadows, suburbs, parks and brushy forest edges. Occasionally found in heavily wooded areas.

OTHER SIGNS:
Scat: Woodchucks usually defecate underground, using one of the many chambers of their extensive burrow system as a latrine. They sometimes deposit scat near the entrance to their burrow, but usually bury it when they do. Scat varies in size, consistency and color depending on diet, but the typical form is a cylinder ½"–¾" in diameter and 1½"–2½" long.

Burrows: Most woodchuck burrows have many entrances, each measuring 6"–12" across. Main entrances usually have large, obvious throw mounds of dirt in front of them, while others, used for a quick escape, may be inconspicuous. Burrows may be very large—up to 5' deep and 30' long—and contain multiple tunnels and chambers.

ACTIVITY:
Hibernates though the winter, often emerging in spring while there is still snow on the ground. Diurnal. Usually most active in early morning and late afternoon. May sun itself through midday.

SIMILAR SPECIES:

The raccoon's bounding gait pattern (pg. 207) looks very similar to the woodchuck's, but raccoons have 5 toes on their front feet. Other squirrels have much smaller tracks.

NOTES:

Whether you call it a groundhog or a woodchuck, this large burrowing member of the squirrel family has a prominent place in popular culture. The name groundhog marks the only U.S. holiday to honor a rodent, while the name woodchuck gives us a well-known tongue-twister. Despite the tongue-twister, the name woodchuck has nothing to do with either wood or chucking, but instead comes from *wuchak*, the Algonquin Indian name for the animal.

Woodchucks are semi-fossorial, digging large, elaborate burrows that they never stray far from and in which they spend the majority of their lives. Though not territorial, they are solitary and defend their burrows from other woodchucks. Frequently, however, these burrows are used by other species after they have been vacated, and sometimes while the original owners are still using them.

Woodchucks are herbivores, and feed primarily on grasses and herbs, such as clover, alfalfa and common plantain. They are good swimmers and capable climbers, and often climb high into shrubs or trees to forage or view the surroundings. In fall, they put on a heavy layer of fat to sustain them through winter hibernation. While they usually spend summers in meadows, pastures and fields, winter hibernation dens are often dug on higher ground that is less susceptible to spring flooding. When hibernating, their body temperature falls to 40°F, their heart rate drops to 4 beats per minute, and breathing may slow to just 10 breaths per hour. They emerge from hibernation in early spring, often when there's still snow on the ground.

Woodchucks are preyed on by foxes and other medium-sized predators, but it's likely more are killed by cars.

max. 1¾"

min. ⅞"

FRONT

FRONT TRACK
typical size

max. 3¼"

min. 1¼"

HIND

HIND TRACK
typical size

Cottontail Rabbits

Sylvilagus spp.

Famously prolific breeders, cottontails are among the most common and well-known mammals in the Midwest. Found almost everywhere, their bounding gait leaves a distinctive and easily recognizable pattern of tracks.

FRONT TRACK

LENGTH: $7/8$"–$1^3/4$", AVERAGING: $1^1/4$"; WIDTH: $5/8$"–$1^1/4$", AVERAGING: $3/4$"

Four toes with small claws sometimes showing. Foot is heavily furred making palm pads indistinct and giving the track a uniform egg-shaped appearance. Toe pads are frequently indistinct as well, but usually show in good substrate. Toes are arranged asymmetrically, with the outermost toe set much farther back than the others. A tiny fifth toe occasionally registers far back on the inside of the track. Often much shorter than the hind track.

HIND TRACK

LENGTH: $1^1/4$"–$3^1/4$", AVERAGING: N/A; WIDTH: $3/4$"–$1^5/8$", AVERAGING: $1^1/8$"

Four toes with small claws sometimes showing. Front edge of the track is often pointy, except when the toes are spread, making the track somewhat egg-shaped. Foot is heavily furred, making the palm pads indistinct. Toe pads may be indistinct as well. The outermost toe is set the farthest back, but much less than on the front track. The furry heel registers inconsistently, making track length range widely, whereas the width measurement is more consistent.

GAITS

Bounds almost exclusively, creating one of the most recognizable gait patterns. Front feet typically register one in front of the other. When they register side by side, they usually touch. The hind feet generally register

QUICK ID TIPS:

- Typical rabbit group pattern: egg-shaped tracks with indistinct pads forming triangular groups
- Larger hind tracks often come to a sharp point in the front, except when toes are spread
- Smaller front feet are usually either touching or register one in front of the other

in front of the front feet, giving the group a triangular shape. Occasionally walks for short distances.

HABITAT:
Can be found anywhere with a mix of dense cover and grass (for food). Ideal habitat is the edge between dense scrub and grass. Found in heavily wooded areas, they prefer farmland, pastures, hedgerows and brushland.

OTHER SIGNS:
Scat: Small, round, slightly flattened pellets composed entirely of plant material. Usually found widely scattered, unlike deer pellets. Especially abundant where rabbits feed, a single individual may produce hundreds of pellets a day. Pellets typically measure about ¹/₄"–³/₈" across.

Forms: Cottontails do not dig dens, but instead rest in shallow depressions in the ground, snow or vegetation, called forms. Usually found at the base of shrubs or in heavy vegetation, forms measure about 7" long by 5" wide.

Feeding: Cuts off vegetation at a 45° angle using its sharp incisors. Often feeds on budding twigs during the winter.

BOUND (fronts together)

ACTIVITY:

Active year-round. Predominantly crepuscular and nocturnal; most active from dusk to dawn. Seen at all times of the day and night. Especially prominent during the summer when long days necessitate daytime feeding and dense vegetation provides abundant food and cover.

SIMILAR SPECIES:

Snowshoe hares (pg. 141) and Black-tailed jackrabbits (pg. 145) leave longer hind tracks, and their tracks and track patterns are larger overall. Tree squirrels (pgs. 109–127) leave similar track patterns, but usually place their front feet side by side and farther apart. Their hind tracks have 5 toes and a less pointed shape.

NOTES:

Well adapted to humans, eastern cottontails are common in suburban and even urban areas. All cottontail species prefer to stay in or near thick cover, rarely venture far from thickets, and travel almost exclusively along well-established trails, even when chased. These trails become especially obvious in the snow as they get packed down with repeated use.

Cottontails share their distinctive gait with other members of the rabbit family. They bound almost exclusively, producing a triangle-shaped track group. Like other rabbits, the length of the hind track is highly variable, as the heel may or may not register. Hind track width and front track measurements are often better measurements for distinguishing cottontail tracks from other rabbits.

Cottontails are prolific breeders; females have a four-week pregnancy and can become pregnant again immediately after giving birth. Pups emerge from the nest at two weeks, weighing 20 percent of their adult weight, and are weaned at four weeks—by this time, the mother is ready to give birth again. A female may have an average of 3–4 litters of 4–6 pups each year. This abundance makes cottontails a primary prey for many predators; they make up the largest portion of the diet for bobcats and coyotes, and are an important food source for cougars, weasels, foxes and raptors.

The prolific breeding makes juvenile rabbits common. Cottontail habitat is often full of the tracks of immature rabbits, which can be distinguished from tracks of small rodents by track shape, gait and trail patterns.

BOUND (fronts together)

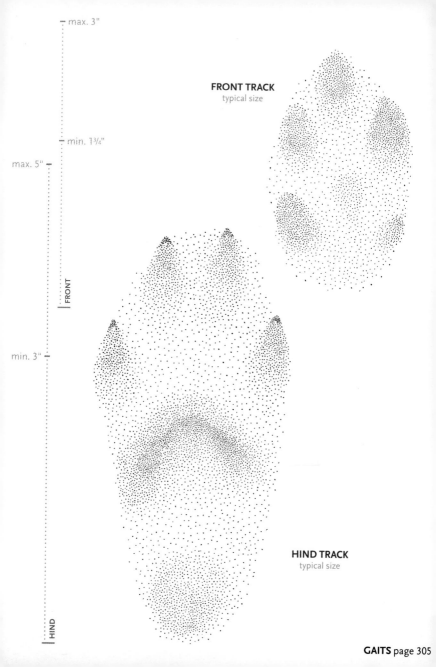

max. 3"

min. 1¾"

FRONT TRACK
typical size

max. 5"

FRONT

min. 3"

HIND

HIND TRACK
typical size

Snowshoe Hare
Lepus americanus

RANGE

The snowshoe hare is a large member of the rabbit family particularly adapted for winters with heavy snow cover. They are best known for their oversize hind feet, which can splay widely to support the animal on top of the snow.

FRONT TRACK
LENGTH: 1¾"–3", AVERAGING: 2¼"; WIDTH: 1¼"–2¼", AVERAGING: 1⅝"

Four toes with small claws sometimes showing. Foot is heavily furred making palm pads indistinct and giving the track a uniform egg-shaped appearance. Toe pads are also often indistinct, but usually show in good substrate. Toes are arranged asymmetrically, with the outermost toe set much farther back than the others. Has a tiny fifth toe on the inside of the foot whose claw occasionally registers. Usually much smaller than hind track.

HIND TRACK
LENGTH: 3"–5", AVERAGING: N/A; WIDTH: 1½"–4½", AVERAGING: N/A

Four toes with small claws sometimes showing. Foot is heavily furred making the palm pads indistinct. Toe pads may be indistinct as well. Usually much larger than front track, the hind track is typically rounder than in other rabbits. The heel may or may not register, causing the length to vary greatly. Width is even more variable as toes may spread far apart, especially in soft substrate.

GAITS
Bounds almost exclusively, leaving the distinctive rabbit group pattern. Front feet typically register one in front of the other. Hind feet register in front of front feet, giving the group a triangle shape. Occasionally walks for short distances.

> **QUICK ID TIPS:**
> • Distinctive rabbit group pattern: egg-shaped tracks with indistinct pads forming triangular groups
> • Front edge of hind track is rounder than for other rabbits
> • Hind track may be much larger than front track when toes are spread

BOUND >>>>>>>>>>>>>>>>>>>>>>>>>>>>

HABITAT:

Snowshoe hares prefer northern forests with continuous winter snow cover and low, dense vegetation. Ideal habitat has a low understory of conifers for cover and winter browse. When populations swell, hares may expand into marginal habitats and areas with less cover or more variable snow cover.

OTHER SIGNS:

Scat: Small, round, slightly flattened pellets. Usually widely scattered and especially abundant where hares feed; a single individual may produce hundreds of pellets a day. Typically measures about 3/8"–1/2" across.

Forms: Snowshoe hares do not dig dens, but rest in shallow depressions in the ground, snow or vegetation, called forms. Usually found under branches or in heavy cover, these forms measure about 9" long by 6" wide.

Feeding: Cuts off vegetation at a 45° angle using sharp incisors and strips bark from branches and tree trunks. Hares often stand on hind legs to browse; look for feeding signs up to 2' above the peak winter snowpack.

ACTIVITY:

Active year-round. Predominantly crepuscular and nocturnal. Most active at dusk and before dawn. Seen at all times of the day and night, especially during the summer when populations swell, and long days necessitate daytime feeding and lush vegetation provides abundant food and cover.

SIMILAR SPECIES:

Jackrabbits (pgs. 145–151) typically show less difference in size between front and hind tracks, but may leave similar tracks and trails, making range and habitat important clues. Black-tailed jackrabbits are unlikely to overlap in range. White-tailed jackrabbits prefer open habitats, and usually leave longer gait patterns due to their longer legs. Cottontail tracks (pg. 137) are generally smaller and toes come to a sharper "point."

NOTES:

The snowshoe hare gets its name from its feet, which are specially adapted for deep snow cover; these hares are seldom found in regions without a continuous winter snowpack. In soft substrates, such as loose snow, a snowshoe hare may spread its toes to nearly three times their normal width, leaving tracks the size of a large dog.

Snowshoe hares are remarkably well adapted to their northern range. Their coats change color with the seasons, from dirty brown in the summer to snow white in the winter. They also subsist remarkably well on meager winter browse. In the spring and summer, snowshoe hares feed primarily on herbaceous plants, supplemented with the buds and emerging leaves of trees and shrubs. In the winter, when succulent vegetation has died back or is buried in snow, they browse on conifer needles and tree bark.

Like other members of the rabbit family, snowshoe hares are prolific breeders. Females become sexually mature at one year of age and typically give birth to two or three litters of 3–6 pups a year. The young begin to disperse in mid to late summer, often moving into more marginal habitats with less cover. The hare's prolific reproduction makes it an important food source for many predators, especially lynx, fox, coyote, weasels, bobcats and owls. They rely primarily on stealth and camouflage for safety and generally stay in dense cover, especially during daytime. Newborn pups leave the birth nest within a few days and find a hiding place nearby. Snowshoe hares are solitary, but may live in close proximity, and frequently have overlapping ranges. Local populations appear to have a dominance hierarchy, with dominant hares occupying the best habitat—but hares display little overt territoriality.

BOUND (fast)

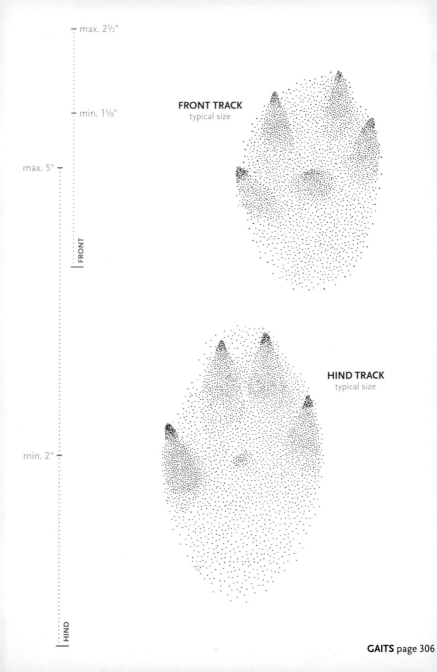

max. 2½"

min. 1⅝"

FRONT TRACK
typical size

max. 5"

FRONT

HIND TRACK
typical size

min. 2"

HIND

Black-tailed Jackrabbit
Lepus californicus

A creature of the open plains, the black-tailed jackrabbit depends on speed and dexterity for survival. Its long, supple legs and fluid movement leave behind a remarkable variety of gait and trail patterns.

FRONT TRACK
LENGTH: 1⁵/₈"–2¹/₂", AVERAGING: 2"; WIDTH: 1¹/₄"–1³/₄", AVERAGING: 1¹/₂"

Four toes with small claws usually showing. Foot is heavily furred, making palm and toe pads indistinct, though toes usually show in good substrate. Toes are arranged asymmetrically, with the outermost toe set much farther back than the others. A tiny fifth toe occasionally registers on the inside of the track. Smaller than hind track, but may have similar dimensions in shallow substrate.

HIND TRACK
LENGTH: 2"–5", AVERAGING: N/A; WIDTH: 1¹/₄"–2¹/₂", AVERAGING: 1³/₄"

Four toes with small claws often showing. Heavily furred foot makes palm and toe pads indistinct, though toes generally show in good substrate. The outermost toe is set the farthest back. Track's front edge is pointy, except when toes spread. Heel usually doesn't show in shallow substrates but sometimes registers.

GAITS
Typically uses a modified bound where one hind foot touches down just before the other, creating distinct variations on the typical rabbit bounding pattern. Because the hind feet don't land at the same time, the hind tracks are offset and this gait may be more properly considered a gallop. Black-tailed jackrabbits create a remarkable diversity of bounding and galloping gait patterns and a tremendous variety of trails. They frequently alternate

QUICK ID TIPS:
- Heavily furred feet make palm, and sometimes toe pads, indistinct
- Tracks are asymmetrical, with the outer toes set farthest back
- Displays a range of gait patterns, varying widely from the typical rabbit trail

BOUND/GALLOP

long, fast bounds with shorter, higher jumps. These so-called "spy jumps" help them get a better view of the surroundings. Occasionally walks for short distances.

HABITAT:

Arid plains and brushland with sparse vegetation. Prefers open environments with some shrubs, such as sagebrush or juniper, for cover.

OTHER SIGNS:

Scat: Small, round, slightly flattened pellets. Usually widely scattered, but may be abundant in feeding locations. A single individual may produce hundreds of pellets a day. Typically measures about 3/8"–1/2" across.

Forms: Jackrabbits don't dig dens, but rest in shallow depressions in the ground called forms. Usually found under low branches or in heavy vegetation, forms measure about 12" long by 6" wide and are sometimes excavated a few inches deep.

Feeding: Cuts off vegetation at a 45° angle using sharp incisors and strips bark from branches and tree trunks.

ACTIVITY:

Active year-round. Predominantly crepuscular and nocturnal. Can be seen at any time, however. Typically beds down during the hottest, coldest or windiest weather.

SIMILAR SPECIES:

White-tailed jackrabbits (pg. 149) and snowshoe hares (pg. 141) have similar tracks and trails, making range and habitat important clues. White-tailed jackrabbits usually leave slightly larger tracks and prefer habitats with more vegetation and colder winters with lasting snow cover. Snowshoe hares are unlikely to overlap in range with black-tailed jackrabbits and the front and hind tracks vary more greatly in size. Cottontail tracks (pg. 137) are generally smaller with the toes coming to a sharper "point." Gaits are usually more compact.

NOTES:

Black-tailed jackrabbits are well adapted for life in the desert and on arid plains. Like all members of the rabbit family, they are prolific breeders and an important food source for many predators, especially coyotes.

Black-tailed jackrabbits prefer open habitats and rely heavily on speed, evasion and their acute senses to escape predators. Their long, loose limbs allow them to move at high speeds with remarkable dexterity. Black-tailed jackrabbits have been clocked running as fast as 40 mph.

They also display some of the most fluid body movements of any species in the Midwest, moving seamlessly between various bounds and gallops. These many gaits leave an amazing variety of trail patterns but often leave indistinct tracks. Because of this, prints are easily confused with those of other animals, especially members of the dog family. Individual tracks can easily resemble a canine's and some galloping trail patterns look similar to a diagonal trot.

Black-tailed jackrabbits feed on grasses, herbs, scrub and cacti. Even on this apparently meager diet, they produce 2–7 litters of 2–5 pups each year. Unlike cottontails, black-tailed jackrabbit pups may leave the nest after 24 hours, but are not fully weaned for about 3 months. More territorial than cottontails, both males and females are sometimes seen charging and sparring. Courtship rituals are also quite vigorous, with one animal leaping high into the air as the other runs underneath.

BOUND/GALLOP

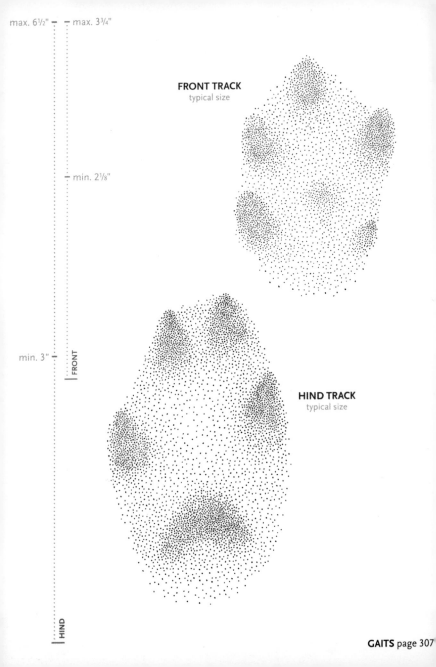

max. 6½" — max. 3¾"

min. 2⅛"

FRONT TRACK
typical size

min. 3"

FRONT

HIND TRACK
typical size

HIND

White-tailed Jackrabbit

Lepus townsendii

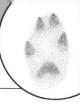

White-tailed jackrabbits are the largest member of the rabbit family in the Midwest, and exceptionally well adapted to cold weather. Their often indistinct tracks can be easily confused with those of other species.

FRONT TRACK
LENGTH: 2⅛"–3¾", **AVERAGING:** 2½"; **WIDTH:** 1½"–2½", **AVERAGING:** 1⅞"

Four toes with small claws usually showing. Foot is heavily furred making palm and toe pads indistinct, though toes usually show in good substrate. The outermost toe is set much farther back than the others, giving the track an asymmetrical appearance. A tiny fifth toe high on the inside of the foot occasionally registers. Smaller than hind track, but may have similar dimensions, especially in shallow substrates.

HIND TRACK
LENGTH: 3"–6½", **AVERAGING:** N/A"; **WIDTH:** 1½"–3", **AVERAGING:** 2"

Four toes with small claws often showing. Heavily furred foot makes pads indistinct, though toe pads usually show in good substrate. The outermost toes are set the farthest back. Front edge of the track is pointy, except when toes are spread. While the heel generally does not register in shallow substrate, it does sometimes show. Also, toes may splay widely, creating a wide range of track sizes.

GAITS

Uses a modified bound almost exclusively where one hind foot touches down just before the other, leaving a variation on the typical triangular rabbit group pattern. Because the hind feet do not land at the same time, the hind tracks are slightly offset and this gait may technically be a gallop

QUICK ID TIPS:
- Heavily furred feet make heel, and sometimes toe pads, indistinct
- Tracks are asymmetrical, with the outer toe set farther back
- Displays variations on the typical rabbit trail pattern with front feet placed one in front of the other and hind feet slightly offset

BOUND/GALLOP

rather than a bound. Sometimes lopes, which is unusual among rabbits. Occasionally walks for short distances.

HABITAT:
Grassland, shrubland and open forest of the northern plains, including cultivated fields and old pastureland. White-tailed jackrabbits are well adapted to open habitat with cold winters and persistent snow cover.

OTHER SIGNS:
Scat: Small, round, slightly flattened pellets measuring about $3/8"$–$3/4"$ across. Especially abundant where the hare feeds. Each hare may drop hundreds of widely scattered pellets each day.

Forms: Jackrabbits do not dig dens, but instead rest in shallow depressions in the ground, called forms. Usually found near low, brushy vegetation, such as sagebrush or low juniper branches, these forms are about 14" long by 8" wide and typically 2"–4" deep.

Feeding: Cuts off vegetation at a 45° angle using its sharp incisors. Strips bark from branches and tree trunks. Hares often stand on their hind legs to browse, so look for feeding sign up to 2' above peak winter snowpack.

ACTIVITY:

Active year-round. Predominantly crepuscular and nocturnal, and most active from about an hour after sunset to an hour before dawn. Can be seen at all times, especially during the spring and summer when there is abundant food, populations swell and long days necessitate daytime feeding.

SIMILAR SPECIES:

Black-tailed jackrabbits (pg. 145) and snowshoe hares (pg. 141) have similar tracks and trails making range and habitat important clues. Black-tailed jackrabbits usually leave slightly smaller tracks and prefer warmer, more arid habitat with less vegetation and less winter snowcover. Snowshoe hares usually show more size difference between the front and the hind track, tend to have more compact gait patterns because of their shorter legs, and prefer wooded areas with abundant, low cover. Cottontails (pg. 137) generally leave more compact gaits and smaller tracks with toes coming to a sharper "point."

NOTES:

White-tailed jackrabbits are the largest member of the rabbit family in the Midwest, and are well adapted to the cold. In winter, these residents of the northern plains grow a thick coat of fur that provides exceptional insulation. In the northern parts of their range, their winter coat turns even whiter than the snowshoe hare's. White-tailed jackrabbits are so well adapted to the cold that they become more active during snowstorms and high winter wind conditions—a behavior that appears to help them avoid predators that bed down during such inclement weather.

The white-tailed jackrabbit's diverse trail patterns and indistinct tracks can easily be confused with those of other animals, especially coyotes. Individual tracks can easily resemble those of a canine, and some galloping trail patterns can look surprisingly similar to a diagonal trot.

White-tailed jackrabbit populations breed synchronously, about once every 6 weeks, beginning in February or March. At breeding times, both males and females will become more mobile, and will take part in dramatic courtship displays that involve chasing and leaping. Over the course of the year, each female will produce about 3–4 litters of 4–6 pups each. Unlike cottontails, which may overlap with the jackrabbit's range, pups are born with their eyes open and may leave the nest within a few days.

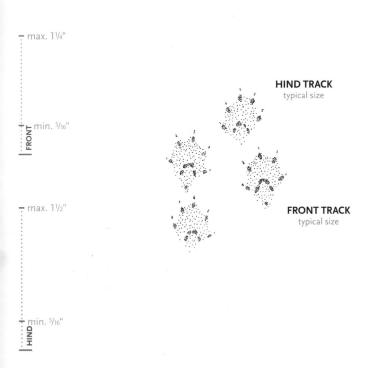

max. 1¼"

min. ⁵/₁₆"

FRONT

max. 1½"

min. ⁵/₁₆"

HIND

HIND TRACK
typical size

FRONT TRACK
typical size

Weasels
Mustela spp.

These three small species of weasels are energetic and inquisitive carnivores. Rarely seen, even though they are active by day, their erratic trails and twisted, rope-like scat often give away their presence.

FRONT TRACK
Least: LENGTH: 5/16"–1/2", AVERAGING: 3/8"; WIDTH: 5/16"–1/2", AVERAGING: 3/8"
Short-tailed: LENGTH: 7/16"–5/8", AVERAGING: 1/2"; WIDTH: 7/16"–5/8", AVERAGING: 1/2"
Long-tailed: LENGTH: 3/4"–1 1/4", AVERAGING: 7/8"; WIDTH: 5/8"–1", AVERAGING: 3/4"

Five toes with thin claws. Loosely connected palm pads form a "C" shape behind the toes. Toe and palm pads are small and often don't register clearly—especially the smallest, innermost toe. A single heel pad rarely shows. The bottom of the foot is furry, particularly in winter.

HIND TRACK
Least: LENGTH: 5/16"–1/2", AVERAGING: 3/8"; WIDTH: 5/16"–1/2", AVERAGING: 3/8"
Short-tailed: LENGTH: 7/16"–5/8", AVERAGING: 1/2"; WIDTH: 7/16"–5/8", AVERAGING: 1/2"
Long-tailed: LENGTH: 3/4"–1 1/2", AVERAGING: 7/8"; WIDTH: 5/8"–1", AVERAGING: 3/4"

Five toes with thin claws. Loosely connected palm pads form an asymmetrical arc behind the toes. The foot is heavily furred and the small pads may not register clearly. The innermost toe is the smallest, set the farthest back, and often does not register. The furry heel rarely shows. Front and hind tracks for a given animal are generally the same size and are roughly as long as they are wide. Size is useful for distinguishing between species, but there is a wide range within each species and overlap between species.

GAITS
Typically travels in a 2x2 lope, mixing long and short bounds. In deep snow, shorter bounds often show foot drag. Also "dives" into deep snow,

QUICK ID TIPS:
- Small tracks and narrow trail width
- Typically travels in a 2x2 lope with highly variable strides
- Adventurous and nosy, their winding trails explore every nook and cranny

LOPE TO BOUND

tunneling for some distance before emerging. Occasionally walks. Away from snow, may leave a 3x4 lope pattern.

HABITAT:
  Least: Primarily meadows, brushland and marshes. Occasionally forests.
  Short-tailed: Primarily coniferous or mixed deciduous-coniferous forests.
  Long-tailed: Found in forests, brushland and fields, including farmland.

OTHER SIGNS:
  Scat: Long, slender, rope-like scat made up mostly of small rodent parts. Scat is usually heavily twisted with pointy ends. Unlike scat from larger members of the weasel family, it rarely contains fruit or plant material. Scat ranges in size from 1/8"–3/8" in diameter and 3/4"–3" in length. All three species commonly form latrines near den sites and deposit scat on raised surfaces along trails.

  Caches: When prey is abundant, weasels cache excess food. Piles of mice, voles or shrews are a good sign of weasel activity.

  Snow Dives: Weasels occasionally dive into deep snow, emerging some distance away. Tunnel entrances measure about 1" in diameter.

ACTIVITY:

Active year-round. May be active at any time of day or night.

SIMILAR SPECIES:

There is a great deal of size overlap between the three weasel species, especially because males are nearly twice the size of females. Trail width, track size, range and habitat provide some clues, but it is often not possible to link weasel tracks to a specific species. Mink (pg. 157) are generally larger, but a small mink will overlap with a large long-tailed weasel. Mink may show webbing and associate more strongly with water; the bottoms of their feet have much less fur.

NOTES:

Least weasels, short-tailed weasels and long-tailed weasels are the smallest members of the weasel family. Their tracks, sign and behavior are quite similar and members of all three species are often referred to simply as "weasels." All weasels are energetic, inquisitive and voracious carnivores. Their diet consists almost entirely of small- and medium-sized mammals, supplemented with amphibians, birds and reptiles. Small but feisty predators, they may take prey up to 5 times their size. They are such an important control of local rodent populations that their genus was named *Mustela*, which means "mouse hunter."

Weasels move eagerly and erratically about the landscape, leaving twisting, winding trails. They move quickly, often stopping and standing on their hind legs to look around them, or turning sharply to head off in a new direction. Though they generally forage on the ground, weasels are capable climbers and swimmers and their trails may begin or end at the edge of a pond or the base of a tree or shrub. In winter, weasels spend much of their time foraging under the snow, where most of their prey is active.

Weasels are active off and on throughout the day and night, alternating periods of hunting with periods of resting in one of their many dens. Dens may be natural cavities or the burrows of small rodents, and usually contain a small nest made of vegetation, fur or feathers. While formidable, weasels are small and are vulnerable to predation by hawks, owls, snakes, foxes, cats and other medium-sized predators.

2X2 LOPE

FRONT TRACK
typical size

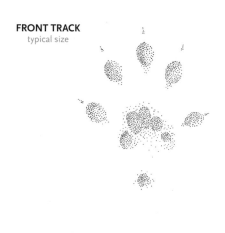

HIND TRACK
typical size

American Mink
Neovision vision

Mink can be found in aquatic habitats throughout the Midwest. Equally at home in the water and on land, they leave twisting trails that may wind across nearly every feature of the landscape.

FRONT TRACK
LENGTH: 1"–1³/₄", AVERAGING: 1³/₈"; WIDTH: ³/₄"–1⁵/₈", AVERAGING: 1³/₈"

Five toes with thin claws. Five loosely connected palm pads form a "C" shape behind the toes. Toes often splay widely. The innermost toe is smallest and may not register. A single heel pad rarely shows. Toes are webbed, and webbing may show in track. Bottom of foot is less furry than in similarly sized members of the weasel family. Slightly larger than hind track.

HIND TRACK
LENGTH: ³/₄"–1¹/₂", AVERAGING: 1¹/₈"; WIDTH: ⁷/₈"–1⁵/₈", AVERAGING: 1¹/₈"

Five toes with thin claws. Four loosely connected palm pads form an asymmetrical arc behind toes. The innermost toe is smallest, set farthest back and often does not register clearly. The heel rarely shows in the track. The foot is less furry than in other weasels and the toes are connected by webbing, which may show in the track. Slightly smaller and usually less splayed than the front track.

GAITS
Typically travels in a lope. Generally uses a 2x2 lope in deeper snow. Occasionally walks.

QUICK ID TIPS:
- Feet are less furry than other similarly sized weasels
- Commonly moves about in a 2x2 or 3x4 lope
- Closely associated with water, especially muskrat habitat

WALK

HABITAT:
Similar to muskrat habitat. Associated with wetland systems, lakes, rivers and streams, especially in forested areas. May travel long distances between bodies of water.

OTHER SIGNS:
Scat: Ranges from ¼" to nearly ½" in diameter and 1"–4" in length. Long, twisted, rope-like scat made up mostly of muskrat or small rodent parts. Less commonly contains large amounts of fruit and berry seeds, scales, feathers or crayfish shells. These scat tend to be more tubular with smoother surfaces and less twisting. Commonly deposited on rock, logs or vegetation next to water, near muskrat burrows or on beaver lodges.

Slides: Sometimes slides downhill on the snow like an otter, but does not slide on flat ground. Slides are typically 3"–5" wide.

Dens: Mink commonly den in stream banks. The entrances to these dens are typically 4" across. May also den in hollow logs or abandoned muskrat burrows. All dens are temporary as mink change dens frequently.

Snow Dives: As with the smaller weasels, mink occasionally dive into deep snow and explore under the surface, emerging some distance away. Tunnel entrances measure about 2" in diameter.

ACTIVITY:

Active year-round. Predominantly crepuscular and nocturnal. May be active during the day as well.

SIMILAR SPECIES:

Marten tracks (pg. 161) are usually larger and much more heavily furred. Marten are also highly arboreal with trails frequently beginning or ending at trees and do not generally associate with water. Weasel tracks (pg. 153) are usually smaller and the feet are more heavily furred making pads less distinct. Also, smaller weasels are less closely associated with water and tend to show more variation in their stride when loping.

NOTES:

An amphibious member of the weasel family, mink are equally at home in water and on land. They live close to water, and trails usually begin or end at the water's edge. Mink spend most of their time foraging in water but are also adept climbers and hunt on land and occasionally in trees. Their preferred prey is muskrat, but mink are opportunistic carnivores and feed on fish, frogs, crayfish, turtles, small rodents, cottontails, waterfowl, eggs, worms and insects.

Like all members of the weasel family, mink are energetic and inquisitive. Their trails explore every nook and cranny across a wide variety of terrain; a trail may weave through underbrush, cross swamps, follow streams, disappear into lakes or ponds, or even lead up a tree.

Mink are solitary and intolerant of intruders. As they move about their home ranges, mink mark their territories with a discharge from their anal glands. This discharge is nearly as strong as a skunk's, though it does not carry as far and is not quite as objectionable. Mink tolerate human habitation fairly well, and are fairly common in suburban areas with adequate open space.

Highly prized for their fur, mink were once heavily trapped. Today, most mink fur comes from farms. Though no longer trapped in significant numbers, mink are preyed upon by foxes, coyotes, wolves, fishers, bobcats, lynx and great horned owls.

3X4 LOPE

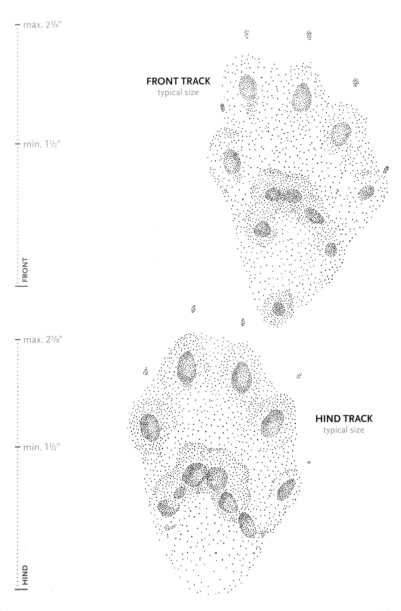

max. 2¾"

min. 1½"

FRONT

FRONT TRACK
typical size

max. 2⅝"

min. 1½"

HIND

HIND TRACK
typical size

American Marten
Martes americana

The marten is a semi-arboreal weasel of the northern boreal forests. Their trails usually display both the characteristic lopes and the erratic routes typical of members of the weasel family.

FRONT TRACK
LENGTH: 1½"–2¾", AVERAGING: 2¼"; WIDTH: 1⅜"–2½", AVERAGING: 2⅛"

Five toes with claws usually showing. The innermost toe is smallest, set farthest back and may not register. The bottom of the foot is heavily furred so toes and palm pads appear relatively small and indistinct, especially in winter. Several palm pads form an arc behind the toes. Palm pads are small and vary considerably in size and shape from one individual to the next. Pads may be fused or register individually, and are often larger on one side of the track than the other. One or two small heel pads may also register.

HIND TRACK
LENGTH: 1½"–2⅝", AVERAGING: 2"; WIDTH: 1⅜"–2½", AVERAGING: 1⅞"

Five toes with claws usually showing. The innermost toe is smallest, set even farther back than in the front track, and may not register. Heavily furred with even less developed pads than the front track. Furry heel often registers, but does not show any pads. Has a slightly different shape than the front track, but is roughly the same size.

GAITS
Travels in a 3x4 lope or a 2x2 lope, preferring the latter in deep snow. Sometimes slows to a walk.

QUICK ID TIPS:
- Commonly moves about in a 2x2 lope, especially in snow
- Arboreal, trails often begin and end at the base of trees
- Heavy fur on the bottom of the foot blurs the track and exaggerates the small size of toe and palm pads

WALK

$>>>>>>>>>>>>>>>>>>>>>>>>>>>>$

HABITAT:

Mature coniferous forests and mixed deciduous-coniferous forests with snags, deadfalls and leaf litter that provide habitat for small rodents.

OTHER SIGNS:

Scat: Long, slender, rope-like scat often made up mostly of small rodent parts. Usually heavily twisted and tapered with pointy ends. In season, martens eat large amounts of fruits and berries and produce scat that is more cylindrical with little or no twisting. Scat ranges in size from $\frac{1}{4}$" to nearly $\frac{3}{4}$" in diameter and 2"–5" in length. Martens commonly leave scat on elevated surfaces along well-used trails.

Snow Dives: Like smaller members of the weasel family, martens occasionally dive into deep snow and explore under the surface, emerging some distance away. Tunnel entrances measure about 3" in diameter.

ACTIVITY:

Active year-round. Predominantly crepuscular and nocturnal, but may be active at any time.

SIMILAR SPECIES:

Mink tracks (pg. 157) are generally smaller and show much less fur on the bottoms of the feet. Mink rarely climb trees and prefer to stay near water. Fisher tracks (pg. 165) are usually larger and show less fur. Fishers are much heavier than martens, even when track size overlaps, and are more likely to walk in deep snow, leaving a trough. Finally, fishers leave wider trails: most fisher trails are over 4", while most marten trails measure under 4". Fox tracks (pg. 217–227) can resemble marten tracks when the inner toe doesn't register, but the gait and trail patterns are quite different.

NOTES:

American martens are a highly arboreal member of the weasel family. Similar to fishers, but on a smaller scale, they are adept climbers and hunt both on the ground and in trees. Their hind feet can rotate 180°, enabling them to move down the trunks of trees headfirst like squirrels. Frequently, they jump from tree trunks rather than climb to the ground, leaving a whole-body "sitzmark" some distance away. While martens move about in the open, they rarely stray far from the forest edge, and trails usually begin or end at the base of a tree. During daylight, they usually rest in trees, sometimes using an abandoned squirrel's nest or a woodpecker's hole.

Like other members of the weasel family, martens are inquisitive, voracious predators. Their diet consists primarily of voles, snowshoe hares, squirrels and ruffed grouse. They vigorously explore root cavities, crevices, boulder jams, and other hiding places. In winter, martens also spend time foraging under snow, where much of their smaller prey is active. More omnivorous than mink or smaller members of the weasel family, martens also eat eggs, fruits, nuts, reptiles, amphibians, invertebrates and carrion. This varied diet can help distinguish marten scat.

Compared to other members of the weasel family, martens have large feet, which give them extra buoyancy in snow. Marten tracks are similar in size to fishers', even though martens weigh significantly less. Marten feet are also heavily furred, especially in winter, when their pads may almost disappear. In spring, their fur thins out and tracks may closely resemble a fisher's. Careful measurements can help distinguish between marten and fisher tracks, but be careful when measuring tracks in a 2x2 lope. In this gait, each print is an imperfect double register (a hind print superimposed on a front print) and tracks may appear larger than they actually are.

3X4 LOPE

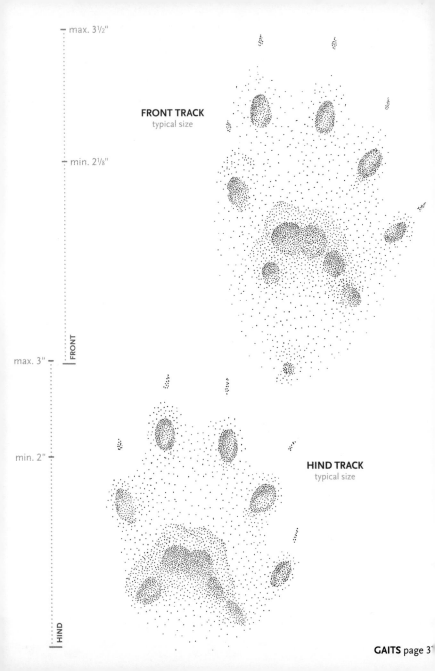

max. 3½"

min. 2⅛"

FRONT TRACK
typical size

FRONT

max. 3"

min. 2"

HIND

HIND TRACK
typical size

RANGE

Fisher

Martes pennanti

Fishers are large forest-dwelling weasels. Like most weasels, they are energetic, inquisitive predators. Their trails tend to zigzag across the landscape, as the fishers investigate every nook and cranny.

FRONT TRACK

LENGTH: 2⅛"–3½", **AVERAGING:** 2¾"; **WIDTH:** 2"–3¼", **AVERAGING:** 2½"

Five toes with claws usually showing. Palm pads form a "C" shape behind the toes. The inner toe is smallest, set farther back on the foot, and may not register. Two small heel pads sometimes register. The bottom of the foot is furred, which may blur the track's appearance somewhat. The front toes can splay widely, sometimes leaving a print as much as 4" across.

HIND TRACK

LENGTH: 2"–3", **AVERAGING:** 2½"; **WIDTH:** 1¾"–3", **AVERAGING:** 2¼"

Five toes with claws usually showing. Palm pads form an irregular "C" shape behind the toes. Smaller than front track, and less likely to splay widely. The inner toe is smallest, set even farther back than on the front foot, and may not register. There are no heel pads, but the furry heel may register. The bottom of the foot is furred and may blur the track's appearance. Slightly smaller than the front track, and less likely to splay.

GAITS

Commonly walks or lopes using either a 3x4 or a 2x2 lope. In deep snow usually uses a 2x2 lope or walks, leaving a trough. More likely than other members of the weasel family to show a variation of the 2x2 lope with one pair of feet landing far in front of the other, sometimes almost one in front of the other.

QUICK ID TIPS:

- Typical weasel track form: 5 toes with the smallest inner toe set much farther back than the others
- Commonly moves about in a 2x2 or 3x4 lope
- Arboreal: trails often begin and end at the base of trees

WALK 〉〉〉〉〉〉〉〉〉〉〉〉〉〉〉〉〉〉〉〉

HABITAT:

Forests, especially mature coniferous forests and mixed deciduous-coniferous forests with a closed canopy and abundant deadfalls.

OTHER SIGNS:

Scat: Long, slender, rope-like scat often made mostly of rodent parts. The typical form is heavily twisted and tapered with pointy ends. In season, fisher may eat large amounts of fruits and berries and produce scat that is more cylindrical with little or no twisting. Occasionally, scat contains some porcupine quills. Scat ranges in size from 1/4" to 3/4" in diameter and 2"–7" in length. Fishers commonly leave scat near den sites and in raccoon latrines. Unlike martens, they do not tend to mark prominent trails.

Scent Posts: Fishers mark small evergreen saplings along heavily used travel corridors. They bite and roll on these saplings, urinating on them as they scent, often leaving them trampled and defoliated.

ACTIVITY:

Active year-round, but activity is hindered by deep, soft snow. Predominantly nocturnal, but may be active any time of day or night.

SIMILAR SPECIES:

Mink tracks (pg. 157) are smaller. Marten tracks are usually smaller, more heavily furred, and have smaller, less defined pads. Marten also weigh less than half as much as fishers, have trails narrower than 4", and rarely walk in deep snow. Otter (pg. 169) show more difference in size between front and hind tracks, often show webbing between the toes, but not fur, and their inner hind toe is larger than the others. Otters weigh about twice as much as fishers, often show a tail drag, and frequently slide while traveling. The raccoon's (pg. 207) walk is distinctive and their tracks have longer toes and a more clearly developed inner toe and palm pad. If the fifth toe fails to register, a fisher track can resemble a bobcat track (pg. 243), but bobcat claws don't usually register. Also, bobcats rarely lope and almost never produce a 2x2 loping trail pattern.

NOTES:

Despite its name, the fisher does not fish. It is a semi-arboreal weasel similar to the American marten, but on a larger scale. Like all members of the weasel family, fishers are energetic, inquisitive predators.

Once prized for their pelts, they were nearly wiped out of during the fur trade. In recent years, they have made a significant recovery. Forest dwellers, fishers prey mostly on small- and medium-sized forest mammals, especially snowshoe hares. Voracious foragers, fishers will tear apart dead snags and rotting logs looking for squirrels, mice and other small rodents. Like martens, they are quite omnivorous and supplement their diet with birds, frogs, eggs, insects, nuts, fruits and berries. Aside from cougars, fishers are the only animals that actively prey on porcupines. While fishers kill few porcupines, each one can feed a fisher for several days.

Fishers are solitary except for mating and raising young. They travel and forage widely across large home ranges (50–150 square miles) resting in the open or taking shelter in natural cavities. They tend to follow their own well-established routes, ignoring roads and trails made by other animals. Like martens, fishers are adept climbers and females spend considerable time in trees. Larger males take to the trees less often and are much less likely to travel through the treetops.

3X4 LOPE

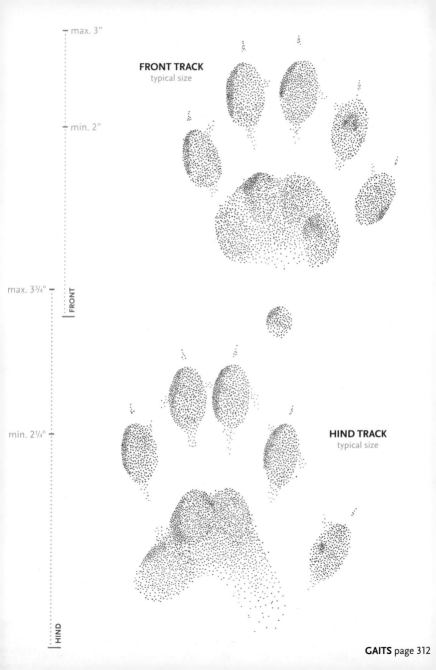

max. 3"

min. 2"

FRONT TRACK
typical size

max. 3¾" — | FRONT

min. 2¼" —

HIND TRACK
typical size

| HIND

Northern River Otter
Lontra canadensis

Famous for its playful nature, the semi-aquatic otter is the largest member of the weasel family in the Midwest. Naturally inquisitive, they will sometimes come investigate small boats they encounter.

FRONT TRACK

LENGTH: 2"–3", AVERAGING: 2½"; WIDTH: 1⅞"–3", AVERAGING: 2½"

Five toes with claws usually showing. The innermost toe is smallest and set the farthest back. Webbing may be evident between toes, but is usually more obvious on the hind tracks. Palm pads are fused together and usually show two leading lobes and two prominent trailing lobes. A small heel pad sometimes registers. Smaller than the hind track.

HIND TRACK

LENGTH: 2¼"–3¾", AVERAGING: 2⅞"; WIDTH: 2⅛"–3½", AVERAGING: 2¾"

Five toes with claws usually showing. The innermost toe may be the largest and is set much farther back than the other four. Webbing is often evident between toes. Palm pads are fused together and show two trailing lobes with the inner lobe extending much farther back than the outer lobe. Larger than the front track.

GAITS

Typically travels in a 3x4 lope, often sliding when the surface permits. Sometimes slows to a walk. May use a 2x2 lope in deep snow.

QUICK ID TIPS:
- Characteristic slides are common on otter trails, especially in the snow; may even slide uphill for short distances
- Typically travels in a 3x4 lope
- Thick, heavy tail often leaves a drag line

WALK

HABITAT:

Lakes, ponds, streams, rivers, marshes, and reservoirs with adequate shoreline cover and abundant fish. Much more common in less developed areas. When waterways freeze, otters inhabit areas with open water accessible from land.

OTHER SIGNS:

Scat: Typically found as a loose, crumbly pile of fish scales. Consistency depends on diet. Scat may range from a loose, liquid patty to a tubular scat measuring ³/₈"–1" in diameter and 3"–6" long. Scat consisting of amphibian remains are the most liquid, while scat made of crustacean remains are cylindrical and most likely to hold together.

Scent Rolls: Otters create scent posts near the water's edge in their territories. Here the otter rolls, matting down the vegetation and often forming a shallow depression. Scat is often deposited on the edges of these rolls. Frequently, otters mound or twist together vegetation that is then scented or used as a post to deposit scat.

Slides: Otters are well known for sliding down hills, and even across level ground when surfaces permit. Slides are typically 6"–10" wide and limited in length only by the terrain. On longer slides, an otter may give itself an extra push, as if swimming across the ground.

White Secretion: Otters deposit a white, sticky secretion with a strong musky odor. These secretions are usually less than 1" wide and often found near scat.

ACTIVITY:
Active year-round. Predominantly crepuscular and nocturnal. Least active around midday.

SIMILAR SPECIES:
Mink, weasel and marten tracks (pgs. 153–163) are smaller. The fisher's front and hind tracks (pg. 165) are more similar in size, do not show webbing, and the fisher's inner toe is smaller than its other toes. Fishers weigh about half as much as otters and rarely show tail drag. Raccoon (pg. 207) toes are more elongated and don't show any webbing; the raccoon's walking gait is also distinctive.

NOTES:
A famously playful and adventurous member of the weasel family, otters are completely at home in the water. They hunt in water exclusively, but come to land to den, mate and move from one water body to another. While their lives revolve around water, otters have been known to cross mountains and travel miles between bodies of water.

While widespread and fairly common, they can be quite secretive, and tend to avoid areas with significant human impact. Otters eat mostly fish, usually preferring the most abundant slow-moving fish in the area. Their diet also includes aquatic crustaceans such as crayfish, large aquatic insects, amphibians, turtles, and occasionally muskrats, beavers and waterfowl.

Efficient hunters, otters have a great deal of time and energy to play. They seem to delight in swimming and play frequently on land too, often sliding on their bellies as they travel. Otters are sometimes seen sliding down hills repeatedly—apparently out of sheer enjoyment. Otters are highly mobile and may move miles across their ranges each day—usually by water—to find optimal foraging, seek a mate, or simply to swim and play.

Tracks and sign are usually concentrated at scent roll sites and along runs between water systems. Runs are most apparent at the narrowest point between two bodies of water.

3X4 LOPE

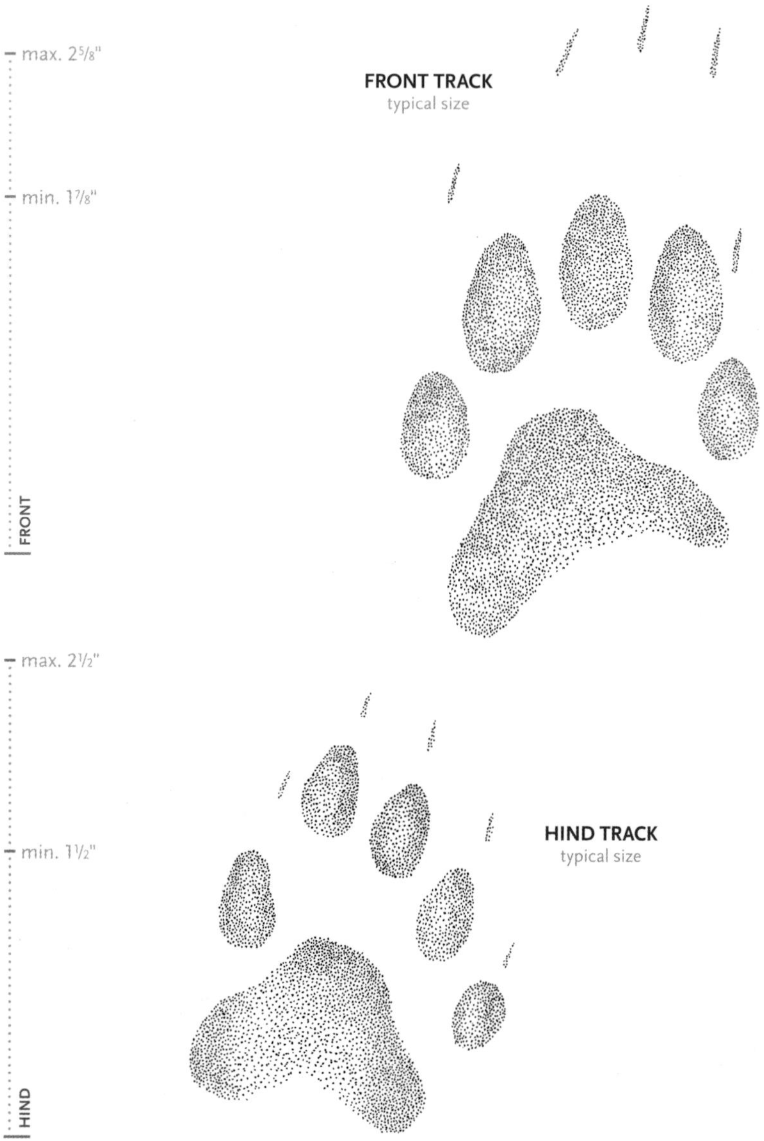

max. 2⁵/₈"

min. 1⁷/₈"

FRONT TRACK
typical size

FRONT

max. 2¹/₂"

min. 1¹/₂"

HIND TRACK
typical size

HIND

RANGE

American Badger
Taxidea taxus

The badger is the most fossorial carnivore in the Midwest, spending much of its time underground. Though generally nocturnal, their prominent burrows, which have wide entrances and large mounds of earth outside, reliably give away their presence.

FRONT TRACK
LENGTH: 1⁷/₈"–2⁵/₈", AVERAGING: 2³/₈"; WIDTH: 1¹/₂"–2³/₄", AVERAGING: 2¹/₈"

Five toes with large, prominent claws. The innermost toe is smallest and may not register. A single large palm pad with two trailing lobes is wider than it is tall. Toes rarely splay. Much larger than the hind track. Prominent claws may add 1" or more to the length of the track.

HIND TRACK
LENGTH: 1¹/₂"–2¹/₂", AVERAGING: 2"; WIDTH: 1¹/₄"–2¹/₄", AVERAGING: 1³/₄"

Five toes with claws usually showing. The innermost toe is set much farther back than the other four and often doesn't register. A single large palm pad has two trailing lobes. Much smaller than the front track.

GAITS
Walks when foraging. Often travels in a trot. Lopes when alarmed. Walks and trots with feet pointed sharply inward (toed-in)—a defining characteristic of the species. Walks in deep snow, leaving a prominent trough.

QUICK ID TIPS:
- Walks with toes turned in sharply
- Long claws leave prominent marks
- Front track is significantly larger than hind track

WALK

HABITAT:
Open plains and prairies, and occasionally the edge of open woodlands.

OTHER SIGNS:
Scat: Badger scat is easy to confuse with that of other similarly sized carnivores; look for other badger sign associated with it. Scat varies in size from ³/₈"–³/₄" in diameter and 3"–6" long. Usually twisted, pointy and partially segmented, it's generally deposited near den entrances, along travel routes, or near the entrance to a ground squirrel or prairie dog burrow.

Burrows: The quintessential badger sign, burrows have an elliptical entrance, about 8"–12" across, to accommodate the animal's squat profile. Entrances are surrounded by a large mound of excavated earth, often littered with bones, fur, droppings, and in some locations, rattlesnake rattles. There are frequently other elliptical holes nearby where the badger dug in search of food.

ACTIVITY:
Active year-round, but may become torpid during the coldest parts of the winter, remaining in its burrow for days or even weeks at a time. Predominantly nocturnal, but sometimes active during the day.

TROT

SIMILAR SPECIES:

No other animal besides a porcupine (pg. 189) walks toed-in and leaves such prominent claw marks. Porcupine trails may look similar in deep snow, but show quill-drag marks, don't show toes clearly, and lead to a tree, not a burrow.

NOTES:

Badgers are consummate burrowers, and their lives revolve around burrows and burrowing. The badger's squat, stocky body, powerful forelimbs and long claws make it supremely adapted for a life of digging. They dig to hunt and to escape danger, using burrows for shelter from the heat and cold, for denning, and to store food. Badgers keep many active burrows, and dig new burrows frequently. In summer, badgers sometimes dig a new burrow every day. In cold weather, badgers may retreat to dens for extended periods, plugging the entrance to keep out the cold. Not surprisingly, burrows are the most conspicuous and reliable sign of badger activity. Though primarily burrowers, badgers swim well and often rest in shallow water on hot days.

Badgers prey primarily on burrowing rodents, including ground squirrels, pocket gophers, rats and mice. They forage by digging out burrows and can quickly destroy an entire colony of ground squirrels. In the winter, they also dig up animals hibernating underground. Badgers also eat insects, birds, carrion and reptiles, and seem to have a particular fondness for rattlesnakes. Badgers are well protected by thick fur and a tough hide, and appear to be highly tolerant of rattlesnake venom. As with many other members of the weasel family, badgers cache excess food for later consumption. Caches, of course, are located in underground burrows.

Badgers do not have any natural enemies. They are formidable fighters with strong claws, a tough hide and a powerful neck. Nonetheless, they rarely pick a fight and generally retreat to a burrow if threatened. If a burrow isn't close enough at hand, a badger may dig one on the spot, throwing dirt into its attacker's face and disappearing underground with remarkable speed.

FRONT TRACK
typical size

– max. 1³⁄₈"

– min. 1"

FRONT

– max. 1¹⁄₄"

– min. ³⁄₄"

HIND

HIND TRACK
typical size

GAITS page 314

Eastern Spotted Skunk
Spilogale putorius

Like all skunks, spotted skunks are well known for their foul-smelling spray. Smaller and much less common than the stripped skunk, they are also more agile and show greater diversity in their gaits and trails.

FRONT TRACK
LENGTH: 1"–1³/₈", **AVERAGING:** 1¹/₈"; **WIDTH:** ³/₄"–1", **AVERAGING:** ⁷/₈"

Five toes with prominent claws. The innermost toe is the smallest and set farther back than others. The three middle toes form an arc. Toes rarely splay. Palm pads are partially fused, sometimes showing some separation and often appearing as a single pad. There are two small heel pads, and one or both may register in the track.

HIND TRACK
LENGTH: ³/₄"–1¹/₄", **AVERAGING:** 1"; **WIDTH:** ⁵/₈"–1¹/₈", **AVERAGING:** ⁷/₈"

Five toes with short, stout claws often showing. The innermost toe is the smallest and set farther back than the outermost toe. The tips of the middle toes typically form a straight line, helping to distinguish between the front and hind tracks. A large, smooth palm pad is prominent in the track. Two distinct heel pads usually register behind the palm pad. Similar in size to the front track.

GAITS
Typically travels in a lope or a bound and walks when foraging or moving about in cover. Often uses a highly irregular "puttering" gait when walking, with tremendous variation in stride from one step to the next.

QUICK ID TIPS:
- Small, delicate tracks with prominent claws
- Tracks have a clean, compact appearance
- Often displays a highly irregular walking gait

WALK

HABITAT:
Mixed woodlands, brushlands, rocky areas and farmland.

OTHER SIGNS:
Scat: Varies with the diet. Typically a smooth cylinder with blunt ends measuring ¼"–¾" in diameter and 2"–5" long. Scat tends to break apart easily, and often contains insect remains. Skunks drop scat randomly as they walk and may also form latrines near den sites or on a regular travel route.

Odor: The skunk's odor is perhaps its most distinctive sign. The odor of a skunk spraying may carry for up to a mile. Catching a whiff of skunk may mean the animal is nearby, or may mean that one sprayed in that location recently. Note that foxes and weasels have an odor that is similar to that of a skunk, but it does not carry as far.

ACTIVITY:
Active year-round. Nocturnal.

SIMILAR SPECIES:
Striped skunk tracks (pg. 181) are larger and have a single, fused heel pad. Striped skunks do not bound and their walking gaits tend to be more regular. Weasels and mink (pgs. 153–159) have smaller claws, smaller palm and

heel pads, and heels often don't register in tracks. When loping, they tend to have more elongated strides, with more compact track groups. Squirrels (pgs. 101–127) and other rodents have four toes on the front foot and usually have smaller, more separated palm pads.

NOTES:

The eastern spotted skunk is smaller, faster and more agile than the striped skunk. Unlike their larger cousins, spotted skunks are active hunters and feed mostly on small mammals. They supplement their diet with insects, birds, eggs, corn and fruits and berries. Spotted skunks can also climb and may scale trees to escape danger or occasionally to forage.

Their most notable characteristic, of course, is the noxious spray common to the skunk family. When threatened, spotted skunks charge in and swing their hindquarters around so their nose and rump are facing their attacker. While it cannot spray quite as far as the striped skunk, the spotted skunk can still spray its noxious fluid more than 8' with pinpoint accuracy. The stream cay carry twice as far and the mist can drift 30'. A direct hit to the eyes can cause temporary blindness, and the powerful odor is enough to drive away nearly any would-be predator. Their only significant threat comes from owls, especially the great horned owl, which seem not to be driven off by the skunk's odor.

Spotted skunks do not keep a territory. They wander freely, generally following existing trail systems and sometimes roads. They will den in any convenient cavity, sometimes seeking shelter in buildings or under porches. Generally solitary, but more social than other skunks, they sometimes gather together in winter dens.

Spotted skunks are completely nocturnal, highly secretive, and rarely seen. They are quite rare, especially compared to striped skunks, and there is evidence their numbers are declining throughout much of their range.

FRONT TRACK
typical size

HIND TRACK
typical size

Striped Skunk
Mephitis mephitis

The striped skunk's famous odor makes it one of the most well-known animals in the Midwest. Though nocturnal, they are not particularly secretive and are often seen at night, particularly on roadsides.

FRONT TRACK
LENGTH: $^7/_8"$–$1^3/_4"$, AVERAGING: $1^3/_8"$; WIDTH: $^7/_8"$–$1^1/_4"$, AVERAGING: $1^1/_8"$

Five toes with long, sturdy claws. Toes are short, stout and partially fused together so they cannot splay. The innermost toe is smallest and set farther back than the others. A large, smooth palm pad is prominent in the track and a small heel pad sometimes registers as well. Prominent claws may add up to $^3/_4"$ to the track length.

HIND TRACK
LENGTH: $1"$–$1^3/_4"$, AVERAGING: $1^3/_8"$; WIDTH: $^7/_8"$–$1^1/_4"$, AVERAGING: $1^1/_8"$

Five toes with sturdy claws often showing. Toes are short, stout and partially fused together so they cannot splay. The innermost toe is the smallest, set farther back than the others and often does not register. A prominent heel pad usually registers behind the large, smooth palm pad. Palm and heel pads are clearly separate. Similar in size to the front track.

GAITS
Typically travels and explores in a lope or an overstep walk. Usually walks when foraging. Tends to direct register walk in deep snow.

QUICK ID TIPS:
- Long, prominent claws on the front foot
- Tracks and trail patterns often resemble a bear in miniature
- Small, compact tracks with toes that never splay

WALK

HABITAT:

Open woodlands, brushlands, grasslands, suburbs. Usually close to water.

OTHER SIGNS:

Scat: Varies with the diet of this opportunistic omnivore. Commonly, scat consists mostly of insect parts and breaks apart easily. The typical form is a smooth cylinder with blunt ends measuring ³/₈"–⁷/₈" in diameter and 2"–5" long. Skunks drop scat randomly, but may also form latrines near den sites or in a prominent location on a regular travel route.

Odor: The skunk's odor is its most distinctive sign and may carry for up to a mile. Catching a whiff may mean a skunk is near or one sprayed recently. Foxes and weasels have a similar odor that doesn't carry as far.

Digs: Striped skunks frequently dig for insects, making small, shallow holes about 1¹/₂"–3" in diameter. Digs look similar to marks made by other animals; look for scat or tracks nearby to determine the source.

ACTIVITY:

Active year-round in warm climates. In cold climates, spends much of winter holed up in its den. Does not hibernate and may emerge on warm winter days to forage. Primarily nocturnal.

SIMILAR SPECIES:

Spotted skunk tracks (pg. 177) are usually smaller, show two distinct heel pads, and the innermost toe on the hind foot is set farther back than the outermost toe. Also, spotted skunk gaits are generally more random. Weasels (pg. 153) have smaller claws, smaller palm and heel pads, and the heels often don't register in tracks. They also have more elongated strides and more compact track groups when loping.

NOTES:

Common, widespread and abundant, the striped skunk's chemical defense is infamous. When threatened, skunks may spray their noxious musk up to 15' with remarkable accuracy. Mist may drift three times that far and the foul smell can carry for a mile. A direct hit to the eyes can temporarily blind an attacker and consuming musk glands can be fatal. Unlike most mammals, which have coloration allowing them to blend in with the surroundings, the skunk's bold white-on-black pattern advertises its presence and its formidable chemical weaponry.

Striped skunks are omnivorous, and primarily eat insects and other invertebrates, which they dig for with their long front claws. Their diet also includes eggs, fruits and berries, carrion, some vegetable matter, and occasional birds or small mammals.

Skunks neither chase their food nor flee predators and are generally docile foragers. They have evolved a relaxed, confident disposition. This is reflected in their trails, which resemble small versions of bear trails. They move about freely, following established trails, including roadways, and can often be seen in late evening foraging along roadsides where, to the detriment of all involved, many are struck by cars. Their only significant predator is the great horned owl, which seems not to be driven off by the skunk's odor.

Generally solitary, but not territorial, they range freely and den in nearly any available shelter, including abandoned burrows, natural cavities and under buildings. They often line their dens with grasses to make a nest. In the winter, skunks sometimes den communally, and may congregate in areas with abundant food, such as a dump.

Striped skunks are the primary vector of rabies in the U.S. Although few people need an extra reason to avoid a skunk, one displaying unusual behavior, such as daytime activity, may be infected.

LOPE

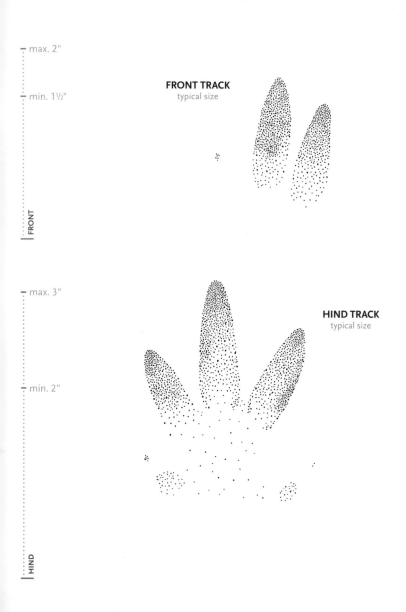

max. 2"

min. 1½"

FRONT TRACK
typical size

FRONT

max. 3"

HIND TRACK
typical size

min. 2"

HIND

Nine-banded Armadillo
Dasypus novemcinctus

The armadillo's signs are as distinctive as its appearance. Their tracks can seem almost bird-like and their scat, as a result of consuming soil while rooting for insects, looks like balls of clay.

FRONT TRACK
LENGTH: 1½"–2", AVERAGING: 1¾"; WIDTH: 1"–1¾", AVERAGING: 1¼"

Four toes with stout claws. The outer two toes are smaller, set higher on the foot and often do not register. Palm is nondescript and usually does not register. The typical track, showing only two long toes, has a bird-like or hoof-like appearance. Smaller and usually shallower than the hind track.

HIND TRACK
LENGTH: 2"–3", AVERAGING: 2½"; WIDTH: 1½"–2¼", AVERAGING: 1¾"

Five toes with stout claws. The outer toes are smaller, set higher on the foot, and often do not register. The center toe is the largest and extends farther forward than the others. Palm is nondescript and does not usually register clearly. The track typically shows three toes and has a distinctly bird-like appearance. Larger than the front track.

GAITS
Typically lopes when traveling, slowing to a walk to forage.

QUICK ID TIPS:
- Tracks have a "bird-like" appearance unique among North American mammals
- Outer toes often do not show in tracks
- Nondescript palm lacks pads and rarely registers

WALK

HABITAT:
 Wooded areas, fields, and brushland. Prefers areas with soft, sandy soils and abundant downed wood. Less common in area with clay soils, where digging is more difficult.

OTHER SIGNS:
 Scat: Armadillos dig for insects and consume a large quantity of soil as they forage. Scat is round or oval and may resemble deer pellets, but composed mostly of clay. Individual pellets measure $1/2$"–1" in diameter and $3/4$"–$1\frac{1}{2}$" in length. Armadillos often bury scat, but sometimes form exposed latrines.

 Burrows: Armadillos are excellent diggers and may excavate large burrows. Entrances are 6"–8" in diameter with a large mound of excavated earth usually evident. Burrows are commonly located along streambanks or in the root system of a large tree. Active burrows have abundant tracks in and out of the entrance and trails radiating from it.

 Nests: Armadillos usually nest in borrows, but in areas subject to flooding, they will rest in aboveground nests, which look like miniature haystacks.

 Feeding Signs: Armadillos root for ground-dwelling insects and also break apart ant hills. Rooting may look similar to skunk or even raccoon activity. Look for tracks or scat to help identify the sign.

ACTIVITY:

Active year-round. Changes its periods of greatest activity with the seasons to avoid exposure to extreme heat and cold. Predominantly nocturnal during hot summer weather and diurnal during cold winter weather.

SIMILAR SPECIES:

Tracks are unlike any other North American mammal. They are more likely to be confused with those of a bird than with another mammal.

NOTES:

Armadillos were named by the Spanish conquistadors who called this unusual animal the "little man in armor." They are the only mammal found in North America that is covered with heavy, bony plates. The armadillo's U.S. range once covered only southern Texas, but in the past century, they have been introduced to Arkansas and Florida, and have considerably expanded their range northward into the southern parts of the Midwest.

Though they appear clumsy, armadillos are surprisingly swift. They will generally run when threatened, and have a habit of jumping straight up in the air when startled. If cornered, they will curl their bodies to protect their soft underparts, but they do not roll into a ball. They are excellent diggers and can disappear into loose soil quite quickly. Armadillos are capable swimmers, and gulp air to increase buoyancy. They are also known to walk along the bottom of streams and ponds for short distances.

Armadillos are generally solitary, but are not territorial. They are nearsighted and can often seem oblivious to their surroundings. They spend much of their time rooting for insects, which are their primary food. They also eat crayfish, amphibians, reptiles, eggs, fruits and carrion.

In addition to their unusual habits and appearance, armadillos exhibit another distinctive trait: each year they give birth to a single litter, and they are always identical quadruplets. The young are born well developed, but with soft armor that hardens over time. When traveling, the babies trail behind their mother like piglets.

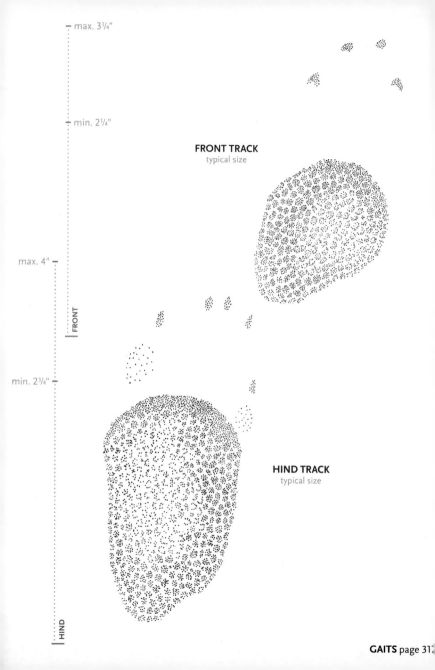

max. 3¼"

min. 2¼"

FRONT TRACK
typical size

max. 4"

FRONT

min. 2¾"

HIND

HIND

North American Porcupine
Erethizon dorsatum

Clear porcupine tracks are unmistakable, and their unique trails feature a toed-in gait and quill drag marks. But it is usually their abundant scat and prominent feeding sign that give away their presence.

FRONT TRACK
LENGTH: 2¼"–3¼", **AVERAGING:** 2¾" (INCLUDES CLAWS); **WIDTH:** 1¼"–1⅞", **AVERAGING:** 1½"

Four toes with very long, stout claws. Claw marks are usually pronounced, and register close together, far in front of the palm. Toes rarely show in the track, and do not splay. Palm and heel pads are fused together into a single large pad that has a distinctive, pebbly texture. Notably smaller than hind track. Because porcupine toes often do not register, their track length typically includes the claws.

HIND TRACK
LENGTH: 2¾"–4", **AVERAGING:** 3⅜" (INCLUDES CLAWS); **WIDTH:** 1¼"–2", **AVERAGING:** 1⅝"

Five toes with long, stout claws. The innermost toe is much shorter than the other four and its claw may not register. Like the front track, the toes do not usually register, but the claws are prominent. Palm and heel pads are fused into a single pad with a distinctive, pebbly texture. Larger and more oblong than the front track.

GAITS
Walks almost exclusively in a distinctive toed-in gait. Most common pattern is an overstep walk. May lope for a short distance if startled. Direct register walks in deep snow, plowing a deep trough with quill drag marks often evident.

QUICK ID TIPS:
- Oval-shaped prints with toes rarely showing
- Long, prominent claws
- Tracks have a unique "pebbly" texture

WALK

HABITAT:
Predominantly arboreal. Common in deciduous, coniferous and mixed forests. In the West, can be found in arid brushland.

OTHER SIGNS:

Scat: Irregular fibrous pellets measuring ¼"–½" in diameter and ½"–1¼" in length. Pellets have round or pointy ends and most are slightly curved. Scat often accumulates in large quantities wherever porcupines feed, travel or rest.

Debarked Trees: During the winter, porcupines feed heavily on the inner bark of trees. They strip large, irregular patches of bark from a wide variety of hardwoods and conifers. Freshly bared wood is usually bright yellow and fades over time. While bark may be stripped from any part of the tree, it is most commonly done high off the ground where the bark is more succulent and the porcupine is safer from predators.

Nip Twigs: When feeding, porcupines bite off branches too thin to support them to reach nuts or succulent growth; these branches fall to the ground or lodge in the canopy.

WALK

ACTIVITY:
Active year-round, but may hole up for days during inclement winter weather. Primarily nocturnal. Occasionally active during the day.

SIMILAR SPECIES:
Clear prints are unmistakable. In soft, loose substrate the walking gait may resemble a badger trail (pg. 173), but badger trails show clear toe marks, don't have quill drag marks and lead to a hole, not a tree.

NOTES:
Porcupines are large rodents best known for the sharply barbed quills covering their body and tail. When threatened, a porcupine contracts muscles under its skin causing its quills to stand firmly on end. Porcupines are not aggressive and cannot throw their quills, but if provoked they can strike with their barbed tail with surprising speed and force. The quills easily come loose, working their way into skin where they can cause infections.

The porcupine has few natural enemies and has developed a very relaxed manner. They move about slowly, and have very small home ranges that they rarely stray from. Porcupines are herbivores, feeding on the buds of trees in spring, tree leaves and herbaceous plants in summer, nuts and fruits in fall, and the inner bark of trees in winter.

Porcupines are excellent climbers and spend a great deal of time in the trees. Their long claws are well adapted for climbing, as is their stout tail, which they use as a brace. They tend to stay close to the trunk, as thinner branches cannot support their weight, and they are heavy enough to injure themselves if they fall.

When walking, porcupines sometimes hold their tail straight out behind them and sweep it side to side along the ground, brushing away their tracks.

Porcupines create well-worn runs between denning sites and preferred feeding areas. In warm weather, they sleep on branches high in trees. In cold weather, they rest in a variety of cavities and shelters, including rock ledges, root tangles and underground burrows. Porcupines are generally solitary, but may gather in large numbers at good feeding or denning sites.

WALK

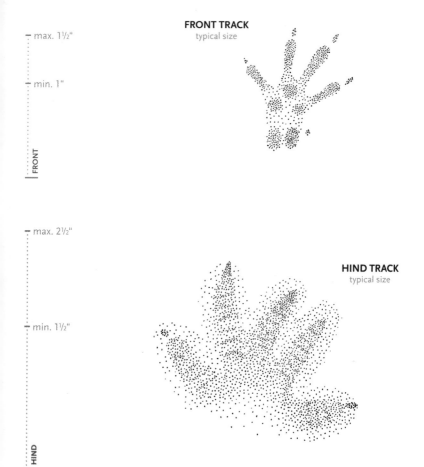

FRONT TRACK
typical size

max. 1½"

min. 1"

FRONT

max. 2½"

HIND TRACK
typical size

min. 1½"

HIND

RANGE

Muskrat
Ondatra zibethicus

Muskrats are common in waterways throughout the Midwest, even in some cities. In addition to their unusual hind tracks, their distinctive signs can include lodges and feeding platforms made of reeds.

FRONT TRACK
LENGTH: 1"–1½", **AVERAGING:** 1¼"; **WIDTH:** 1"–1½", **AVERAGING:** 1¼"

Four slender toes with prominent claws. The inner- and outermost toes point to the sides; the two center toes point forward. Toe pads are slightly bulbous, but toes usually connect to the palm in the track. A tiny fifth toe on the inside of the foot may register as a tiny dot. Three palm pads are partially fused and form a triangular shape. Two round heel pads often register as well. Much smaller than the hind track.

HIND TRACK
LENGTH: 1½"–2½", **AVERAGING:** 2"; **WIDTH:** 1⅜"–2¼", **AVERAGING:** 1⅞"

Five wide, ribbed toes with claws often showing. The innermost toe is the smallest and set a bit farther back than the others. The middle three toes have similar proportions and usually register closest together. Each toe is connected to the palm and is surrounded by a shelf of stiff hairs that exaggerate its width. Palm pads are fused together. There are two heel pads that rarely register. Tracks typically register strongly toed-in. Much larger than the front track.

GAITS
Usually walks with an indirect register. Hind feet fall behind, in front of, or mostly on top of the front feet. Lopes or bounds when threatened. Walks in snow, often showing foot and tail drags. Plows a trough in deep snow.

QUICK ID TIPS:
- Hind foot is much larger than the front, which it often partially covers
- Distinctive hind toes are long, stout and surrounded by a shelf of stiff hairs
- Usually found close to water, especially ponds and wetlands

WALK

HABITAT:

Marshes, ponds, streams, lakes, rivers and canals. Generally avoids strong currents. Especially common in shallow cattail marshes and beaver ponds.

OTHER SIGNS:

Scat: Generally an oblong pellet ranging from ¹³/₁₆" to 1" in diameter. Dry, hard pellets are smaller and more distinct. Wetter, soft pellets are larger and clump together more often. Very wet scat may be amorphous. Often accumulates on elevated surfaces near the water's edge, including beaver lodges.

Lodges: Similar to beaver lodges, but smaller. Instead of wood, they are constructed out of softer, lighter materials. Reeds, cattails and similar plants are mixed with mud and piled into a mound reaching 1½'–4' above the waterline. Mounds are excavated from the inside, creating dens that are accessible via underwater entrances.

Burrows: Muskrats frequently create burrows in stream and pond banks. Entrances to burrows may be above or below the waterline and typically measure 3½"–6" across. While burrows are sometimes small, they may be large and complex, with many tunnels, chambers and entrances.

Feeding Stations: In winter, muskrats push mud and plant matter up though holes in the ice. These debris help keep the hole open and provide some protection from predators. In summer, muskrats create feeding platforms of cut vegetation, creating a somewhat solid surface in a marsh. These vary widely in size and may even resemble a lodge.

Scent Posts: Muskrat scent posts are small mats of cut vegetation where males deposit musk and scat.

ACTIVITY:

Active year-round. Particularly active in the spring. Predominantly nocturnal and crepuscular, but may be active at any time.

SIMILAR SPECIES:

Clear hind tracks are unmistakable. Beaver tracks (pg. 197) have some similar characteristics, but are much larger.

NOTES:

Muskrats are highly aquatic rodents with habitat and behavior similar to beavers. Like beavers, muskrats frequent ponds and wetlands and build lodges, spend most of their time in the water, and often make their homes in beaver ponds. They may even move into an occupied beaver lodge. They do not fell trees or gnaw sticks, but instead build lodges and feeding platforms out of cattails, reeds and aquatic plants.

While muskrats do not build dams, they create open water in marshy wetlands by consuming large quantities of cattails and other plants. This supports wetland diversity, providing habitat for waterfowl. Muskrats are primarily herbivores but also eat clams, and clamshells sometimes accumulate at feeding platforms or near burrows.

Muskrats are essentially a wetland species, yet have flourished even as wetlands have declined, as they are highly adaptable and have adjusted well to human land uses. They have become quite abundant in rural, suburban and even urban streams, ponds and canals. Males are generally territorial, especially during breeding. A lodge or burrow is usually shared by a breeding pair and offspring. Young disperse in spring and may travel some distance to find homes. In winter, males are less territorial, and several may share a lodge or burrow.

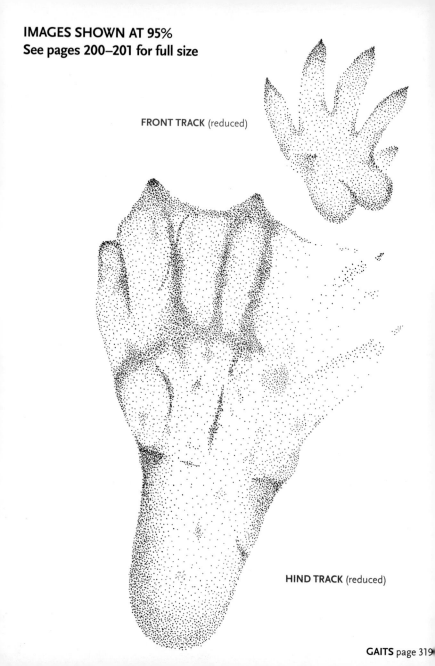

FRONT TRACK (reduced)

HIND TRACK (reduced)

American Beaver
Castor canadensis

Found throughout the Midwest, beavers are best known for their remarkable lodges and dams. Not all beavers build these structures, but all beavers fell trees and leave behind large, unmistakable tracks.

FRONT TRACK
LENGTH: 2"–3½", **AVERAGING:** 2¾"; **WIDTH:** 1½"–3", **AVERAGING:** 2¼"

Five strongly curved toes with blunt claws. The innermost toe is small and often doesn't show. The outermost toe may also fail to register. Palm pads are fused and blend together with the base of the toes. Two distinct heel pads sometimes register. Much smaller than the hind track.

HIND TRACK
LENGTH: 4½"–7", **AVERAGING:** 5¾"; **WIDTH:** 3"–5", **AVERAGING:** 4"

Five toes with stout, blunt claws. Webbing between toes is usually visible. When walking, the foot is toed-in and the two innermost toes do not register reliably. Large palm pads are usually indistinct. The heel almost always registers. Usually registers on top of the front track. Much larger than front track.

GAITS
Generally walks on land in a direct register or, sometimes, indirect register. May bound when alarmed. Plows though snow, creating a wide trough.

> **QUICK ID TIPS:**
> - Extremely large, toed-in hind tracks; clear prints are unmistakable
> - Trails usually lead directly to or from a body of water
> - Tracks may be completely obscured by heavy tail drag

WALK

197

HABITAT:
 Swamps, rivers, streams, marshes, lakes and ponds in wooded areas.

OTHER SIGNS:
 Scat: Beavers defecate in water and scat is rarely seen. If found, the typical form is an oval pellet ¾"–1½" around made of wood and plant fibers.

 Lodges: Easily recognizable, beaver lodges are large domes of sticks and mud with underwater entrances. Carefully built and maintained, lodges are quite sturdy and may be used for many generations. If abandoned, they may be reclaimed by other beavers or persist for years. Look for other beaver sign to identify active lodges.

 Dams: Impressive structures constructed of wood and mud. Far from being haphazard piles of debris, dams are engineered with large anchor poles and a lattice of sticks to hold mud in place. Dams are nearly waterproof and may be as large as 10' high or hundreds of yards long. Beavers often build a series of dams along a waterway.

 Chews: When beavers feed, they leave behind sticks and small logs stripped of bark with ends gnawed to a point. Tooth marks on chews range from ⅛" to ¼" wide. Beavers also chew on the bark of standing trees.

Canals: Beavers sometimes dig canals from ponds to provide safer travel and to float logs to the lodge or dam. Canals can measure 2' wide and 2' deep and may be several hundred yards long.

Scent Posts: Beavers mark piles of vegetation and mud with a substance called castorem, secreted from a specialized scent glad. The odor, reminiscent of a barn, is evidence of current beaver activity.

ACTIVITY:

Active year-round. In northern climates, spends most of winter in its lodge or under the ice. Predominantly nocturnal and crepuscular.

SIMILAR SPECIES:

Unmistakable in our region; its distinctive signs minimize confusion.

NOTES:

Common and widespread, beavers are best known for dramatically altering their landscape. The largest rodent in the Midwest, this highly aquatic animal leaves prominent signs of its presence. While it can be uncommon to find clear beaver tracks, other signs of their presence are easy to spot. The distinctive lodge, dam, felled trees and chewed sticks all point unmistakably to this animal. Beavers also make trails between feeding areas or bodies of water and clip them clear of protruding branches.

The beaver's reputation as highly industrious is well earned. Lodges and dams can reach enormous proportions and undergo constant maintenance. While beavers primarily eat green plants and roots during summer, in the winter they rely on the inner bark of trees such as aspen, cottonwood, birch, maple and willow. They cut trees down with remarkable speed by gnawing through the trunk with their sharp incisors. They can down a 5" willow in three minutes, regularly drop trees over 6" in diameter and have been known to fell trees over 2' across. Trees are cut into small sections to transport. Larger pieces are used in construction, while smaller branches may be stored underwater for food in winter. Where natural water levels are high, such as large streams and rivers, beavers forgo building and simply burrow into the bank. Such "bank beavers" still fell trees to feed on in winter.

Beavers are preyed on by otters, wolves, coyotes, bobcats and red foxes.

FRONT TRACK
shown typical size

max. 3½"

min. 2"

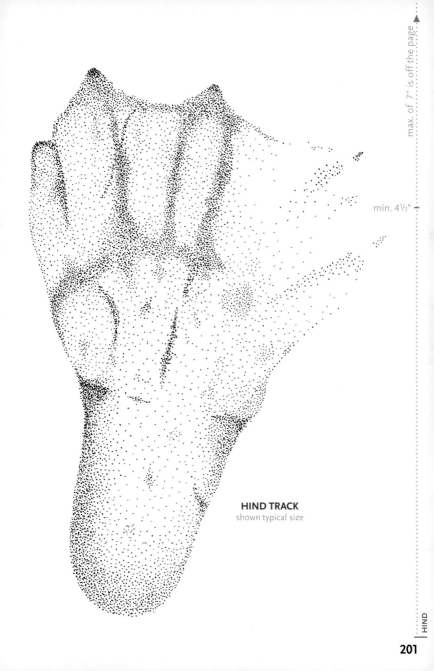

min. 4½"

HIND TRACK
shown typical size

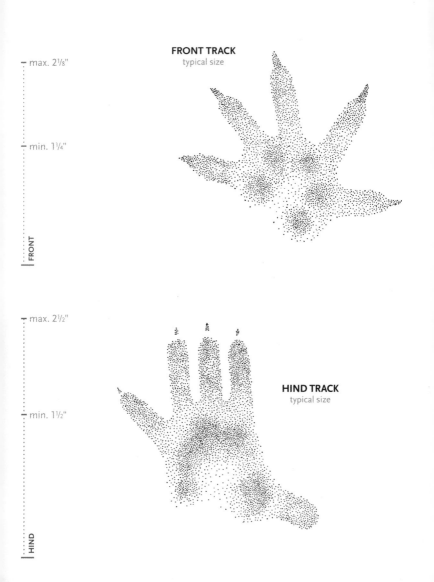

FRONT TRACK
typical size

max. 2⅛"

min. 1¼"

FRONT

max. 2½"

HIND TRACK
typical size

min. 1½"

HIND

Virginia Opossum
Didelphis virginiana

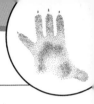

Virginia opossums are common in the southern parts of the Midwest and their range continues to expand northward. Their distinctive star-shaped front track and hand-like hind track are unmistakable.

FRONT TRACK
LENGTH: 1¼"–2⅛", **AVERAGING:** 1¾"; **WIDTH:** 1½"–2¼", **AVERAGING:** 1⅞"

Five toes with small claws sometimes showing. Long toes radiate out from a semicircle of 6 palm pads, which may not all register clearly. Toes are usually widely splayed and give the print a star-like appearance. Usually wider than it is long.

HIND TRACK
LENGTH: 1½"–2½", **AVERAGING:** 2"; **WIDTH:** 1½"–2⅝", **AVERAGING:** 1⅞"

Five toes with small claws often showing on the four outer toes. Has a distinctive appearance, resembling a human hand. Innermost toe, which lacks a claw, extends sideways away from other toes, like a human thumb. The outermost toe is also separated slightly from the middle three toes. Six pads form a shape similar to a human palm.

GAITS
Walks when exploring and trots when traveling. Usually walks in a direct register or double register, but sometimes displays the extreme overstep walk common to raccoons. Bounds when chasing prey or escaping. Walks in deep snow, dragging its feet with each step.

QUICK ID TIPS:
- Front track has a unique, star-like shape with five widely splayed toes radiating outward
- Hind track resembles a human hand and has an opposable thumb
- Toes on the hind track point outward from the direction of travel while the thumb points inward

WALK

HABITAT:

Forests, open woods, farmlands, suburban and urban areas.

OTHER SIGNS:

Scat: Because the opossum's diets is so diverse, their scat varies widely and cannot be readily distinguished. Scat also tends to break down quickly and is rarely found. Scat may range in size from ³⁄₈"–1¹⁄₈" in diameter and from 1"–4¹⁄₂" in length and be composed of nearly anything.

ACTIVITY:

Doesn't hibernate, but reduces activity in cold weather and may hole up for days at a time in the winter. Nocturnal.

SIMILAR SPECIES:

Clear tracks are unmistakable. Unclear prints may resemble a raccoon's. Raccoons (pg. 207) never show tail drag and use their distinctive overstep walk more consistently.

TROT

NOTES:

One of the most common arboreal animals in the southern part of the Midwest, the Virginia opossum is North America's only marsupial. Like other marsupials, opossums climb to their mother's pouch shortly after birth, where they nurse for two months before venturing outside. The Virginia opossum migrated to the United States at about the same time European settlers first arrived and has been expanding its range northward ever since.

Remarkably hardy, opossums tolerate a wide range of climate conditions. While they are poorly adapted to deal with extreme cold and prone to frostbite on their naked feet and tails, they continue to expand their range northward. In cold climates, opossums greatly reduce their activity in winter, but do not hibernate and need to leave their dens to forage. In the northern portions of their range, it's not uncommon to see an opossum that has lost toes or part of its tail to frostbite or to find blood in their trails in winter.

Opossums adjust well to human habitation and can eat nearly anything. Their highly varied diet includes carrion, insects, frogs, birds, eggs, snakes, small mammals, worms, fruits and berries, corn and garbage. They often forage along streams and have been known to raid henhouses. As nocturnal carrion eaters, many are also struck by cars while feeding on the remains of other roadkill.

Opossums are solitary, non-territorial and semi-nomadic. They den up during the day and forage at night across a constantly shifting home range. They commonly travel along roads and established trails and den up in almost any convenient shelter, including abandoned burrows, hollow logs, rock crevices and buildings. They may line their den with leaves, which they carry with their prehensile tail.

Opossums are also excellent climbers and spend much of their time in trees, often using their tail like a fifth leg—occasionally hanging or swinging from it as they move through the branches. When threatened, an opossum may hiss and bare its teeth, or it may play "possum," falling limp, drooling, and excreting a foul-smelling substance from its anus. This unique display is apparently unusual enough, or revolting enough, to dissuade most predators.

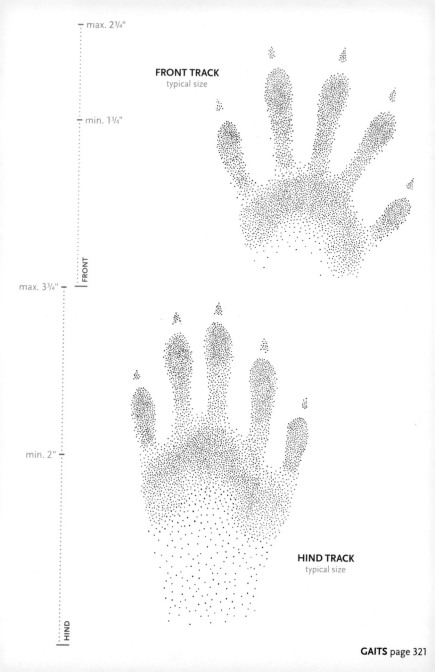

max. 2¾"

min. 1¾"

FRONT TRACK
typical size

FRONT

max. 3¾"

min. 2"

HIND TRACK
typical size

HIND

Northern Raccoon
Procyon lotor

The well-known raccoon is common throughout the Midwest, even in our largest cities. While its tracks and gait are usually distinctive, partial or obscured prints can be easy to mistake for those of other animals.

FRONT TRACK
LENGTH: 1³/₄"–2³/₄", **AVERAGING:** 2¹/₄"; **WIDTH:** 1¹/₂"–2³/₄", **AVERAGING:** 2"

Five long toes with claws often showing. The innermost toe is set farther back than others and may register more lightly. In most tracks, the toe pads connect to the prominent, "C"-shaped palm pad. A smaller heel pad occasionally registers. Toes often splay widely, but may be held close together, creating significant variation in track appearance. Typically registers more lightly than the hind track.

HIND TRACK
LENGTH: 2"–3³/₄", **AVERAGING:** 2⁷/₈"; **WIDTH:** 1¹/₂"–2³/₄", **AVERAGING:** 2¹/₈"

Five long toes with claws usually showing. The innermost toe is set farther back than the others. Toes usually connect to the prominent palm in the track, and splay less often than in the front track. The heel registers more often than in the front track. Similar in size to the front track, though typically longer.

GAITS
Travels in a distinctive overstep walk, nearly unique to this species. Sometimes bounds. Flees in a gallop. May direct register walk in deep snow.

QUICK ID TIPS:
- Distinctive overstep walking pattern with the hind track beside the front track
- Tracks often resemble human hand prints with long fingers and a prominent palm
- Dexterous fingers result in a wide range of track shapes and sizes

WALK

HABITAT:

Varied and wide ranging. Most common in wetlands, damp woods and along waterways. Also common in urban and suburban areas.

OTHER SIGNS:

Scat: Usually tubular in shape and breaks apart easily. Often made up of invertebrate remains, seeds and grain. Typically ranges from ¼"–1¼" in diameter and 3½"–7" in length. **Warning**: Raccoons often carry a parasitic roundworm called *Baylisascaris procyonis*, which can be fatal in humans. Use caution when handling raccoon scat.

Latrines: Look for communal latrines near dens or along well-used routes.

Feeding: Raccoons have a tremendously varied diet, but look for signs of favorite foods, such as crayfish along the shores of streams or ponds. In cornfields, look for broken stalks with chewed cob ends and scattered kernels. In urban areas, look for toppled trash cans or scattered garbage.

Dens: Raccoons use many types of denning sites, but commonly inhabit hollow trees. Look for cavities formed where a large tree limb has fallen away, with scratch marks in the bark and accumulated scat near the base.

ACTIVITY:

Inactive during the coldest winter weather. Not a true hibernator, but may sleep for days or weeks. May be active on warmer winter days. Predominantly nocturnal, but occasionally active during the day.

SIMILAR SPECIES:

The raccoon's dexterous toes lead to a wide variety of track shapes, and raccoon prints are frequently confused with other animal tracks. However, few other animals use the raccoon's distinctive overstep walk, and none use it as often. Otter (pg. 169) and fisher tracks (pg. 165) are generally rounder with shorter toe pads that are clearly separate from their asymmetrical palm pads. Opossum front tracks (pg. 203) splay more widely than raccoon tracks and have a rounder palm pad. The innermost toe on the hind track points far to the inside, away from the other four. Opossums may also show tail drag.

NOTES:

Raccoons are one of the most common medium-sized mammals in North America. They adapt well to human habitation and thrive in suburban and urban areas, reaching their highest population densities in some of the Midwest's largest cities.

Omnivorous opportunists, raccoons have a widely varied diet. They eat fruits, berries, nuts, seeds and grain, especially sweet corn, as well as carrion, eggs and small animals. They commonly forage along ponds or streams for crayfish, frogs, fish, clams, and other aquatic creatures. They also forage in trees and root for insects. The raccoon's dexterous fingers are capable of untying knots, unscrewing jar lids, and turning door knobs. In developed areas, they commonly climb into garbage cans and compost bins and may raid food stores.

Raccoons are excellent climbers and often take refuge in trees. They may sleep on branches in mild weather, and commonly den in hollow cavities of large trees. They also den up in rock crevices, abandoned buildings, culverts, brush piles, and the abandoned dens of other animals.

Raccoons usually make their own trail systems, connecting dens to good foraging sites. Raccoons sometimes follow roads, but more often cross them, and many are killed while doing so.

BOUND

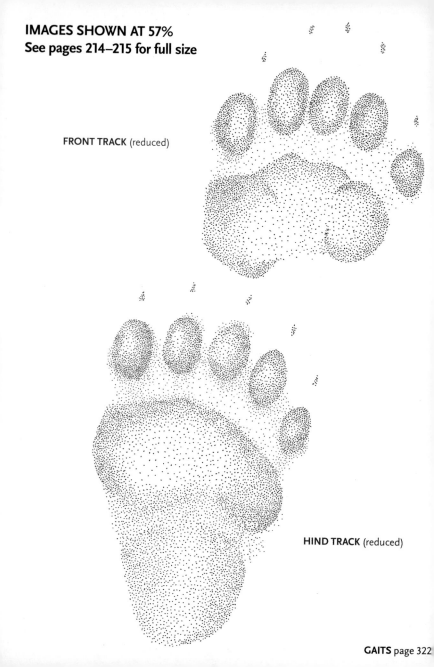

FRONT TRACK (reduced)

HIND TRACK (reduced)

RANGE

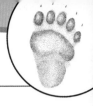

Black Bear
Ursus americanus

Black bears are found along the northern and southern edges of the Midwest. Though their large tracks are distinctive, it is the scat and feeding sign of this enormous omnivore that often give it away.

FRONT TRACK
LENGTH: 3½"–6", **AVERAGING:** 4¼"; **WIDTH:** 3½"–5½" **AVERAGING:** 4½"

Five toes with very long, sturdy claws usually showing. The innermost toe is the smallest and doesn't always register. The single, robust palm pad is much wider than long and dominates the track. A small, round heel pad sometimes registers. The spaces between pads are filled with dense fur. Claws are usually prominent, but sometimes fail to register. Front claws are longer than hind claws and vary greatly in length. Extremely long claws may register so far in front of the toes that they are easily overlooked.

HIND TRACK
LENGTH: 5"–8", **AVERAGING:** 6½"; **WIDTH:** 3½"–5¾", **AVERAGING:** 4½"

Five toes with stout claws usually showing. Similar to the front track, the innermost toe is the smallest and may not register strongly. Has a single, large palm pad. The heel pad is larger than in the front track and registers more often. When it does, it is connected to the palm pad along the outer edge of track and there is a wedge-shaped indentation on the inside edge, between the heel and the palm. Similar in size to the front track, though typically longer.

GAITS
Typically walks, using a direct register or an overstep walk, with feet slightly toed-in. Sometimes trots or lopes. May flee in a gallop. Usually direct register walks in deep snow.

QUICK ID TIPS:
- Among the largest tracks in our region, clear prints are unmistakable
- Each foot has five toes and a very wide, robust palm pad
- When heel pads register, hind tracks have a "Bigfoot-like" appearance

WALK

HABITAT:
Forests and swamps.

OTHER SIGNS:

Scat: Bear scat varies greatly with diet. The general form is a wide, segmented cylinder with blunt ends measuring 1"–2½" in diameter and 5"–12" in length. Segments may be linked together or completely separate, and formless plops are also common. Scats often include easily recognizable insect remains, nut shells, fruit or berry seeds, grasses, or fur and bones. Most contain little fibrous material and break apart easily. Bears deposit scat 6–8 times per day, apparently at random. Scat often accumulates along travel routes, near den sites or areas with abundant food.

Bear Trees: As they mark territory and feed, black bears damage trees. Bears pull branches down to mouth level to feed. Bear "nests" are accumulations of broken branches discarded by a bear foraging in the canopy. Bears also break branches or small trees by biting them; bear bites often leave a mark that looks like a .22 rifle shot. Also look for claw marks where a bear has scratched or climbed a tree.

Feeding: Black bears frequently dig, overturn rocks, and break apart logs while foraging. The size and scope of these disturbances are a good clue they were created by a bear.

Cached kills: When a black bear kills a large animal, it often covers the un-eaten portion with debris. Bears may be highly protective of cached kills, which are best left alone.

ACTIVITY:

In northern climates, black bears hibernate in winter. When not hibernating, bears may be active at any time. Generally diurnal in wilderness areas, but nocturnal near human habitation.

SIMILAR SPECIES:

Clear tracks are unmistakable. Cougar tracks (pg. 253) are somewhat similar, but cougars have four toes with claws rarely showing, and their palm pads have a trapezoidal shape.

NOTES:

The black bear is common and the largest carnivore in our region. Although classified as a carnivore, their varied diet is mostly plant-based and includes leaves, fruits and berries. They have relatively poor eyesight and forage using their excellent sense of smell. While their lumbering overstep walk looks clumsy, black bears are remarkably quiet and can move up to 35 mph. Strong swimmers and good climbers, bears often forage in trees and climb to escape perceived threats.

Black bears are generally solitary, except when raising cubs. Litters of 1–3 cubs are born in January or February in the winter den and stay with their mother until fall or sometimes until the following spring. In areas with abundant food, including garbage dumps, bears may congregate, forming a social hierarchy.

Black bears have few natural enemies today, but they evolved during the last ice age when they faced predators. As a result, bears behave almost like a small omnivore, such as a raccoon, rather than a dominant carnivore. According to bear expert Lynn Rogers, the lives of black bears are ruled by fear and food, in that order. Though usually relaxed, they are shy and are easily startled; when surprised (even by a domestic cat) they usually run away or climb a tree. While generally timid, black bears are formidable; they are extremely strong, with powerful jaws and long claws.

max. 6"

FRONT TRACK
shown typical size

min. 3½"

min. 5"

HIND TRACK
shown typical size

max. 1½"

min. 1"

FRONT

max. 1½"

min. 1"

HIND

FRONT TRACK
typical size

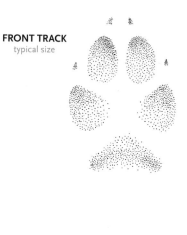

HIND TRACK
typical size

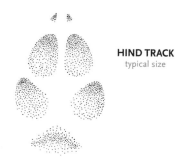

Swift Fox
Vulpes velox

The smallest fox in the Midwest, swift fox leave delicate versions of the familiar canine tracks and trails. A western species, its range is slowly expanding again after being nearly wiped out of our region.

FRONT TRACK
LENGTH: 1"–1½", **AVERAGING:** 1¼"; **WIDTH:** 1"–1½", **AVERAGING:** 1¼"

Four toes with claws usually showing. The triangular palm pad shows three trailing lobes. Rounder than hind track with a more robust palm pad. In some individuals, fur on the bottom of the foot may reduce the apparent size of the pads and make them appear less distinct.

HIND TRACK
LENGTH: 1"–1½", **AVERAGING:** 1¼"; **WIDTH:** ⅞"–1¼", **AVERAGING:** 1⅛"

Four toes with claws usually showing. The small, triangular palm pad usually registers quite lightly and does not show in some cases. Typically shows the same amount of fur as the front track, varying significantly from one individual to the next. Narrower than front track, but may splay in loose sand or other soft surfaces.

GAITS
Commonly moves about in a lope or a trot, sometimes slowing to a walk. As with most other canines, uses both direct register trots and side trots regularly.

> **QUICK ID TIPS:**
> - Typical canine track showing four symmetrical toes, claws and a triangular heel pad
> - Smallest wild canine track in the Midwest
> - Hind palm pad registers very lightly and may not show at all

HABITAT:
Arid lands including short-grass prairie and open shrubland.

OTHER SIGNS:

Scat: One or more long droppings ranging from $3/16$"–$5/8$" in diameter and 2"–$4^1/2$" in length, often containing bone fragments encased in hair. Unlike other fox scat, it is not likely to contain fruit or berry seeds. Often deposited in latrines at the base of prominent shrubs.

Dens: Swift foxes inhabit dens year-round. Entrances measure about 8" wide and are often keyhole-shaped. Each fox uses multiple dens and each den typically has two or three entrances. Each den's main entrance often has an obvious mound of excavated dirt in front of it. Tracks, hair and bones may be evident in the disturbed soil near the entrance.

Urine: Swift fox urine has a pungent odor, reminiscent of a skunk or of red fox urine.

ACTIVITY:
Active year-round. Mostly nocturnal, but sometimes active during the day.

SIMILAR SPECIES:

Gray fox front tracks (pg. 221) are rounder, show more negative space between the toes and the palm pad, and are usually larger, though there is some overlap in size. Gray fox are less likely to be seen in open, arid country. All other wild canid tracks are larger.

NOTES:

The swift fox is the smallest of the region's foxes and leaves the most delicate tracks and trails. An animal of the arid grasslands, it is also our most carnivorous fox; its diet consists primarily of small mammals, rabbits, birds, insects and lizards. Only a small fraction of their diet consists of plant material, and it is not usually evident in scat. In the winter, swift fox cache excess food under the snow.

Once widespread in the West, the swift fox has suffered from habitat loss and from hunting and trapping for its pelts. Less wary than other foxes, and just as curious, they are especially vulnerable to human hunters. With recent conservation efforts and the collapse of the fur industry, their range is expanding. They have been reintroduced to the grasslands in the western portion of our region, but remain an endangered species.

Swift fox inhabit their dens year-round, using them as shelter from the weather and from predators. Each fox has several dens in its home range, and each den has several entrances. Swift fox are remarkably fast for such a small animal, hence their common name. They are able to run at 25 mph for short distances and are quite agile. Nonetheless, they are vulnerable to both coyotes and domestic dogs on the open prairie, and usually try to escape underground when threatened.

Swift foxes may pair for life, but travel and hunt individually. Litters of 3–6 young are born in an underground chamber in the den in late winter or early spring. Pups stay in their den for the first month, are weaned at three months and disperse by the end of summer.

max. 1¾"

min. 1¼"

FRONT

FRONT TRACK
typical size

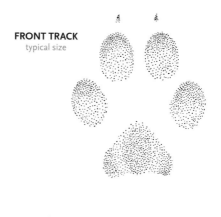

max. 1¾"

min. 1⅛"

HIND

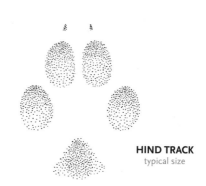

HIND TRACK
typical size

Gray Fox

Urocyon cinereoargenteus

The only canine that regularly climbs trees, the agile gray fox has semi-retractable claws that often do not register in their tracks. This can give their delicate prints an almost cat-like appearance.

FRONT TRACK

LENGTH: 1¼"–1¾", AVERAGING: 1½"; WIDTH: 1¼"–1¾", AVERAGING: 1½"

Four toes with semi-retractable claws sometimes showing. A fused palm pad may look like a rounded triangle, three merged dots, or a single large dot with "wings." There is often more "negative space" between the toes and the palm pad than in other foxes. Larger and rounder than the hind track with a more robust palm pad.

HIND TRACK

LENGTH: 1⅛"–1¾", AVERAGING: 1½"; WIDTH: 1"–1⅝", AVERAGING: 1¼"

Four toes with semi-retractable claws that register less often than in front tracks. The triangular palm pad registers more lightly than in front track and the side lobes may fail to register, leaving a round dot similar in size and shape to a toe pad. Narrower and more oval than front track.

GAITS

Usually travels in a direct register trot. Commonly speeds up into a straddle trot, rather than the side trot typical of other canines. Sometimes walks. Lopes or gallops when chasing or fleeing. Avoids deep snow when possible.

QUICK ID TIPS:

- Typical canine track with four symmetrical toes and a triangular heel pad
- Semi-retractable claws may not show in tracks
- A capable climber, a gray fox trail may begin or end at the base of a tree

HABITAT:

Prefers broken habitats and higher levels of cover than the red fox. Adapts to areas near people if there is sufficient cover.

OTHER SIGNS:

Scat: Typically one or more long droppings ranging from ⅜"–¾" in diameter and 3"–6" long. Structure varies with diet and often contains bone fragments. In summer, scat may include grasses, fruit or berry seeds and insect remains. Often deposited at trail junctions or on raised surfaces. Easily confused with smaller red fox or coyote scat.

Dens: Gray foxes typically use natural cavities as dens; entrances vary in size and shape and are sometimes marked by hair, small bones or scraps. When pups begin to emerge from den, the ground becomes packed down from continuous play and feeding and is littered with tiny scat.

Caches: Buries excess food, typically covering it with loose dirt, turf or moss. Excavated caches are wide, shallow depressions.

ACTIVITY:

Active year-round. Predominantly nocturnal or crepuscular. Sometimes active during the day, but usually retires to shelter.

SIMILAR SPECIES:

Domestic cat and bobcat tracks (pgs. 239–245) are less symmetrical, rounder, and have a much larger palm pad. Swift fox tracks (pg. 217) are generally smaller, but overlap in size; they show claw marks more often and front tracks are more oval with less negative space between the toes and the palm pad. Red fox tracks (pg. 225) are larger, may show a "bar" in the palm pad of the front track, and are less distinct because of the fur-filled negative space between the pads. Small domestic dogs rarely direct register and typically show round, blunt claw marks.

NOTES:

The only true tree climber in the dog family, gray foxes possess cat-like agility. Their trails often travel up angled tree trunks, along logs, walls and fences, and disappear into the branches of shrubs and trees. A canid trail that begins or ends at the base of a tree is almost certainly that of a gray fox.

More omnivorous than most other canids. While they feed heavily on rabbits and small mammals, especially in winter, their diet also includes insects, birds, corn, apples, berries and nuts. Being adept climbers, gray foxes sometimes forage in trees, especially for fruits or berries. Grasshoppers and crickets are an important part of their diet in late summer and autumn.

Unlike larger canids, gray foxes rarely bed in the open, preferring to find natural cover. Occasionally bed in trees or shrubs during the day. Prefer to avoid deep snow, and may hole up for extended periods when snow conditions make travel difficult. May use roads and packed trails, with short excursions to hunt and forage.

Gray foxes typically travel alone or in pairs. Litters of 1–7 young are born in a natal den in March, April or May. The male helps raise the young, but doesn't occupy the den. Pups are weaned at three months and travel with the mother before dispersing in late fall or early winter.

Like red foxes, gray foxes have few predators but are occasionally preyed on by bobcats. A few are shot or trapped, primarily for pelts. As in red fox, rabies and distemper are common in gray fox.

STRADDLE TROT

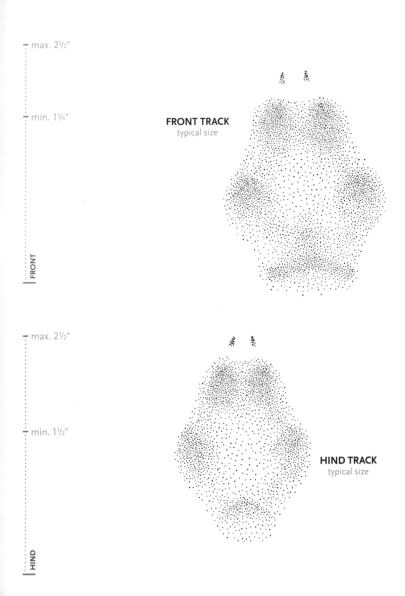

max. 2½"

min. 1¾"

FRONT TRACK
typical size

FRONT

max. 2½"

min. 1½"

HIND TRACK
typical size

HIND

Red Fox
Vulpes vulpes

Common throughout most of the Midwest, red foxes adjust well to human development. Their precise, narrow trails can often be found crossing wilderness trails, farmland and even urban golf courses.

FRONT TRACK
LENGTH: 1³/₄"–2¹/₂", **AVERAGING:** 2"; **WIDTH:** 1¹/₂"–2¹/₈", **AVERAGING:** 1³/₄"

Four toes, with claws usually showing. The bottom of the foot is heavily furred. A triangular palm pad protrudes sharply though the hair and often leaves a straight or boomerang-shaped "heel bar," unique to the red fox. Furred foot may make toe and palm pads appear small and indistinct, greatly exaggerating the negative space between pads.

HIND TRACK
LENGTH: 1¹/₂"–2¹/₂", **AVERAGING:** 1⁷/₈"; **WIDTH:** 1¹/₄"–1⁷/₈", **AVERAGING:** 1¹/₂"

Four toes with claws usually showing. Like the front foot, the hind foot is heavily furred, but the palm pad does not protrude as sharply and rarely leaves a "bar" in the track. Often indistinct, the palm pad usually looks like a tall, narrow triangle, or sometimes a dot. Similar to front track, but usually narrower and more delicate-looking.

GAITS
Typically trots in a direct register or side trot. Direct register trots may leave an extremely narrow trail with all tracks in a single nearly straight line. Lopes or gallops when chasing or fleeing. Often walks when in deep snow, but may bound, leaving a series of whole-body imprints.

QUICK ID TIPS:
- Typical canine track showing four toes, claws and a triangular heel pad
- Heavily furred foot often makes pads appear less distinct than other canids
- Shows a distinctive bar across the heel pad of the front track

TROT

HABITAT:

Prefers a mixture of cover and open space. Adapts readily to human presence and is common in cropland, suburban areas, and even urban areas with enough brush or woods. Favors mixed habitat of brushland and fields.

OTHER SIGNS:

Scat: One or more long droppings ranging from ³⁄₈"–³⁄₄" in diameter and 3"–6" long. Structure varies with diet. Often contains bone fragments. In summer, scat may include grasses, fruit seeds and insect remains. Often deposited at trail junctions or on raised surfaces. Easily confused with gray fox or coyote scat, though coyote scat is usually longer.

Dens: Found on open ground or areas with sparse cover and a good view of the surroundings, dens are often enlarged woodchuck or badger dens. The main entrance measures about 8"–9" in diameter and is usually marked with a fan of excavated earth. Tracks, hair and a distinctive red fox odor are usually evident near the main entrance.

Odor: Red foxes urine has a distinctive, pungent odor similar to a skunk.

Caches: Red foxes store excess food in holes covered by dirt or leaves, which are usually well disguised and difficult to find.

ACTIVITY:

Active year-round. Predominantly nocturnal, sometimes crepuscular. Occasionally active during the daytime, especially in winter.

SIMILAR SPECIES:

No other track shows the distinctive "heel bar" and no other canid track in our region is so heavily furred. Swift fox tracks (pg. 217) are smaller. Gray fox tracks (pg. 221) are usually smaller and often don't show claws. Coyote tracks (pg. 229) are larger and usually longer and narrower. Coyotes also leave wider trails and don't typically direct register. Domestic dog tracks are usually wider with toes splayed more and blunter claws pointing outward. Bobcat tracks (pg. 243) are rounder, show two lobes on the leading edge of the palm pad and rarely show claws.

NOTES:

Well adapted to human habitation, red foxes are the most common wild canid in most of our region. They are abundant in farmland and suburbs and can even be seen in our largest cities. Like all foxes, they are quite agile. While they do not climb, they commonly walk along fallen logs or up angled tree trunks.

Red foxes are omnivorous, eating rabbits, small mammals, birds, berries, fruits, insects and crayfish. They may also feed on carrion and raid garbage cans. Red foxes stalk prey more often than other canids. Their hearing is uniquely sensitive to low frequencies, enabling them to hear small animals digging beneath grass, snow or leaves. Once they locate their prey, they pounce.

Red foxes form long-term pair bonds and frequently mate for life. They hunt and forage individually, but both parents care for young. Litters of 4–10 pups are born March, April or May in an underground den and stay with their parents until fall. Males disperse widely, traveling up to 150 miles from home. Females usually stay closer, sometimes returning to their maternal den to help their parents raise the next year's litter. Dens are abandoned in the fall and the foxes spend the winter in solitude.

While they have few natural enemies, red foxes generally do not compete well with coyotes. Common causes of mortality are cars and disease. Red foxes are one of the most common vectors for rabies, and populations frequently suffer from distemper and mange.

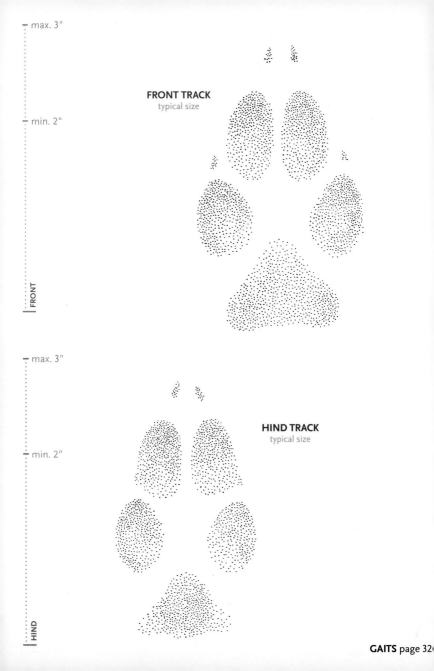

max. 3"

min. 2"

FRONT TRACK
typical size

FRONT

max. 3"

min. 2"

HIND TRACK
typical size

HIND

Coyote
Canis latrans

Coyote tracks and trails can look very similar to those of domestic dogs, but are generally narrower and more precise. Learn to distinguish them and you may find them nearly anywhere—even in our largest cities.

FRONT TRACK
LENGTH: 2"–3", AVERAGING: 2½"; WIDTH: 1½"–2¾", AVERAGING: 2¼"

Four toes with claws. A large, triangular palm pad shows three trailing lobes. Inner and outer claws register close to the middle toes, and are easily overlooked. Middle two claws register close together and often point slightly inward. Rounder than the hind track, with a more robust palm pad.

HIND TRACK
LENGTH: 2"–3", AVERAGING: 2¼"; WIDTH: 1⅜"–2¼", AVERAGING: 1⅞"

Four toes with claws usually showing. The triangular palm pad has three trailing lobes, but often registers lightly and may appear as a round compression. Inner and outer claws register close to the middle toes, and sometimes cannot be distinguished at all. The middle two claws register close together and often point inward. Smaller than front track and usually narrower.

GAITS

Typically trots (including side trot) when traveling, but walks frequently. Usually only lopes or gallops to pursue prey or flee. Exhibits an unusual variety of walks and trots, leaving more variants than other canids.

QUICK ID TIPS:
- Typical canine track showing four symmetrical toes, claws and a triangular heel pad
- Inner and outer claws usually register close to the middle toes and sometimes do not show
- Tracks are narrow; the inner and outer toes are nearly tucked behind the middle two toes

OVERSTEP WALK

HABITAT:
Wide ranging and adaptable. Prefers open brush, but range and habitat have expanded with the gray wolf's decline. Now ubiquitous in region.

OTHER SIGNS:
Scat: One or more long droppings range from ³/₈"–1¹/₄" in diameter. Similar to red fox scat in composition, but can be much larger. Structure varies with diet. Often contains bone fragments. In summer, scat may include grasses, fruit or berry seeds and insect remains. Often deposited at trail junctions or on prominent, raised surfaces.

Dens: Coyote den entrances measure about 12"–24" in diameter, larger than fox dens, but smaller than most wolf dens. Typically have two entrances. The main entrance often has a mound of dirt in front. Tracks and hair are usually evident in disturbed soil near the entrance.

ACTIVITY:
Predominantly crepuscular, but may be active at any time.

SIMILAR SPECIES:
Gray fox tracks (pg. 221) are smaller, rounder and usually don't show claws. Gray wolf (pg. 233) tracks are larger. Red fox tracks (pg. 225) are more

TROT

heavily furred, have a chevron-shaped bar in the palm pad and less-distinct toe and palm pads. Red fox strides and trail widths are generally smaller. Bobcat tracks (pg. 243) have two lobes on the leading edge of the palm pad, and usually don't show claws. Coyote tracks can usually be distinguished from wolf and fox tracks, but may be confused with those of domestic dogs. Dog tracks are usually wider with splayed toes splayed and blunter claws that point outward. Dog trails tend to be less precise. When in doubt, look closely at both front and hind tracks. It's often the case that one, but not both, of a dog's tracks closely resembles a coyote's.

NOTES:

Coyotes have adapted extremely well to modern human land use. Despite dedicated eradication efforts for many years, coyotes have increased in numbers and expanded their range. Coyotes do not compete well with wolves, but coyotes are more resilient than wolves in the face of widespread predator control. While wolf populations shrank as the result of extermination policies, coyote populations actually grew, and coyotes expanded into many areas where they were once excluded by wolves.

Once almost exclusively a western species, coyotes are now common throughout the Midwest. Eastern coyotes are larger on average than their western counterparts—likely as a result of interbreeding with wolves in the Northeast.

Coyotes are opportunistic foragers and their diverse diet consists primarily of small mammals, but it also includes insects, fruits, berries, grasses, fish, crayfish, reptiles and birds. Coyotes rarely kill large mammals, but readily feed on animals that have died of other causes. Occasionally coyotes will kill fawns, or even adult deer that have been severely weakened.

The most common social structure for coyotes is a mated pair or a small family group of 3–5, though solitary individuals aren't rare. Coyotes may also form packs, which have a complex social structure similar to a wolf pack. Groups usually disperse to hunt and forage, engaging in group yip-howls before separating and after reuniting.

FRONT TRACK (reduced)

HIND TRACK (reduced)

GAITS page 32

Gray Wolf
Canis lupus

Gray wolf packs typically travel 25 miles or more each night—frequently following dirt roads or crossing frozen lakes. Almost anywhere there are wolves, there are abundant tracks and sign for us to find.

FRONT TRACK
LENGTH: 3¼"–4½", **AVERAGING:** 3¾"; **WIDTH:** 2¾"–4", **AVERAGING:** 3⅜"

Large, robust track with four toes, stout claws and a large triangular palm pad with three trailing lobes. Width is highly variable. Toes may splay widely, making the track appear round, or be pulled in tight leaving a narrow, almost rectangular, print. Strong toes can pull soil between the pads into a dome slightly higher than the surrounding surface. Larger than the hind track, with a longer palm pad and less space between pads.

HIND TRACK
LENGTH: 3"–4¼", **AVERAGING:** 3½"; **WIDTH:** 2½"–3¾", **AVERAGING:** 3⅛"

Four toes with stout claws. A single, triangular palm pad shows three trailing lobes. Less likely to splay than the front track, it has a more consistent width and shape with the side toes and claws usually pointing straight forward. The negative space between the toes and the palm pad looks like a five-pointed star and may be pulled up into a dome by the animal's powerful toes. Smaller and typically narrower than the front track.

GAITS
Typically trots, but may lope or gallop without apparent need. Displays a wide variety of trots. Side trots are often irregular, with the hind foot sometimes landing directly in front of the front foot. Usually walks in deep snow, but may trot or bound at times.

QUICK ID TIPS:
- Typical canine track showing four symmetrical toes, claws and a triangular heel pad
- Largest wild canine track in our region; difficult to mistake for anything other than a large domestic dog
- Powerful toes may pull soil up into a dome in the space between the pads

TROT

HABITAT:

Historically found in nearly all habitats. Eradication efforts nearly wiped them out, but populations are now recovering. Found primarily in sparsely populated, heavily forested areas with populations of large ungulates.

OTHER SIGNS:

Scat: One or more long droppings ranging from ½"–1⅞" in diameter and 6"–18" in length. Frequently deposited along travel routes and near kill sites. Accumulates near dens and rendezvous sites. Overlaps in size considerably with coyote scat. Consistency depends on diet. When a pack makes a kill, it first feeds on organ meat, leaving scat full of blood meal with little or no hair or bones. Dark, smooth, and wet, this scat is often loose and poorly formed. As the pack eats the rest, they consume more hair and bone and scat becomes firmer and lighter in color and persists much longer.

Dens: Natal dens typically have two or more entrances that measure about 20"–25" in diameter. The main entrance usually has an obvious mound of excavated dirt in front of it. If left undisturbed, a pack may use the same den for many years.

ACTIVITY:

Active year-round. Mostly crepuscular or nocturnal, but may be active during the day. Often travels long distances at night when hunting.

SIMILAR SPECIES:

All other wild canines leave smaller tracks. Domestic dog tracks are rarely as large, exhibit more splayed toes, and don't show the raised negative space. Dogs usually have shorter strides, and tend to leave more erratic trails. Cougar tracks (pg. 253) are rounder, less symmetrical and don't show claws. No other large track has a triangular palm pad.

NOTES:

The gray wolf was once one of the most widely distributed predators in the world, ranging across much of Europe, Asia and North America. Heavily persecuted in the United States until the 1960s, wolves were nearly wiped out in the Lower 48 states. Under the protection of the Endangered Species Act, wolves rebounded and healthy populations once again inhabit our northern forests.

Wolves are highly social and typically live in packs of 2 to more than 15 individuals (usually 5–7). Packs generally avoid one another, and clearly define their territories by placing scat and urine along major travel routes, including roads. These territories can range from 20–250 square miles. When prey is abundant, packs can maintain stable territory boundaries for many generations.

Wolves may travel farther and more often than any other land animal in the world, making them both masters of efficiency and remarkably strong. Packs typically cover over 25 miles each night, making use of smooth travel routes such as roads, packed trails, and frozen lakes. When traveling in snow, they often line up single-file and walk exactly in each others' footprints. Their strong toes leave clean, consistent tracks and often pull the soil between them up into a small dome.

Wolves may eat beavers, small mammals, and occasionally birds, fish, insects and berries, but they specialize in hunting large ungulates. Despite eating mostly deer, wolves have little impact on the population. Even in wolf-rich northern Minnesota, wolves kill only about one-quarter as many deer as hunters do.

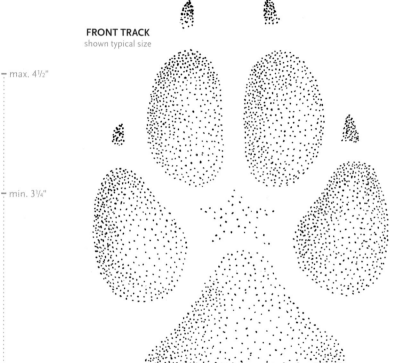

FRONT TRACK
shown typical size

max. 4½"

min. 3¼"

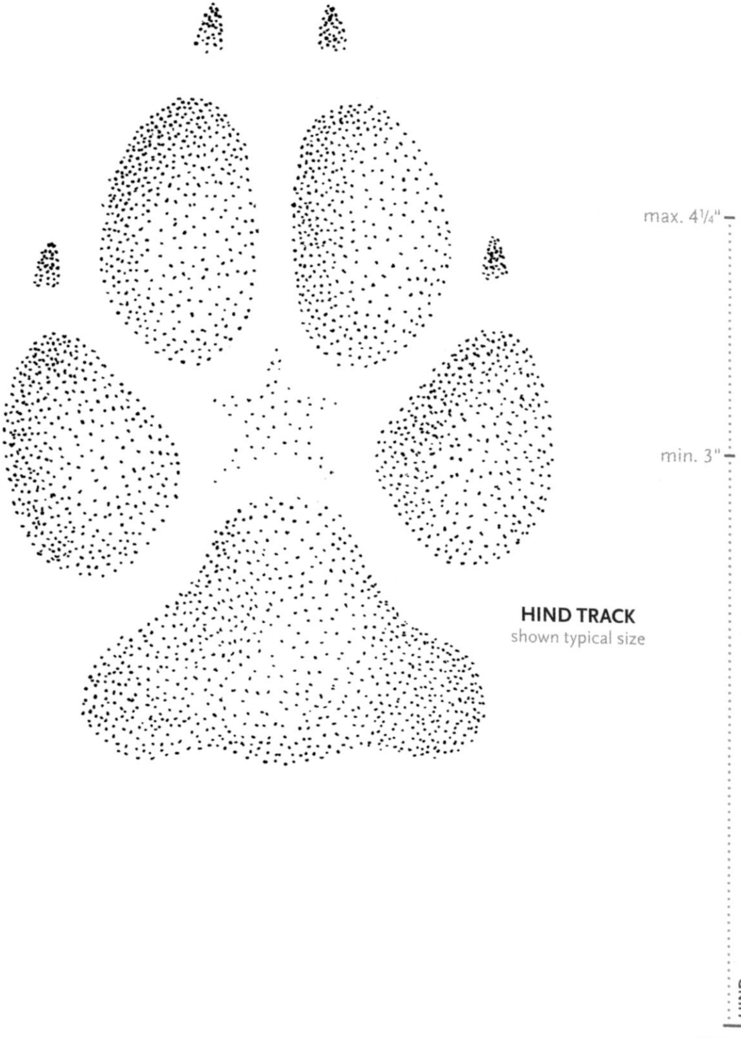

max. 4¼" –

min. 3" –

HIND TRACK
shown typical size

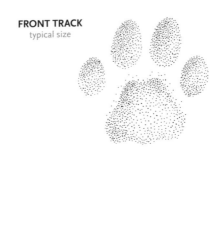

FRONT TRACK
typical size

- max. 1⁵/₈"

- min. 1"

FRONT

HIND TRACK
typical size

- max. 1⁵/₈"

- min. 1¹/₈"

HIND

GAITS page 328

Domestic Cat
Felis catus

Domestic cats can be found in cities, suburbs and farmsteads, and even in remote wilderness areas. Feral cats can be highly secretive, but in good substrate their distinctive round tracks give them away.

FRONT TRACK

LENGTH: 1"–1⁵⁄₈", AVERAGING: 1³⁄₈"; WIDTH: 1"–1³⁄₄", AVERAGING: 1³⁄₈"

Four toes and a large trapezoidal palm pad with two leading lobes and three trailing lobes. Retractable claws rarely show. The space in between the toes and the palm pad forms a "C" shape. A small fifth toe high on the foot may occasionally register on soft substrate or at high speeds. Usually larger, rounder and less symmetrical than the hind track, with a larger palm pad.

HIND TRACK

LENGTH: 1¹⁄₈"–1⁵⁄₈", AVERAGING: 1³⁄₈"; WIDTH: ⁷⁄₈"–1⁵⁄₈", AVERAGING: 1¹⁄₄"

Four toes and a large trapezoidal palm pad. Usually smaller, more oval and more symmetrical than the front track, with longer toes and a smaller palm pad.

GAITS

Usually walks, but may trot when feeling exposed or excited. Gallops when chasing prey or fleeing. Stalks prey in a slow, understep walk.

QUICK ID TIPS:
- Overall track shape is typically round
- Claws rarely show in tracks
- Large palm pad relative to track size

WALK

covered
scat

HABITAT:

Most common in urban, suburban, and rural areas, but may be found almost anywhere with sufficient cover and abundant small prey. Prefers transitional areas.

OTHER SIGNS:

Scat: Long, cylindrical scat, usually segmented, with blunt ends and no twisting. Measures about $3/8$"–$7/8$" in diameter and 2"–5" long. Frequently deposited in a scrape and usually covered. Most commonly left on soft substrates, which makes the scat easier to cover.

Spray/Scent Posts: Cats spray urine onto marking posts to define territory and communicate with each other. Usually visible only in the winter, but can be smelled at any time of year and has the distinctive "litter box" smell of cat urine.

ACTIVITY:

Active year-round. Predominantly nocturnal. Activity patterns depend on how accustomed the individual is to humans. A neighborhood stray regularly fed by people may be quite active during the day, while a completely feral cat is likely to be fully nocturnal and highly elusive.

SIMILAR SPECIES:

Bobcat tracks (pg. 243) are usually larger, but may overlap in size. A bobcat's hind tracks tend to be more oval, its front tracks are wider and more asymmetrical, and its trails are more precise. Bobcats are rare in suburbia, while domestic cats are rare in prime bobcat habitat. Gray fox tracks (pg. 221) are similar in size and shape, but have much smaller palm pads with a single lobe on the leading edge. Small domestic dog tracks show stout claws.

NOTES:

The familiar domestic cat is not as fully adapted to life with people as the domestic dog, and domestic cats retain most of their wild behavior patterns. When living with people, domestic cats appear to retain a number of kitten-like behaviors—tolerating other cats, looking to people for food, and sleeping close to people and other cats. However, even a well-mannered, well-fed lap-cat quickly assumes its wild hunting behavior. Simply dangling a piece of string is enough to awaken most cats' hunting instincts. Away from people, domestic cats easily revert to the wild and may avoid human contact.

Feral cats are common in urban, suburban and rural areas, but also turn up in remote wilderness. They tend to live near transition areas, with a mix of open ground and cover. They prey primarily on small mammals—the reason they were domesticated in the first place—and birds. As with other cats, they are quite secretive and may go unnoticed even when their population numbers are quite high.

Feral cats are generally solitary animals, like the native wildcats of North America. However, in areas where food is concentrated—including garbage dumps and other areas with high rodent populations—they will often form colonies. These colonies are groups of females and juveniles, with roving males moving in and out.

TROT

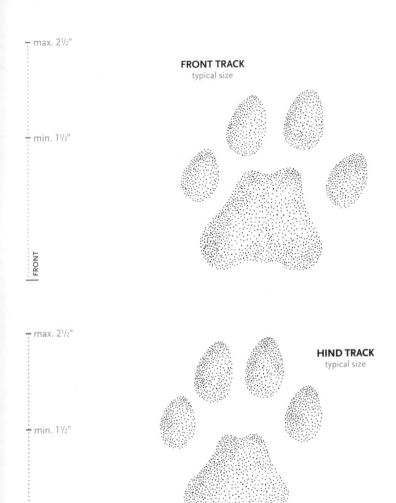

max. 2½"

min. 1½"

FRONT TRACK
typical size

FRONT

max. 2½"

min. 1½"

HIND TRACK
typical size

HIND

Bobcat
Lynx rufus

The most common wildcat in North America, bobcats are found across much of the Midwest. Signs of their presence include not only their tracks, but also their spray, which has the distinctive smell of a litter box.

FRONT TRACK
LENGTH: 1½"–2½", **AVERAGING:** 2"; **WIDTH:** 1½"–2½", **AVERAGING:** 2⅛"

Four toes and a large trapezoidal palm pad with two leading lobes and three trailing lobes. A small fifth toe high on the foot may show in soft substrate or at high speeds. Claws are retractable and rarely show. The space in between the toes and the palm pad forms a "C" shape. The front track is larger, rounder and more asymmetrical than the hind track; it is also usually wider, but can vary greatly in width, even between prints, as the animal flexes or spreads its toes.

HIND TRACK
LENGTH: 1½"–2½", **AVERAGING:** 2"; **WIDTH:** 1¼"–2¼", **AVERAGING:** 1⅞"

Four toes and a large trapezoidal palm pad with two leading lobes and three trailing lobes. Claws are retractable and rarely show. The hind track is usually smaller than the front track and has a smaller palm pad. More symmetrical than the front track, with a smaller palm pad.

GAITS
Usually walks, often in an overstep. May trot when feeling exposed or excited. Gallops when chasing prey or fleeing. Stalks in a slow, understep walk. Direct register walks in deep snow, partially dragging its feet.

QUICK ID TIPS:
- Claws rarely show in tracks
- Large palm pad relative to track size
- Front track is asymmetrical and may be wider than it is long

WALK

HABITAT:
Bobcats are quite widespread and have adapted to a range of habitats. They prefer a mixture of cover and open space and locales with abundant prey, places to climb, and shelter for denning. They also require relatively large home ranges of 1–20 square miles. Rocky outcroppings, mixed forests, and wetlands are common habitats. Bobcats generally avoid suburban developments, despite the abundance of prey.

OTHER SIGNS:
Scat: Long, cylindrical scat, usually segmented, with blunt ends and no twisting. Measures about ½"–1" in diameter and 3"–9" long and may be found at trail junctions or near denning sites. Frequently deposited in a scrape; covered about half of the time. Strict carnivores, bobcat scat consists almost exclusively of animal matter, though grass is found occasionally. Bones are usually encased in scat and do not protrude.

Scratching Posts: Bobcats sharpen their claws by scratching on trees, logs and stumps. Claw marks are generally about 3'–4' off the ground.

Spray/Scent Posts: Bobcats spray urine onto marking posts to define territory and communicate. Stumps, rocks and low-hanging branches along trails are common targets. Posts can usually only be seen in winter, when urine colors the snow, but they can be smelled any time of year. When tracking a bobcat, stay alert for a distinctive "litter box" smell.

Cached Kills: Like other cats, bobcats cover their kills by scraping dirt and debris toward them from many directions, using their front paws. The scrape marks made by a bobcat usually range from 1'–1½' long, as contrasted with the scrape marks of a domestic cat, which are under 1', and those of a cougar, which are 1½'–3'.

ACTIVITY:

Active year-round. Mainly crepuscular and nocturnal, they are most active from late afternoon to midnight and in the hours before sunrise.

SIMILAR SPECIES:

Domestic cat tracks (pg. 239) are usually smaller, with rounder hind prints and less precise trails. Domestic cats are also uncommon in prime bobcat habitat, while bobcats are rare in suburbia. Cougar (pg. 253) tracks are larger. Lynx (pg. 247) tracks are larger and much less distinct. Gray fox (pg. 221) tracks are usually smaller and have a much smaller palm pad with a single lobe on the leading edge.

NOTES:

The bobcat is the most common wild cat in North America. It ranges from southern Canada to central Mexico and is found everywhere in the Lower 48, except for the central portion of our Midwest region. Though common and widespread, it is usually secretive, making sightings rare.

Bobcats are more strictly carnivorous than foxes, subsisting almost exclusively on meat, but occasionally eating small quantities of grass. They feed primarily on rabbits, usually cottontails, and are generally most common where rabbits are abundant. They also feed on small mammals, birds, deer, and porcupines, which they attack on the nose. They ambush deer from above and kill with a bite to the neck. Since they cannot break deer bones, a partially covered deer carcass with its bones intact is a good indication of a bobcat.

Bobcats usually move by walking, pausing frequently to watch and listen. Since they mostly hunt by ambush, they rely heavily on stealth. They typically travel more slowly and spend less time in the open than foxes or coyotes.

IMAGES SHOWN AT 79%
See pages 250–251 for full size

FRONT TRACK (reduced)

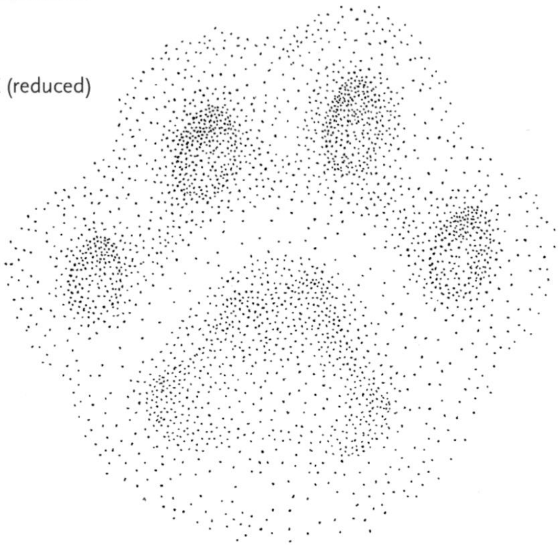

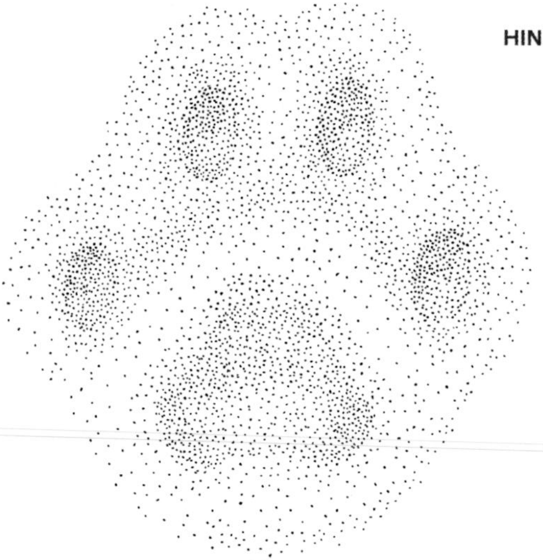

HIND TRACK (reduced)

RANGE

Canada Lynx
Lynx canadensis

Canada lynx are well adapted to deep snow and prey almost exclusively on snowshoe hares. Known Midwestern populations are limited to Minnesota, but their tracks are sometimes spotted in Wisconsin and Michigan.

FRONT TRACK
LENGTH: $2^{3}/_{4}$"–4", **AVERAGING:** $3^{3}/_{8}$"; **WIDTH:** $2^{5}/_{8}$"–$4^{1}/_{2}$", **AVERAGING:** $3^{3}/_{8}$"

Four toes and a single trapezoidal palm pad. Claws are retractable and rarely show. Toe and palm pads are smaller than in other cats. The bottom of the foot has a large amount of fur, making the track somewhat indistinct. Can vary greatly in width, even between tracks, as the animal flexes or spreads its toes. In snow, tracks can measure up to 4" long and $4^{1}/_{2}$" wide. On harder surfaces, lynx rarely spread their toes as much and tracks usually measure less than 3" by 3".

HIND TRACK
LENGTH: $2^{3}/_{4}$"–4", **AVERAGING:** $3^{3}/_{8}$"; **WIDTH:** $2^{1}/_{2}$"–$4^{1}/_{4}$", **AVERAGING:** $3^{1}/_{4}$"

Four toes and a trapezoidal palm pad. Heavily furred with small pads. Toes are longer than on the front foot, resulting in even greater variation in track size for a given animal. In deep snow, inner and outer toes may spread far to the sides, creating a distinctive cross-shaped pattern.

GAITS
Walks in a direct register or overstep when hunting or moving in cover. Usually direct register walks in deep snow. May trot across exposed areas. Gallops when chasing prey or fleeing.

QUICK ID TIPS:
- Heavily furred feet make toe and heel pads look small and often make tracks indistinct
- In deep snow, toes spread to form a cross-shaped compression
- Tracks are much larger in deep snow than on harder surfaces as toes spread to give extra buoyancy

WALK

HABITAT:
Lives primarily in northern coniferous forests. Preys almost exclusively on snowshoe hares, and occupies the same habitats.

OTHER SIGNS:

Scat: Long, cylindrical scat, usually segmented, with blunt ends and no twisting. Measures about ½"–1" in diameter and 3"–10" long. Adults rarely cover their scat, which is often left in exposed or slightly elevated areas. Strict carnivores, lynx scat consists almost exclusively of animal matter, though grass is found occasionally. Bones are usually encased in scat, and do not protrude.

Scratching Post: Lynx sharpen their claws by scratching trees, logs and stumps. Claw marks are generally 3'–4' off the ground, or above peak winter snowpack.

Spray/Scent Posts: Lynx spray urine onto stumps, rocks and low branches to define territory and communicate. These posts can usually only be seen in winter, when the urine colors the snow telltale yellow, but have a distinctive "litter box" smell that can be detected at any time of year.

ACTIVITY:

Active year-round. Predominantly crepuscular and nocturnal. Usually rests during the day under shelter or on a tree limb.

SIMILAR SPECIES:

Compared to cougar prints, (pg. 253), lynx toes and palm pads are very small, though overall track size may be the same. Cougar trail widths may be similar, but cougars take much longer strides. Both animals have wider trails (and longer strides) than bobcats.

NOTES:

Lynx are animals of the far northern forests and highly adapted to cold weather and deep snow. Lynx are more prey-specific than their feline cousin, the bobcat, feeding almost exclusively on snowshoe hare. Not only does the lynx's range and habitat mirror that of the snowshoe hare, their populations rise and fall together in roughly 10-year cycles. When hare populations are high, lynx populations grow in response to the abundant food, then increased predation from the growing lynx population causes hare populations to decline. As food becomes scarce, lynx populations decline. Hare populations then grow again, continuing the cycle.

Lynx generally walk while hunting and tend to stick to cover. They cross open and exposed areas, but often speed up to a trot to do so. They are more apt than other cats to follow trails and little-used roads and are killed on roads more commonly than other cat species.

Lynx do not generally kill large prey, and their caching behavior is much less developed than in other large cats. Most carcasses are not covered, and those that are may be poorly covered.

Like other cats, lynx are solitary, except for the young who usually stay with their mother through their first winter.

FRONT TRACK
shown typical size

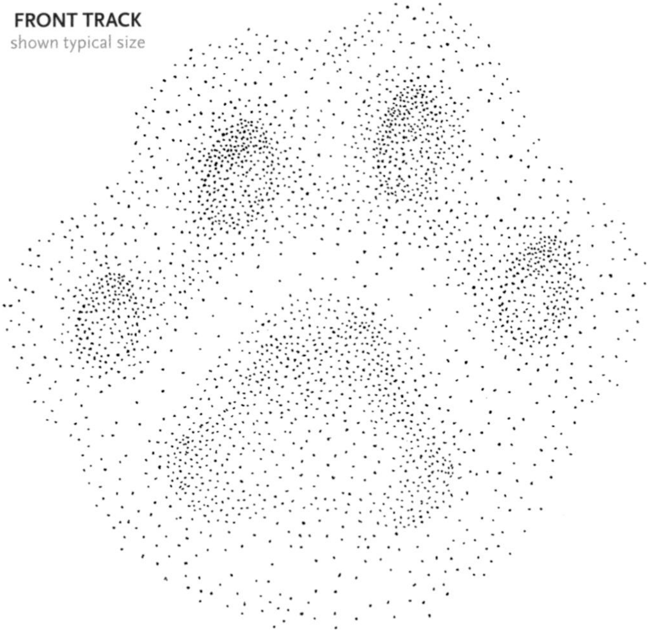

max. 4"

min. 2¾"

HIND TRACK
shown typical size

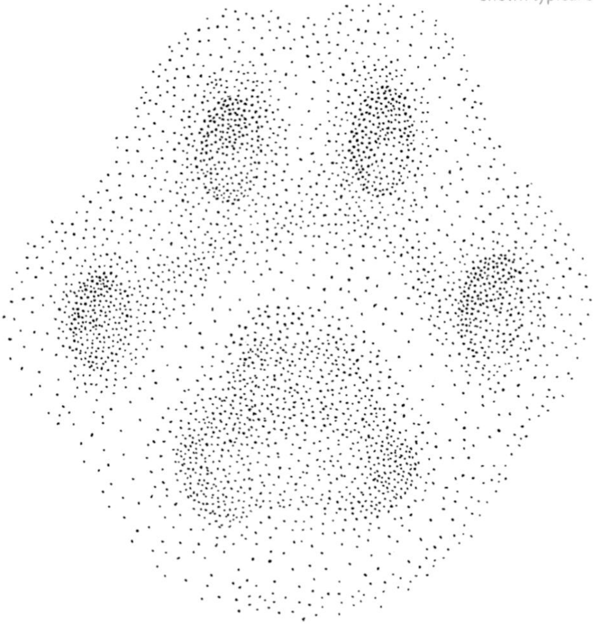

max. 4"

min. 2¾"

FRONT TRACK (reduced)

HIND TRACK (reduced)

Cougar

Puma concolor

Cougars are expanding their range after having been wiped out in the Midwest by predator-control programs. Their huge, distinctly feline tracks are occasionally spotted as far east as Lake Michigan.

FRONT TRACK

LENGTH: 2³/₄"–4", AVERAGING: 3³/₈"; WIDTH: 2³/₄"–4¹/₂", AVERAGING: 3¹/₂"

Four toes and a large trapezoidal palm pad with two leading lobes and three trailing lobes. Retractable claws rarely show. The space in between the toes and the palm pad forms a "C" shape. Front track is larger, rounder and less symmetrical than hind track. Usually noticeably wider than the hind track, but width can vary greatly, even between prints as the animal flexes or spreads its toes.

HIND TRACK

LENGTH: 2³/₄"–4", AVERAGING: 3³/₈"; WIDTH: 2¹/₂"–4¹/₄", AVERAGING: 3¹/₄"

Four toes and a large trapezoidal palm pad. Usually smaller, more oval, and more symmetrical than the front track with a smaller palm pad.

GAITS

Usually walks in a direct register or overstep, often leaving winding trails that snake across the landscape. May speed up to a trot when feeling exposed or excited. Gallops when chasing prey or fleeing. Stalks prey in a slow, understep walk.

QUICK ID TIPS:
- The largest clear print in our region that does not typically show claw marks
- Large palm pad relative to track size
- The space between the toes and the palm pad forms a "C" shape

WALK

HABITAT:

Lives in a wide range of habitats, generally mirroring habitats of deer, their primary food source. Generally stays on steep terrain or close to cover, but crosses exposed areas when traveling. Makes heavy use of exposed ridges because of the safety, sun and view of terrain they provide.

OTHER SIGNS:

Scat: Long, cylindrical scat, usually segmented with no twisting, and often with blunt ends. Measures about $3/4$"–$1\frac{1}{2}$" in diameter and 6"–17" long. May be found on a scrape, near a den, lay or kill site, or along a trail. Sometimes covered. Cats are stricter carnivores than dogs, and their scat consists almost exclusively of animal matter. Bones are usually encased inside the scat and do not protrude.

Scratching Posts: Cougars sharpen their claws by scratching on trees, logs and stumps; claw marks are generally about 5' off the ground.

Scrapes: Cougars mark their presence by scraping up mounds of dirt and debris with their hind feet and depositing urine or scat on top. Scrape marks generally measure 8"–12" wide; bobcat scratches are usually less than 8" in width.

Cached Kills: Typical cougar prey is too large for the animal to eat at one time, and is generally covered and consumed over several days. Like other cats, cougars cover their kills by using their front paws to scrape dirt and debris toward the kill from many directions. Scrape marks usually range from 1½'–3' long; bobcat scrape marks are usually 1'–1½'.

ACTIVITY:

Active year-round. Predominantly nocturnal, but sometimes active in daytime or twilight.

SIMILAR SPECIES:

Lynx tracks (pg. 247) may be the same size, but have much smaller toe and heel pads, and are usually less distinct. Bobcat tracks (pg. 243) are generally smaller, and bobcats take shorter strides. Wolf and large dog tracks (pg. 233) usually show claws and are more symmetrical with smaller, more triangular palm pads. Bear tracks (pg. 211) have 5 toes.

NOTES:

Has the largest range of any North American mammal. In the early 1800s, cougars were found across nearly all of North America. Government-supported hunting wiped cougars out east of the Rockies. Today, many populations are recovering.

Highly secretive and solitary animals, the cougar's distribution is constantly disputed. While the only confirmed breeding populations in our region are in the far western Dakotas, cougar sightings are recorded frequently in Minnesota, Wisconsin, Kansas and Michigan's Upper Peninsula. A male cougar's home range covers 50–175 square miles, with female home ranges half that size. Males without a home range may travel hundreds of miles from where they were born. When traveling, cougars are more likely to cross roads and trails than follow them.

Females raise cubs by themselves, weaning cubs at about 3 months. Cubs may stay with their mother for two years. Cougars are primarily large game hunters, feeding mainly on deer. Cougars can sprint faster than deer, but can't endure a prolonged chase and prefer to stalk to within 20'–30', then pounce. They kill with a bite to the neck, usually severing the spinal cord. Typically, they drag the carcass to a sheltered area, such as a ravine or a thicket, to feed. Cougars also eat porcupines, beaver, raccoons, foxes, coyotes and occasionally livestock.

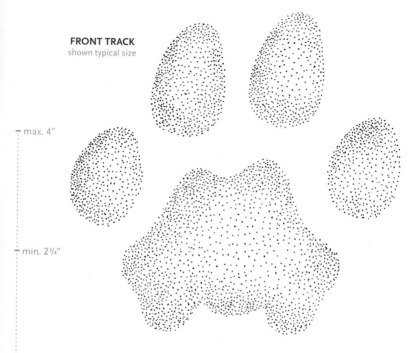

FRONT TRACK
shown typical size

— max. 4"

— min. 2¾"

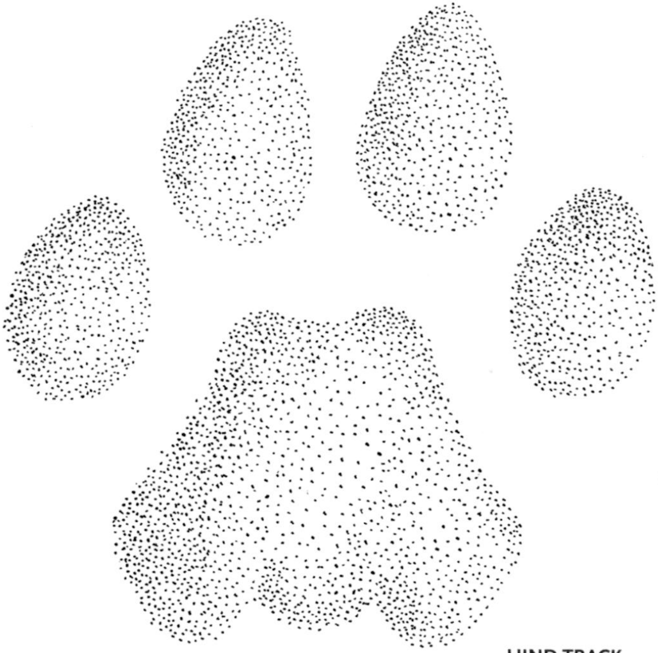

max. 4"

min. 2¾"

HIND TRACK
shown typical size

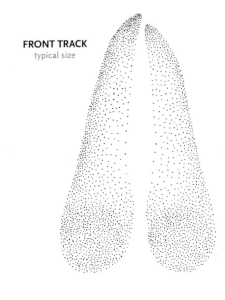

FRONT TRACK
typical size

— max. 3¼"

— min. 2⅛"

FRONT

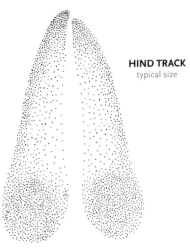

HIND TRACK
typical size

— max. 3"

— min. 2⅛"

HIND

RANGE

Pronghorn
Antilocapra americana

Pronghorn are a migratory animal at home on the open plains. They fare poorly in deep snow or where fences carve up the land, but small herds of these speedy animals are still found in the western Midwest.

FRONT TRACK
LENGTH: 2⅛"–3¼", AVERAGING: 2¾"; WIDTH: 1½"–2⅜", AVERAGING: 2"

Two-toed hoof with no dewclaws. The outer toe is slightly larger than the inner toe and typically protrudes farther forward. Outer hoof walls are straight or slightly concave near the center of the track. Inner hoof walls are concave for the front half of the track, often creating a large raised area in the center of the track. Soft pads on the back edge of the track often create clear, round impressions.

HIND TRACK
LENGTH: 2⅛"–3", AVERAGING: 2½"; WIDTH: 1½"–2⅛", AVERAGING: 1¾"

Two-toed hoof with no dewclaws. Slightly smaller than front track, but otherwise similar. Size difference between front and hind tracks is less pronounced than in other deer species.

GAITS
Walks most of the time in either a direct register or an overstep. The overstep walk is unique among ungulates and diagnostic for the species. Be careful to correctly identify the front and hind feet, as understep walks are common in deer trails. Lopes or gallops when alarmed or threatened.

QUICK ID TIPS:
- Narrow, heart-shaped track points in the direction of travel
- Lacks dewclaws, unlike members of the deer family
- Center of the track often slightly raised

WALK

HABITAT:

Open prairie and brushland with high visibility. Requires low, broken vegetation for birthing.

OTHER SIGNS:

Scat: Varies by season. The basic form of the scat is an oval pellet typically measuring $1/4"$–$1/2"$ in diameter and $3/8"$–$3/4"$ long. Usually has a dimple on one end and a small point on the other. In winter, pellets are typically dry and fibrous. In spring and summer, when pronghorn feed on more succulent browse, pellets are very soft and may clump together into a single large mass.

Territorial Mark: Males urinate and deposit scat to mark territory boundaries, often after scraping the ground with their hooves. Urine or scat may be on top or next to scrapes; they are made in all seasons, but are most frequent during the fall rut and in spring as territories are established.

ACTIVITY:

Active year-round. Predominantly diurnal. Often grazes in mornings and evenings, but may be active any time.

SIMILAR SPECIES:

Deer tracks (pg. 263–269) are wider in the forward half of the track and have a convex outer edge. They have a less distinct rear edge and lack the round pad compressions and raised center area commonly seen in pronghorn tracks. Deer may show dewclaws in deep substrate or when running and never use an overstep walk, though understep walks are common.

NOTES:

The pronghorn is a species of the open plains. An unusual animal, it is the only representative of its family in the world. Once abundant across the West, their distribution is now spotty. Perhaps the most athletic land animal on earth, pronghorns have huge hearts and lungs which, together with an elevated hemoglobin level, allow them to run at high speeds for longer periods than any other animal. Pronghorn cruise at 35–40 mph for miles on end and sprint near 60 mph. No North American predator comes close. Pronghorn appear to know this and seem to playfully flaunt their speed, racing one another, and sometimes even cars on the highway. Despite their athleticism, pronghorn can't jump, and fences on rangeland have seriously inhibited their migration.

Most of the year, pronghorns are found in small bands of females and fawns. In the spring, dominant males associate with these bands and establish territories that they defend through the fall rut. Fawns are born in May and June and are vulnerable for their first month of life, until they can run with the herd. Fawns are preyed upon by coyotes and golden eagles. Dominant males defend fawns against coyotes, and can usually drive off a lone coyote. Young are weaned by 12 weeks, and males usually leave their mother to join a bachelor herd at this time. Bachelors may test the dominance of territorial males, and serious fights resulting in injuries or fatalities are not rare. Such territorial aggression increases with population density. During the winter, large herds form with little aggression evident. Dominant males usually avoid contact with these herds. Adults are generally safe from predators, and most adult mortality is due to winter starvation. Poorly adapted to snow, pronghorn require nearly open ground to access winter browse.

Pronghorns get their name from their unique horn, which bears a pronged sheath of keratin (the material that makes up hooves and human fingernails). The sheath is shed each year shortly after breeding, but the bony core is retained—making the structure a true horn, not an antler.

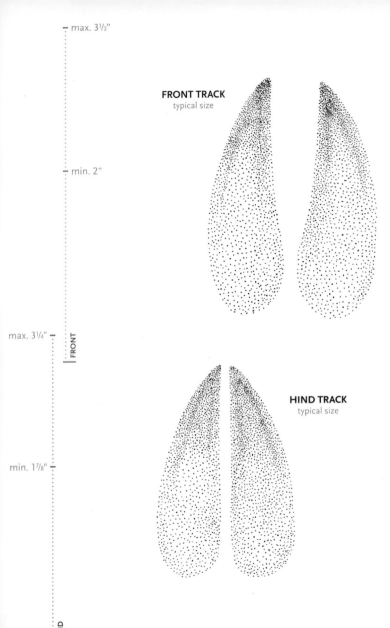

FRONT TRACK
typical size

max. 3½"

min. 2"

max. 3¼" | FRONT

HIND TRACK
typical size

min. 1⅞"

HIND

White-tailed Deer
Odocoileus virginianus

White-tailed deer are the most common large animal in the Midwest. Their familiar heart-shaped tracks can be found almost anywhere, from wilderness to farmlands to suburban back yards.

FRONT TRACK
LENGTH: 2"–3½", AVERAGING: 2⅝"; WIDTH: 1⅝"–2¾", AVERAGING: 2"

Two-toed hoof and two dewclaws, which usually register only in deep substrate or when the animal is running. The outer toe typically protrudes farther forward than the inner toe. Each toe has a thin hoof wall surrounding a large pad. Typically heart-shaped, but the toes may spread widely, especially on soft ground or when running.

HIND TRACK
LENGTH: 1⅞"–3¼", AVERAGING: 2½"; WIDTH: 1½"–2½", AVERAGING: 1¾"

Similar to the front track, but slightly smaller and more symmetrical. The deer's usual walking gait typically places the hind track nearly on top of, or even completely inside, the front track. Dewclaws on the hind foot are higher on the leg and less likely to register than front dewclaws.

GAITS
Walks most of the time. Occasionally trots, usually when mildly alarmed or agitated. Flees in a gallop. Walks in deep snow, dragging its feet as it steps, creating two parallel troughs.

QUICK ID TIPS:
- Distinctive heart-shaped track points in the direction of travel
- Forms well-worn "deer runs" throughout their range
- Extremely abundant in many suburban and exurban areas

WALK >>>>>>>>>>>>>>

HABITAT:
Ranges widely. Prefers woodland edges with trees for cover and open land for food. Especially abundant in some human-altered habitats, including corridors through suburbia or woods adjacent to farmland.

OTHER SIGNS:

Scat: Varies by season. The typical form of the scat is an oval pellet less than ½" in diameter with a dimple on one end and a small point on the other. In winter, pellets are typically dry and fibrous. In spring and summer, pellets are soft and may clump in a single large mass.

Beds: Deer rest most of the night and day in kidney bean-shaped beds, usually found on dry, smooth ground often with some shelter.

Browse: Deer tear their browse, rather than cut cleanly through it. Most deer browse is found between knee and hip height (~15"–36"). Look for twigs and vegetation that appear torn off square with a rough-looking end.

Scrapes: During mating season, bucks create scrapes on the ground with their front hooves, usually urinating on the spot afterward. At the same time, they pull down an overhead branch and rub their forehead and its scent gland against it.

ACTIVITY:

Active year-round. Predominantly crepuscular. They browse at dusk and dawn and usually retire to beds during the night and day.

SIMILAR SPECIES:

Mule deer tracks (pg. 267) are similar and many experienced trackers cannot reliably differentiate them by shape. Habitat is the best clue, as the two species' habitats don't usually overlap. When they do, mule deer tracks are usually larger. Elk and moose tracks (pgs. 271–281) are even larger. Pronghorn tracks (pg. 259) have a large raised area in the center, have no dewclaws, and are much slimmer, especially in front.

NOTES:

White-tailed deer are the most common large mammals in North America, with current populations exceeding those at the time of European settlement. Different subspecies vary greatly in size, with adults ranging from 90 to 300 pounds or more. In the Midwest, white-tails from Kansas, Nebraska, Iowa and Missouri tend to be smaller than their northern and eastern kin.

White-tailed deer are preyed on by coyotes, lynx, bobcats, cougars, black bears and wolves. Nevertheless, human hunting, domestic dogs, and cars cause most deer fatalities. Due to their large size and numerous predators, deer have become masters of stealth and escape. They are capable of standing and lying motionless for long periods of time, and can move almost silently though the woods. Fast and agile runners, they can sprint over 35 mph and jump 7' fences from a standstill.

White-tailed deer typically travel on well-established runs, which become worn over time and are especially obvious in snow. During winter, large numbers of whitetails sometimes congregate in conifer stands for shelter and browse. For most of the year, whitetails feed on herbs, grasses, fruits, acorns, mushrooms, corn, sedges and ferns.

White-tails breed in fall. Bucks create scrapes and rubs to communicate dominance and attract mates. Fawns are born in spring or early summer and spend most of their first month lying hidden near their mother. Fawn tracks, when spotted, can be very small—sometimes only 1/2" in length.

GALLOP

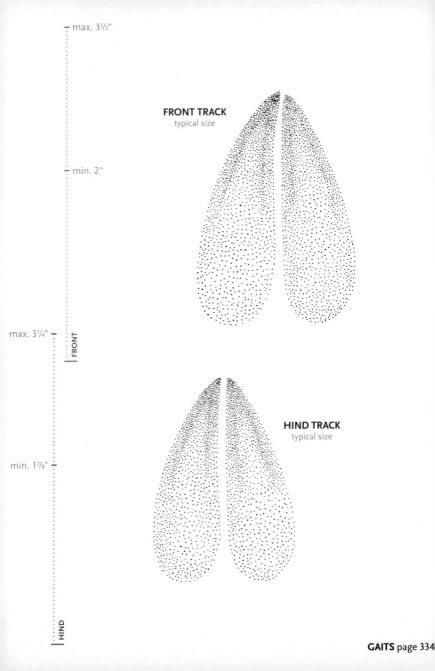

max. 3½"

min. 2"

FRONT TRACK
typical size

max. 3¼" FRONT

min. 1⅞"

HIND TRACK
typical size

HIND

Mule Deer

Odocoileus hemionus

Mule deer are similar to white-tailed deer, but better adapted to dry habitats. Found in the arid, western parts of the Midwest, their tracks and sign may be indistinguishable from those of white-tails.

FRONT TRACK

LENGTH: 2"–3½", AVERAGING: 2½"; WIDTH: 1¾"–2¾", AVERAGING: 2"

Two toes and two dewclaws, which usually register only in soft substrate or when the animal is running. The outer toe typically protrudes farther forward than the inner toe. Each toe has a thin hoof wall surrounding a large pad. Typically heart-shaped, but the toes may spread widely, especially on soft ground or when running.

HIND TRACK

LENGTH: 1⅞"–3¼", AVERAGING: 2⅜"; WIDTH: 1½"–2½", AVERAGING: 1¾"

Similar to the front track but slightly smaller and more symmetrical. The typical walking gait usually places the hind track nearly on top of, or even completely inside, the front track. The dewclaws on the hind foot are higher on the leg and less likely to register than the front dewclaws.

GAITS

Walks most of the time. Lopes, gallops, or pronks when alarmed or threatened. Pronking, also called stotting, is an unusual gait in which the deer leaps and lands with all four feet simultaneously. Trots when mildly alarmed or agitated. Walks in deep snow, usually dragging its feet as it steps, creating two parallel troughs.

QUICK ID TIPS:

- Distinctive heart-shaped track points in the direction of travel
- Leaves tracks and signs that are nearly identical to white-tailed deer; use habitat and range to distinguish between the two
- Found primarily in the West, it prefers drier habitat than white-tailed deer

WALK

HABITAT:

Prairies, farmlands, brushlands and mixed open forests. Avoids dense woods, and open grasslands with no tree cover.

OTHER SIGNS:

Scat: Varies by season. The basic form of the scat is an oval pellet usually less than ½" in diameter, with a dimple on one end and a small point on the other. In winter, pellets are typically dry and fibrous. In spring and summer pellets are softer.

Beds: Deer rest most of the day and night in kidney bean-shaped beds found on dry, level ground with shelter and a view of the landscape.

Browse: Deer tear browse, rather than cutting it. Browse is often found between knee and hip height (~15"–36"). Look for twigs and vegetation that is torn off square with a rough-looking end. Rabbit browse, by contrast, looks as if it were cut by a knife at a 45° angle.

Scrapes: During mating season, bucks create scrapes on the ground with their front hooves, usually urinating on the spot.

ACTIVITY:

Active year-round. Predominantly crepuscular and nocturnal. Often browses around dusk and dawn and retires to beds during the day and parts of the night. Midday feeding is common in fall and winter.

SIMILAR SPECIES:

White-tailed deer tracks (pg. 263) are quite similar and many experienced trackers cannot reliably differentiate their tracks by shape. Where they overlap ranges, the local white-tailed deer are usually smaller than the mule deer. Moose (pg. 277) and elk tracks (pg. 271) are larger. Pronghorn tracks (pg. 259) are much slimmer, especially in the front, and have a large raised area in the center. Also, pronghorns do not have dewclaws.

NOTES:

Found along the western edge of our region, mule deer are quite similar to white-tailed deer. Well adapted to arid conditions, mule deer may be found in sagebrush country and arid plains. Where their ranges overlap with white-tailed deer, mule deer tend to occupy drier habitats, which often have rockier terrain. This terrain can wear down a mule deer's hooves, which then leave blunter, rounder-tipped tracks.

Mule deer tracks and signs are not readily distinguishable from those of white-tailed deer. Range and habitat are usually the best clues for telling the two species apart. One feature that is diagnostic for mule deer is the pronk, a gait used frequently when they are alarmed or threatened. It is never seen in white-tailed deer.

Mule deer generally live alone or in small groups. Bucks are often solitary, especially in summer, but sometimes form small bachelor groups. Does are usually seen with fawns and yearlings. Bucks do not collect harems. A single buck follows a single doe until mating. Dominant bucks, however, mate with many females. Females give birth to 1 or 2 fawns, which stay with the mother for a year.

The mule deer's primary natural predators are wolves and cougars, but human hunting is the largest cause of adult mortality. Cars and domestic dogs also impact populations.

PRONK

FRONT TRACK (reduced)

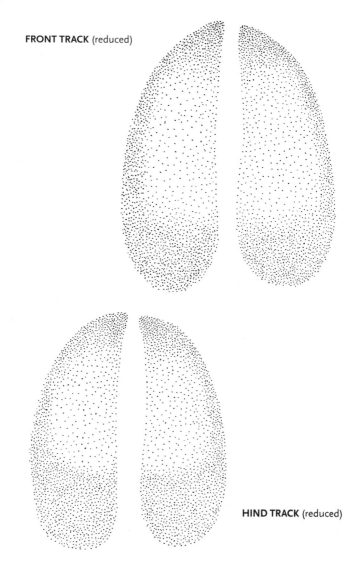

HIND TRACK (reduced)

Elk

Cervus elaphus

Once common in much of the Midwest, elk are now restricted to a few tiny pockets in the north and west. Their large tracks are a distinctly round version of the familiar heart-shape common to the deer family.

FRONT TRACK

LENGTH: $3^{1}/4$"–$4^{3}/4$", AVERAGING: $4^{1}/4$"; WIDTH: $2^{3}/4$"–$4^{1}/4$", AVERAGING: $3^{1}/4$"

Two toes and two dewclaws, which usually register only in deep substrate or when the animal is running. The outer toe typically protrudes farther forward than the inner toe. Each toe has a thin hoof wall surrounding a pad and large area of subunguinis (analogous to the soft material under our fingernails). The pad fills the rear quarter/third of the track and makes a deep impression; subunguinis fills the remainder, appearing as a raised area in the middle of the track. Toes may spread wide, especially on soft ground or when running.

HIND TRACK

LENGTH: $2^{7}/8$"–$4^{1}/4$", AVERAGING: $3^{3}/4$"; WIDTH: $2^{3}/8$"–$3^{3}/4$", AVERAGING: 3"

Similar to the front track, but slightly smaller and more symmetrical with the pad making up more of the total track. The elk's walking gait usually places the hind track on top of, or even completely inside, the front track.

GAITS

Walks most of the time. Lopes or gallops when alarmed or threatened. Trots when mildly alarmed or agitated, often using an overstep "straddle trot" with hind feet spread wider than front feet. This straddle trot is unusual among ungulates and diagnostic for elk. Direct register walks in deep snow, leaving two parallel troughs.

QUICK ID TIPS:
- Rounder than other tracks in the deer family
- Usually found in sizable large herds, though lone bulls are also common
- In our region, found almost exclusively in small pockets on game farms and protected lands

WALK >>>>>>>>>>>>>>>>>>>>>>

HABITAT:

Found primarily in open forest, young conifer stands, young aspen stands, farmlands, prairies and river corridors. Prefers edge habitats with open fields for browse and some cover for relief from the weather.

OTHER SIGNS:

Scat: Scat varies from season to season as diet changes. The basic form of the scat is an oval pellet usually $1/2"$–$3/4"$ in diameter and $1/2"$–$1"$ long. Scat usually has a dimple on one end and a small point on the other. In winter, pellets are dry and fibrous. In spring and summer, pellets are soft and may clump together in a single large mass, sometimes appearing as a formless plop about 6" in diameter.

Beds: Elk rest most of the day in kidney bean-shaped beds. These are usually found on dry, smooth ground, often with some shelter.

Browse: In grasslands, elk are primarily grazers. Where abundant grass and herbs are sparse, they browse woody plants, particularly young aspen. Elk also scrape tree bark with their lower incisors when browse is scarce.

Rubs: Bulls rub their antlers and foreheads against small trees to remove the velvet that covered their antlers, and as a marking behavior.

Wallows: Bull elk scrape shallow depressions with their hooves and antlers, urinate or defecate in them, then roll or wallow in the depression as part of the mating ritual.

ACTIVITY:

Active year-round. They are most active browsing around dusk and dawn and usually retire to beds during the day.

SIMILAR SPECIES:

Tracks of white-tailed deer (pg. 263) and mule deer (pg. 267) are smaller. Moose tracks (pg. 277) are larger. Elk tracks are noticeably rounder in front and on the sides when compared with other members of the deer family—this can help distinguish juveniles. May be most similar in size and shape to domestic calf tracks. Calves generally take much shorter strides and a calf's gait is less regular and precise than an elk's.

NOTES:

The elk was once abundant throughout the U.S. and Canada, but was extirpated from much of its former range by overhunting and habitat loss. In the Midwest, there are a few tiny pockets where elk reside, primarily in game or wildlife reserves.

Elk are herding animals. In the West, herds of cows and calves may grow to over 400 animals. In the Midwest, herds are a fraction of this size. Bulls herd separately in small groups that may live on the outskirts of a cow-calf herd. Lone elk, usually older bulls, are also common. Elk are the most polygamous species in the deer family in North America. During the rut, herd dynamics change as dominant bulls assemble and defend large harems of up to 60 cows.

Elk are grazers, feeding primarily on grasses and herbs, but also browse when given the opportunity. Elk do particularly well after fires, which create favorable young browse and open up densely wooded areas. Elk are particularly fond of aspen, and can do considerable damage to aspen stands, especially in the absence of wolves—their primary natural predator.

Elk travel along regular corridors, but are less likely than other members of the deer family to use the same exact trails. They walk when browsing and speed up to a trot when agitated. Frequently, when mildly alarmed, elk will move in a stiff-legged, overstep straddle trot with head erect, scoping for danger.

STRADDLE TROT

FRONT TRACK
shown typical size

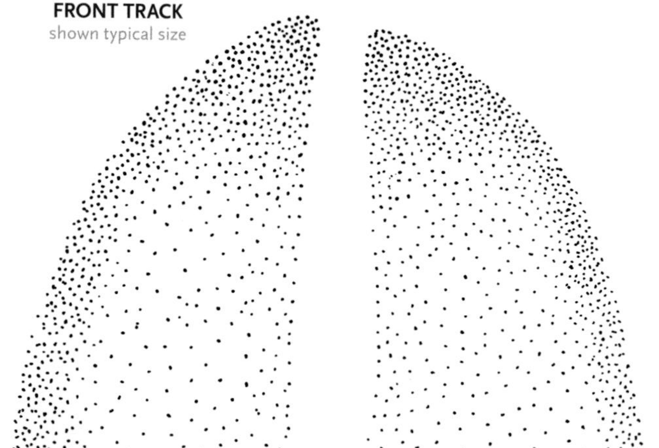

max. 4¾"

min. 3¼"

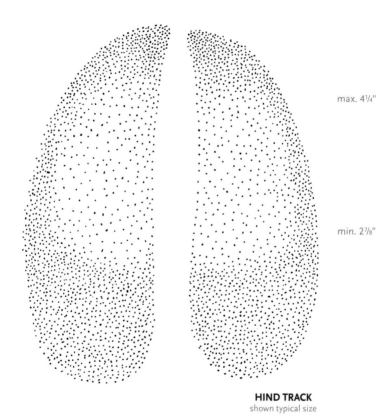

max. 4¼" —

min. 2⅞" —

HIND TRACK
shown typical size

FRONT TRACK (reduced)

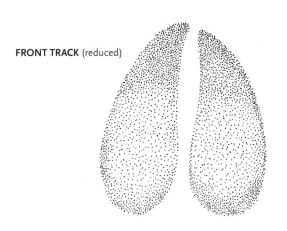

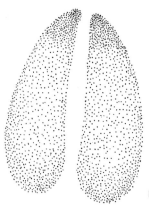

HIND TRACK (reduced)

Moose

Alces alces

Moose are the largest member of the deer family. The gigantic tracks of adult moose are unmistakable. A creature of the far north, they are well adapted to heavy snow, but fare poorly in the heat of summer.

FRONT TRACK
LENGTH: 4½"–7", AVERAGING: 5¾"; WIDTH: 3¾"–5¾", AVERAGING: 4¾"

A two-toed hoof with two dewclaws, which usually register only in deep substrate or when the animal is running. The outer toe typically protrudes farther forward than the inner toe. Each toe has a thin hoof wall surrounding a pad with a distinct band of subunguinis (analogous to the soft material under our fingernails) in between. Typically heart-shaped, but toes may spread widely, especially on soft ground or when running. The pointed front of the track wears with age, becoming rounder.

HIND TRACK
LENGTH: 4¼"–6½", AVERAGING: 5⅜"; WIDTH: 3½"–5", AVERAGING: 4¼"

Similar to the front track, but slightly smaller and more symmetrical than front track. The moose's typical walking gait usually places the hind track nearly on top of, or even completely inside, the front track. Dewclaws on the hind foot are higher on the leg and less likely to register than front dewclaws.

GAITS
Walks most of the time. Lopes or gallops when alarmed or threatened. Occasionally trots, usually when mildly alarmed or agitated. Direct register walks in deep snow, dragging its feet much less than smaller members of the deer family.

QUICK ID TIPS:
- Largest member of the deer family in the world, it has the largest tracks of any deer
- Distinctive heart-shaped track points in the direction of travel
- Large size makes adult moose tracks nearly unmistakable in our region

WALK

HABITAT:

Northern forests with lakes and swamps. Typically associated with willow growth throughout its range.

OTHER SIGNS:

Scat: Scat varies by season as diet changes. The basic form of the scat is an oval or block-like pellet usually $1/2$"–$7/8$" in diameter and 1"–$1 3/4$" long. In winter, pellets are typically dry and fibrous. In spring and summer, when moose feed on more succulent browse, pellets are very soft and may clump together into a single large mass 7"–11" in diameter.

Beds: When not feeding, moose often rest in beds, which have a roughly kidney bean shape. Moose beds are much larger than white-tailed deer beds, but may overlap with elk beds in size.

Winter Browse: Moose scrape the bark and strip small branches from trees as high as they can reach, frequently 7'. Look for incisor scrapes on red maple and aspen, and high browse on willow and balsam fir trees.

Rubs: Bulls rub their antlers and foreheads against small trees to remove the velvet that covered them, and as a marking behavior. These are similar to white-tailed deer rubs, but much higher, ranging from 3' to over 7' off the ground.

Rut Pits/Wallows: Bulls make rut pits by scraping the ground with their front hooves, then urinating in the depression. Cows, and sometimes bulls, wallow in these pits as part of the mating ritual. Pits measure 1½' to 4' long, 1'–4' wide, and 3"–6" deep.

ACTIVITY:

Active year-round. Predominantly nocturnal and crepuscular. Most active at night, but may be seen foraging at any time of day or night.

SIMILAR SPECIES:

White-tailed deer (pg. 263) and mule deer tracks (pg. 267) are much smaller. Elk tracks (pg. 271) have a rounder shape, are generally smaller, and have prominent pads in the rear third to half of the track. The pads on moose hooves are less distinct and extend almost the entire length of the track.

NOTES:

An animal of the far north, moose are well adapted to cold and snow. Their long legs allow them to walk easily in moderate snow cover, while their large bodies and dense hair keep them warm. Moose are so well adapted to cold that they need to expend extra energy to stay cool when temperatures rise above 55°F. Easily stressed by heat, moose spend much of the summer in the water, browsing on willows and aquatic plants. Though generally solitary, moose are not territorial and may congregate to feed during summer.

Like other members of the deer family, moose make prominent trails in the forest. Moose trails are wider and deeper than white-tailed deer or elk trails, and moose are more likely to detour around obstacles. Moose are primarily browsers, not grazers, and their browse sign can often be distinguished from that of deer by its height.

While moose may look ungainly, they can run at up to 35 mph, move almost silently through the forest and be fiercely unpredictable. A huge animal with strong legs and sharp hooves, they have no natural enemies except for wolves, which specialize in hunting moose in some areas. While generally shy and docile, rutting bulls and cows with calves have been known to attack not only people but cars and trucks as well. It is wise to be cautious when tracking moose.

TROT

FRONT TRACK
shown typical size

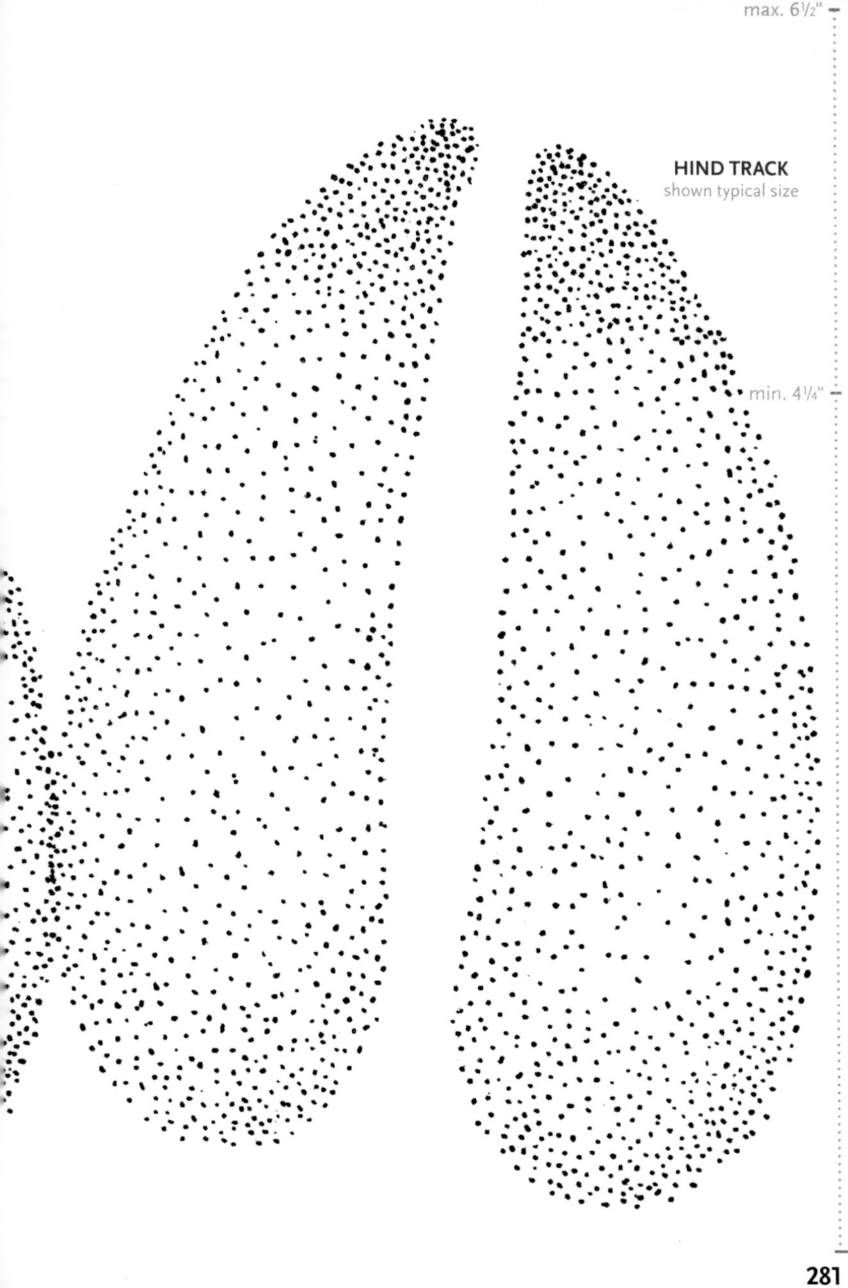

max. 6½"

HIND TRACK
shown typical size

min. 4¼"

HIND

FRONT TRACK (reduced)

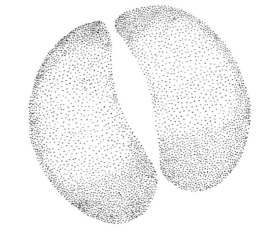

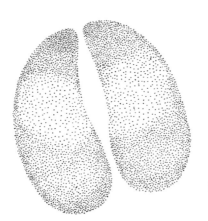

HIND TRACK (reduced)

RANGE (captive)

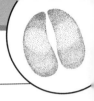

American Bison
Bison bison

Huge migratory herds of bison were once a fixture of the Great Plains. Now, only captive animals remain in the Midwest. The largest land animal in North America, they leave enormous tracks, wallows and scat.

FRONT TRACK
LENGTH: 4½"–6½", **AVERAGING:** 5½"; **WIDTH:** 4½"–6½", **AVERAGING:** 5½"

Two toes and two dewclaws, which usually register only in deep substrate. The outer toe is slightly larger and typically protrudes farther forward than the inner toe. Tracks are round and may be circular or slightly wider than long. Interior hoof wall is concave with a large space between the toes in the middle of the track. Each toe has a soft pad in the center that has a distinct "V" shape along its rear edge.

HIND TRACK
LENGTH: 4"–6", **AVERAGING:** 5"; **WIDTH:** 4"–6", **AVERAGING:** 5"

Two toes and two dewclaws. Interior track walls are concave, but do not create as large a space between the toes as is seen in the front track. Soft pads in each toe have a distinct "V" shape to their rear edge. Slightly smaller and more symmetrical than the front track.

GAITS
Usually walks, often in an understep. May trot or lope for short distances when alarmed or when playing. Stampedes in a full gallop. Walks in deep snow, dragging its feet, sometimes plowing snow aside with its body or head.

QUICK ID TIPS:
- Extremely large, round hoof cannot be mistaken for any other wild animal track in our region
- Typically live and move about in large herds
- Today bison roam freely only in a few parks, reserves and ranches

UNDERSTEP WALK

HABITAT:

Open prairies and grasslands, but ventures into adjacent open forests.

OTHER SIGNS:

Scat: Scat varies from season to season as diet changes. In summer, scat consists of large, amorphous patties measuring 10"–12" in diameter, which are nearly identical to cow patties, though usually larger. In winter, scat are piles or clumps of "chips," each measuring 3"–4½" in diameter.

Rubs: In wooded areas, bison rub their horns and foreheads against trees, wearing the bark smooth and trampling the surrounding ground. Bison also rub against boulders on the open plains and against telephone poles.

Wallows: In open grasslands, bison create large, dusty, saucer-shaped depressions 8'–10' across where they wallow to avoid biting insects. Bison sometimes urinate in these pits and then wallow, caking themselves with mud as protection from insects.

ACTIVITY:

Active year-round. Predominantly diurnal. Most active grazing in the mornings and evenings, but may be seen any time of day or night. Often rest in the open during the day, chewing their cud.

SIMILAR SPECIES:

Moose tracks (pg. 277) have straighter sides and more pointed tips. All other cloven-hoof tracks are much smaller. Bison calf tracks may resemble an elk's (pg. 271), but are even rounder and are generally found with prints of adults. Bison tracks are most likely to be confused with domestic cow tracks, which are generally smaller, but otherwise very similar. On hard ground, a bison's interior hoof walls may not register clearly, and the round, sharp-edged tracks may resemble horse tracks.

NOTES:

The bison is the largest land animal in North America, and was once the most abundant large animal on the continent and a fixture of the Midwestern plains. Bison numbered in the tens of millions when European settlers first arrived. In the 1800s, the great bison herds were hunted to near extinction. By the early 1900s fewer than 1,000 remained. Theodore Roosevelt, one of America's iconic outdoorsmen, wrote of the slaughter, "Never before in all of history were so many large wild animals of one species slain in so short a space of time." An emblem of the American West, the bison was saved from extinction, but no longer ranges in huge wild herds across the Great Plains. The total wild bison population is now estimated to be about 30,000 individuals, scattered across a few large national parks in the West. A much larger number of bison—perhaps half a million—now live in commercial herds on private ranches. Only captive herds live in our region.

Bison normally travel in herds of 5–20, though lone animals are not rare. Males herd separately from females and calves. Where the animals still range freely, herds merge together during the breeding season and may become very large. The breeding season lasts from June to September with a single calf born about 9 months later. Calves can stand 30 minutes after birth, walk within hours, and join the herd after 1–2 days. Bison are hardy animals, well adapted to hard winters on the open plains. They are grazers, feeding on grass and herbs year-round. In the winter, bison use their huge heads to plow even deep snows aside to feed on the plants underneath.

Adult bison are formidable, and a herd is even more so. Their primary defense is stampeding. In our region, they have no natural predators. In the West, only wolves and grizzlies are a threat, and even they only prey upon calves or sick individuals apart from the herd.

max. 6½"

min. 4½"

FRONT TRACK
shown typical size

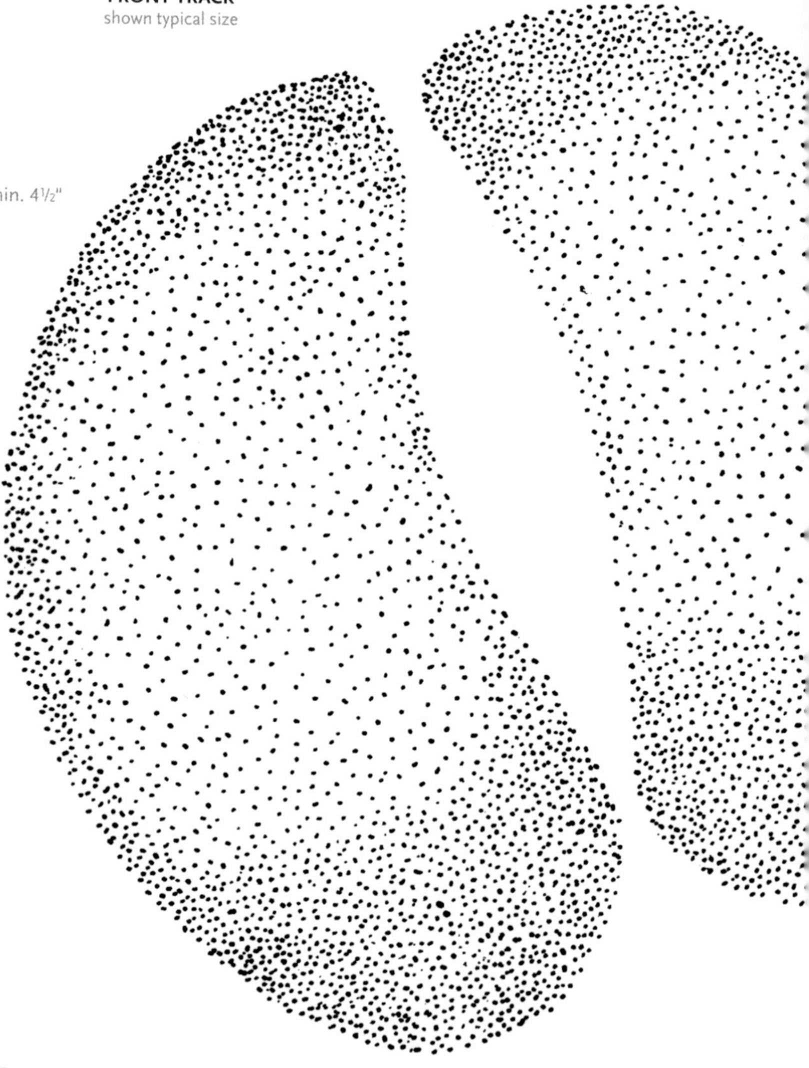

HIND TRACK
shown typical size

max. 6"

min. 4"

Gait Patterns

This section provides detailed information about many of the gaits commonly used by mammals in the Midwest. Each page includes between one and three trail patterns left by each species, together with a description of the animal's usual movement patterns and typical measurements for its trails.

The illustrations show patterns of tracks that are representative of the animal moving in a particular gait. Please note that while these illustrations represent common track patterns left by a given species, they represent only a tiny fraction of the patterns you will see in the field. Each illustrations show a specific example of the given species moving in a straight line at a fairly constant speed. In the field, animals produce a wide variety of track patterns as they twist and turn, stop and start, sit down and get up again. That said, these patterns will help you become familiar with the ways each species typically moves and provide you with a good foundation for identifying trails.

The range of measurements provided below each illustration are generous enough to cover most trails made by adult members of a particular species, but specific enough to help you discern between many species with similar-looking tracks and gait patterns. While we have not included every possible measurement for each gait, we have included the most useful data to help you narrow down the options for what may have left a particular trail.

For detailed information about measuring and interpreting gaits, please see page 22 in the introduction.

Smaller shrews typically bound leaving trails similar to a white-footed mouse trails in miniature. Larger shrews more commonly trot, leaving a vole-like trail. Most shrews bound in deeper snow. Moles travel aboveground in a kind of modified wiggling walk.

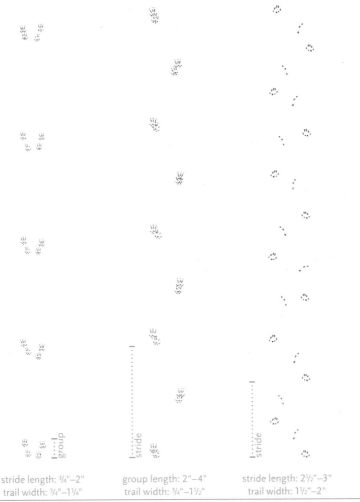

stride length: ¾"–2"
trail width: ¾"–1¼"

group length: 2"–4"
trail width: ¾"–1½"

stride length: 2½"–3"
trail width: 1½"–2"

bound (small shrews)   **trot** (large shrews)   **walk** (moles)

FRONT FOOT • HIND FOOT
STRIDE: hind track to next hind track on same side
GROUP: back edge of rearmost track to the front edge of the foremost track

Bounds when traveling. Like the white-footed mouse, its trail looks like that of a miniature tree squirrel. Slows to a walk when foraging. In snow, front and hind prints may blur together and tail drag may show.

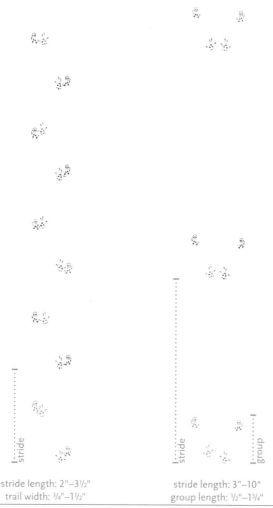

stride length: 2"–3½"
trail width: ¾"–1½"

stride length: 3"–10"
group length: ½"–1¾"

walk   **bound**

FRONT FOOT • HIND FOOT

STRIDE: hind track to next hind track on same side
GROUP: back edge of rearmost track to the front edge of the foremost track

Usually bounds, leaving a trail pattern that looks like that of a tiny tree squirrel. Sometimes walks when foraging. A few species are also known to lope. Often travels on top of deep snow.

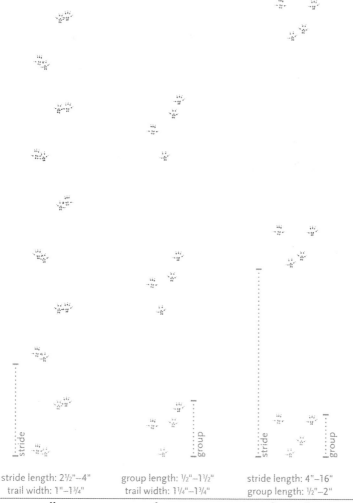

stride length: 2½"–4"
trail width: 1"–1¾"

group length: ½"–1½"
trail width: 1¼"–1¾"

stride length: 4"–16"
group length: ½"–2"

walk   **lope**   **bound**

FRONT FOOT • HIND FOOT
STRIDE: hind track to next hind track on same side
GROUP: back edge of rearmost track to the front edge of the foremost track

Typically travels in a walk or a trot ("scurries"), which are quite difficult to differentiate. May speed up to a bound when threatened or exposed.

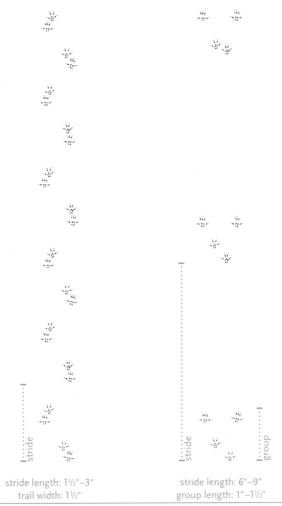

stride length: 1½"–3"
trail width: 1½"

stride length: 6"–9"
group length: 1"–1½"

walk/trot

bound

FRONT FOOT • HIND FOOT

STRIDE: hind track to next hind track on same side
GROUP: back edge of rearmost track to the front edge of the foremost track

Usually travels in a direct register trot. Speeds up to a hop or lope when exposed. Sometimes walks, especially in thick cover. Rarely bounds. Tracks are common in light snow, but when snow is deep, voles generally tunnel under it.

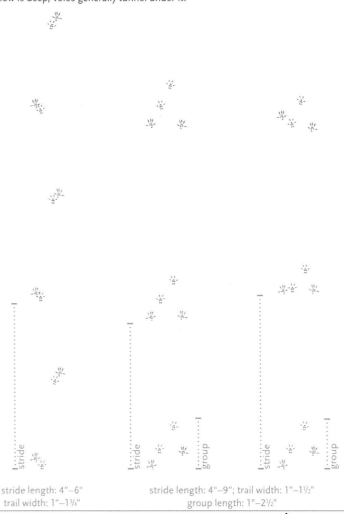

trot	hop	hop/lope
stride length: 4"–6" trail width: 1"–1¾"	stride length: 4"–9"; trail width: 1"–1½" group length: 1"–2½"	

FRONT FOOT • HIND FOOT
STRIDE: hind track to next hind track on same side
GROUP: back edge of rearmost track to the front edge of the foremost track

GAITS: Jumping & Pocket Mice (pgs. 77–83)

These Jumping & Pocket Mouse gaits are in proportion to each other.

Both species nearly always bound. Jumping mice leave more irregular track groups than most other mice. They usually take strides of 4"–10", but are capable of leaping over 3'. Pocket mice typically overlap their front feet.

trail width: 1½"–2"
group length: 1"–2½"

trail width: ¾"–1¼"
group length: 1"–3"

bound (Jumping Mouse) **bound** (Pocket Mouse)

FRONT FOOT • HIND FOOT

GROUP: back edge of rearmost track to the front edge of the foremost track

Travels in a distinctive bipedal bound shared by all kangaroo rats and kangaroo mice. At high speeds, one foot may land in front of the other creating a bipedal gallop. The stride varies greatly with speed, reaching 8' when the animal is fleeing. Sometimes bounds on all four feet when foraging.

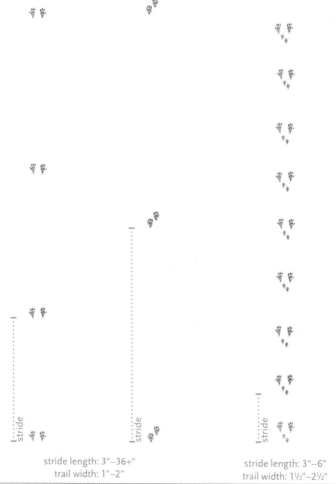

bipedal bound

bipedal gallop

stride length: 3"–36+"
trail width: 1"–2"

bound

stride length: 3"–6"
trail width: 1½"–2½"

FRONT FOOT • HIND FOOT

STRIDE: hind track to next hind track on same side

Usually walks in or near cover, but often bounds when in the open. Generally bounds with its front feet set one in front of the other.

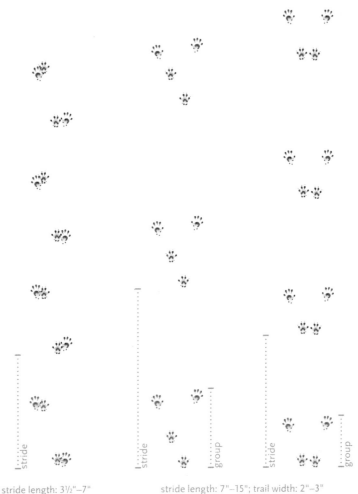

stride length: 3½"–7"
trail width: 1½"–2½"

walk

stride length: 7"–15"; trail width: 2"–3"
group length: 2"–7"

bound

FRONT FOOT • HIND FOOT

STRIDE: hind track to next hind track on same side
GROUP: back edge of rearmost track to the front edge of the foremost track

Typically travels in a walk or a trot. May speed up to a bound when threatened or when crossing open areas. Usually bounds in deep snow, leaving an obvious tail drag.

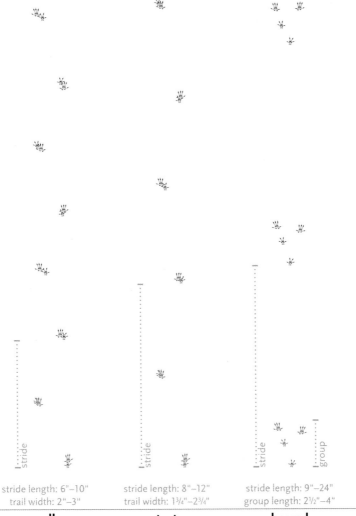

stride length: 6"–10"
trail width: 2"–3"

stride length: 8"–12"
trail width: 1¾"–2¾"

stride length: 9"–24"
group length: 2½"–4"

walk   **trot**   **bound**

FRONT FOOT • HIND FOOT
STRIDE: hind track to next hind track on same side
GROUP: back edge of rearmost track to the front edge of the foremost track

Walks or trots ("scurries") almost exclusively. Pocket gophers can walk and trot equally well forward and backward. Since these "scurrying" gaits keep the spine level, they are ideally suited to life in underground tunnels.

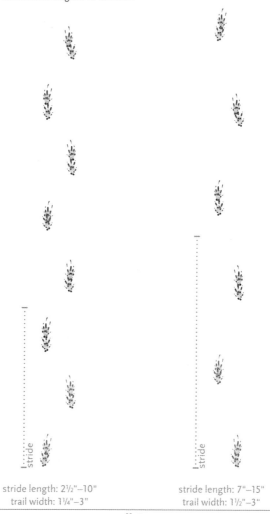

stride length: 2½"–10"
trail width: 1¼"–3"

stride length: 7"–15"
trail width: 1½"–3"

walk/trot

FRONT FOOT • HIND FOOT
STRIDE: hind track to next hind track on same side

Travels in a bound. May walk while foraging. Typically bounds with one front foot in front of the other, though occasionally front feet land side by side.

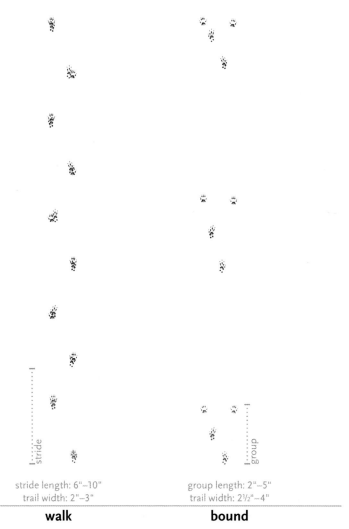

stride length: 6"–10"
trail width: 2"–3"

group length: 2"–5"
trail width: 2½"–4"

walk

bound

FRONT FOOT • HIND FOOT

STRIDE: hind track to next hind track on same side
GROUP: back edge of rearmost track to the front edge of the foremost track

Chipmunks bound almost exclusively, leaving a pattern like that of a tree squirrel. Southern Flying Squirrels normally hop, rather than bound, creating a pattern similar to that of a chipmunk traveling in the opposite direction. Northern Flying Squirrels usually bound with their front feet wide apart, leaving a distinctively "boxy" variation on the typical tree squirrel pattern.

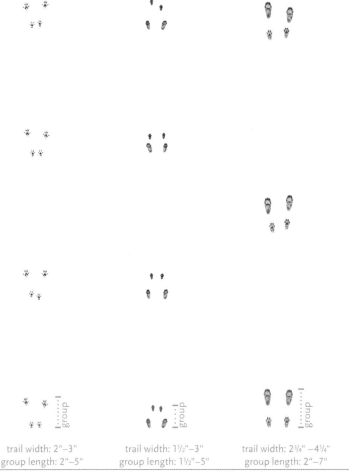

trail width: 2"–3"
group length: 2"–5"

trail width: 1½"–3"
group length: 1½"–5"

trail width: 2¾" –4¼"
group length: 2"–7"

bound (Chipmunk)   **hop** (S. Flying Squirrel)   **bound** (N. Flying Squirrel)

FRONT FOOT • HIND FOOT

GROUP: back edge of rearmost track to the front edge of the foremost track

These three tree squirrels all usually bound. When bounding, front feet generally register side by side with a gap between them, but are sometimes offset. Occasionally walk. In deep snow, may leave a single body print with the feet dragging on the outside of the trail, creating an H-shaped imprint.

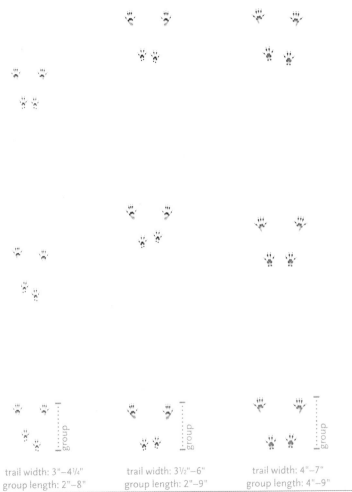

trail width: 3"–4¼"
group length: 2"–8"

trail width: 3½"–6"
group length: 2"–9"

trail width: 4"–7"
group length: 4"–9"

bound (Red Squirrel)   **bound** (E. Gray Squirrel)   **bound** (E. Fox Squirrel)

FRONT FOOT • HIND FOOT
GROUP: back edge of rearmost track to the front edge of the foremost track

GAITS: Black-tailed Prairie Dog (pg. 129)

These Black-tailed Prairie Dog gaits are in proportion to each other.

Walks most of the time with the hind track usually covering or partially covering the front track. May lope when covering open ground and bound when fleeing. Drags its feet when walking in snow.

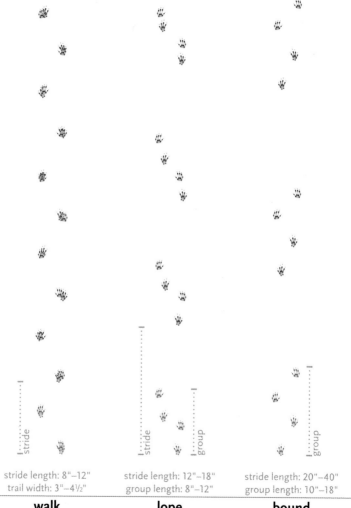

stride length: 8"–12"
trail width: 3"–4½"

stride length: 12"–18"
group length: 8"–12"

stride length: 20"–40"
group length: 10"–18"

walk　　　　　**lope**　　　　　**bound**

FRONT FOOT • HIND FOOT

STRIDE: hind track to next hind track on same side
GROUP: back edge of rearmost track to the front edge of the foremost track

Walks most of the time with the hind track next to or partially covering the front track. May trot or lope to across open ground and may bound when fleeing. Trots look like the walking pattern, but with a longer stride and slightly narrower trail. Bounding pattern is similar to a raccoon's.

stride length: 9"–20"
trail width: 4"–5½"

group length: 5"–12"
trail width: 4¾"–7½"

walk

bound

FRONT FOOT • HIND FOOT
STRIDE: hind track to next hind track on same side
GROUP: back edge of rearmost track to the front edge of the foremost track

303

Bounds almost exclusively, creating one of the most recognizable track patterns. Front feet register one in front of the other or touching one another. Hind feet generally register in front of the front feet, giving the group a triangular shape. Occasionally walks.

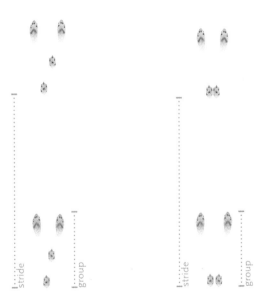

stride length: 10"–48"; trail width: 2⅛"–5"
group length: 4"–18"

bound   **bound** (fronts together)

FRONT FOOT • HIND FOOT

STRIDE: hind track to next hind track on same side
GROUP: back edge of rearmost track to the front edge of the foremost track

Bounds almost exclusively, leaving the distinctive rabbit group pattern. Front feet typically register one in front of the other. Hind feet register in front of front feet, giving the group a triangle shape. Occasionally walks for short distances.

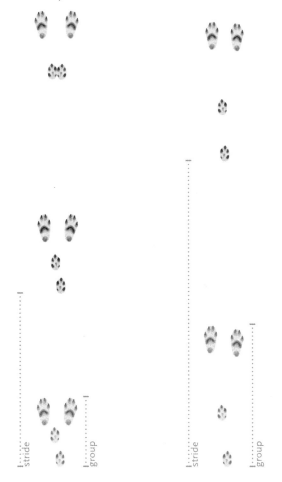

stride length: 18"–72"; trail width: 4"–9"
group length: 8"–20"

bound **bound** (fast)

FRONT FOOT • HIND FOOT

STRIDE: hind track to next hind track on same side
GROUP: back edge of rearmost track to the front edge of the foremost track

GAITS: Black-tailed Jackrabbit (pg. 145)

These Black-tailed Jackrabbit gaits are in proportion to each other.

Typically uses a modified bound/gallop where one hind foot touches down just before the other, creating variations on the typical rabbit trail pattern. Creates a remarkable diversity of bounding and galloping patterns. Occasionally walks.

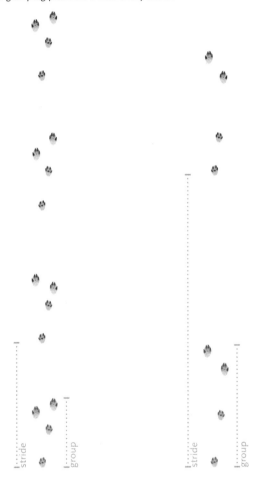

stride length: 10"–120"; trail width: 3"–8"
group length: 10"–24"

bound/gallop

FRONT FOOT • HIND FOOT

STRIDE: hind track to next hind track on same side
GROUP: back edge of rearmost track to the front edge of the foremost track

GAITS: White-tailed Jackrabbit (pg. 149)

These White-tailed Jackrabbit gaits are in proportion to each other.

Uses a modified bound/gallop almost exclusively where one hind foot touches down just before the other, leaving a variation on the typical rabbit group pattern. Sometimes lopes, which is unusual among rabbits. Occasionally walks.

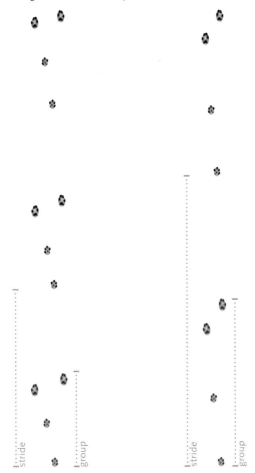

stride length: 24"–120"; trail width: 4½"–9"
group length: 20"–45"

bound/gallop

FRONT FOOT • HIND FOOT

STRIDE: hind track to next hind track on same side
GROUP: back edge of rearmost track to the front edge of the foremost track

Typically travels in a 2x2 lope, mixing long and short bounds. In deep snow, shorter bounds often show foot drag. Occasionally walks. Away from snow may leave a 3x4 lope pattern.

stride length: 4"–45"
trail width: ¾"–3"

lope to bound   **2x2 lope**

FRONT FOOT • HIND FOOT
STRIDE: hind track to next hind track on same side

Typically travels in a lope. Generally uses a 2x2 lope in deeper snow. Occasionally walks.

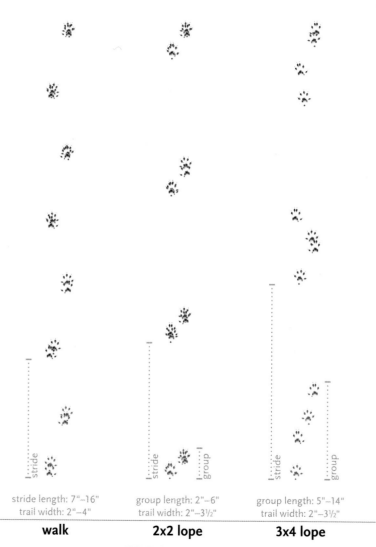

stride length: 7"–16"
trail width: 2"–4"

walk

group length: 2"–6"
trail width: 2"–3½"

2x2 lope

group length: 5"–14"
trail width: 2"–3½"

3x4 lope

FRONT FOOT • HIND FOOT
STRIDE: hind track to next hind track on same side
GROUP: back edge of rearmost track to the front edge of the foremost track

GAITS: American Marten (pg. 161)

These American Marten gaits are in proportion to each other.

Travels in a 3x4 lope or a 2x2 lope, preferring the latter in deep snow. Sometimes slows to a walk.

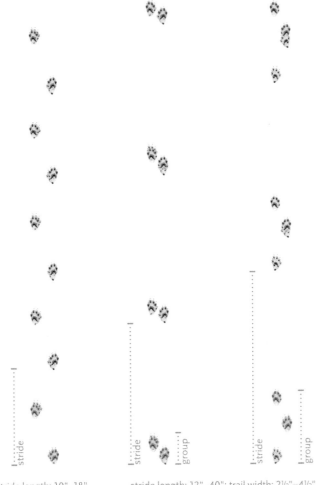

stride length: 10"–18"
trail width: 3"–4½"

stride length: 12"–40"; trail width: 2½"–4½"
group length: 3½"–20"

walk   **2x2 lope**   **3x4 lope**

FRONT FOOT • HIND FOOT
STRIDE: hind track to next hind track on same side
GROUP: back edge of rearmost track to the front edge of the foremost track

Commonly walks or lopes using either a 3x4 or a 2x2 lope. In deep snow usually uses a 2x2 lope or walks, leaving a trough. In a 2x2 lope, one pair of feet will often land far ahead of the other, sometimes almost directly in front.

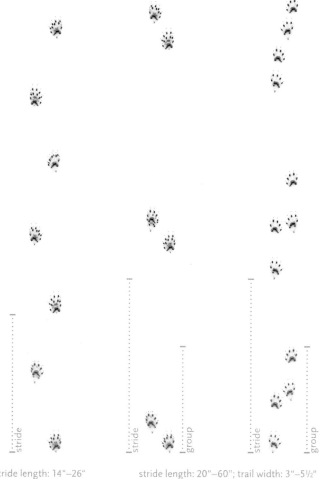

stride length: 14"–26"
trail width: 3½"–6"

stride length: 20"–60"; trail width: 3"–5½"
group length: 6"–24"

walk   **2x2 lope**   **3x4 lope**

FRONT FOOT • HIND FOOT

STRIDE: hind track to next hind track on same side
GROUP: back edge of rearmost track to the front edge of the foremost track

Typically travels in a 3x4 lope, often sliding when the surface permits. Explores in a walking gait. May use a 2x2 lope in deep snow.

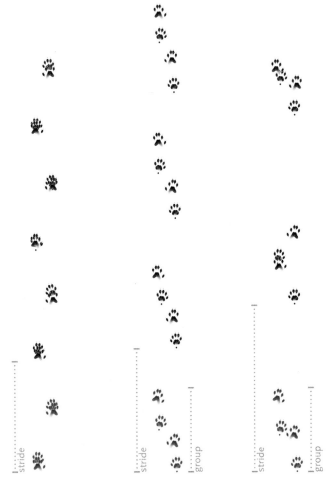

stride length: 12"–28"
trail width: 4"–7"

walk

stride length: 15"–50"; trail width: 4"–7"
group length: 10"–20"

3x4 lope

FRONT FOOT • HIND FOOT

STRIDE: hind track to next hind track on same side
GROUP: back edge of rearmost track to the front edge of the foremost track

Walks when foraging. Often travels in a trot. Lopes when alarmed. Walks and trots with feet pointed sharply inward (toed-in)—a defining characteristic of the species. Walks in deep snow, leaving a prominent trough.

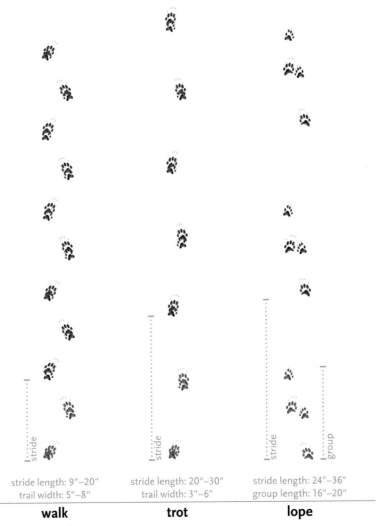

stride length: 9"–20"
trail width: 5"–8"

stride length: 20"–30"
trail width: 3"–6"

stride length: 24"–36"
group length: 16"–20"

walk   **trot**   **lope**

FRONT FOOT • HIND FOOT
STRIDE: hind track to next hind track on same side
GROUP: back edge of rearmost track to the front edge of the foremost track

Typically travels in a lope or a bound and walks when foraging or moving about in cover. Often uses a highly irregular "puttering" gait when walking, with tremendous variation in stride from one step to the next.

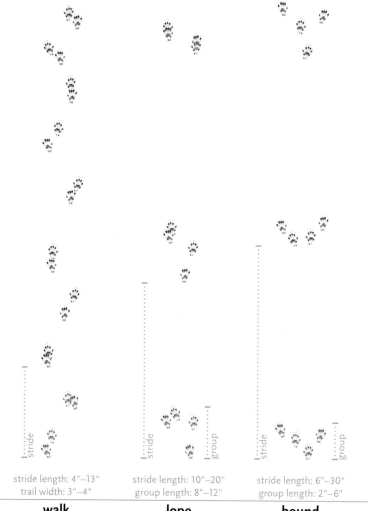

stride length: 4"–13"
trail width: 3"–4"

stride length: 10"–20"
group length: 8"–12"

stride length: 6"–30"
group length: 2"–6"

walk   **lope**   **bound**

FRONT FOOT • HIND FOOT

STRIDE: hind track to next hind track on same side
GROUP: back edge of rearmost track to the front edge of the foremost track

Typically travels and explores in a lope or an overstep walk. Usually walks when foraging. Tends to direct register walk in deep snow.

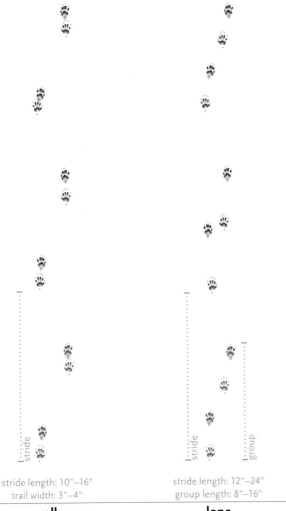

stride length: 10"–16"
trail width: 3"–4"

stride length: 12"–24"
group length: 8"–16"

walk

lope

FRONT FOOT • HIND FOOT
STRIDE: hind track to next hind track on same side
GROUP: back edge of rearmost track to the front edge of the foremost track

Typically lopes when traveling, slowing to a walk when foraging.

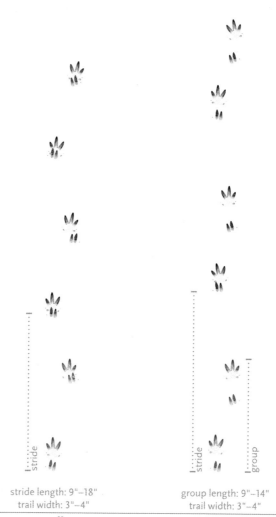

stride length: 9"–18"
trail width: 3"–4"

group length: 9"–14"
trail width: 3"–4"

walk   **lope**

FRONT FOOT • HIND FOOT

STRIDE: hind track to next hind track on same side
GROUP: back edge of rearmost track to the front edge of the foremost track

Walks almost exclusively in a distinctive toed-in gait. Most common pattern is an overstep walk. May lope for a short distance if startled. Direct register walks in deep snow, plowing a deep trough with quill drag marks often evident.

stride length: 12"–22"
trail width: 5"–9"

walk

FRONT FOOT • HIND FOOT
STRIDE: hind track to next hind track on same side

Usually walks with an indirect register. Hind feet fall behind, in front of, or mostly on top of the front feet. Lopes or bounds when threatened. Walks in snow, often showing foot and tail drags. Plows a trough in deep snow.

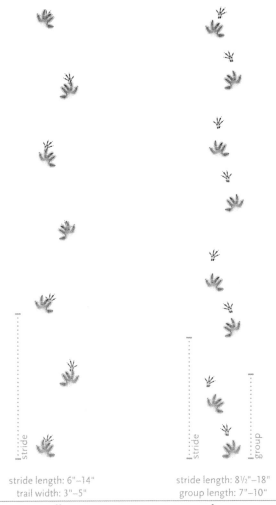

stride length: 6"–14"
trail width: 3"–5"

walk

stride length: 8½"–18"
group length: 7"–10"

lope

FRONT FOOT • HIND FOOT

STRIDE: hind track to next hind track on same side
GROUP: back edge of rearmost track to the front edge of the foremost track

Generally walks on land in a direct register or, sometimes, indirect register. May bound when alarmed. Plows through snow, creating a wide trough.

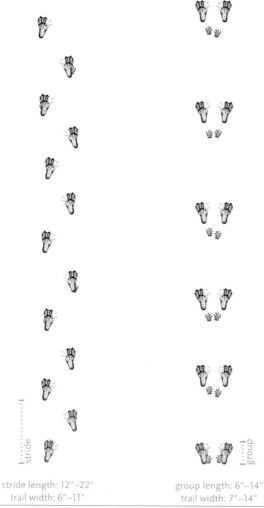

stride length: 12"–22"
trail width: 6"–11"

group length: 6"–14"
trail width: 7"–14"

walk   **bound**

FRONT FOOT • HIND FOOT
STRIDE: hind track to next hind track on same side
GROUP: back edge of rearmost track to the front edge of the foremost track

Walks when exploring and trots when traveling. Usually walks in a direct register or double register, but sometimes displays the extreme overstep walk common to raccoons. Bounds when chasing prey or escaping. Walks in deep snow, dragging its feet with each step.

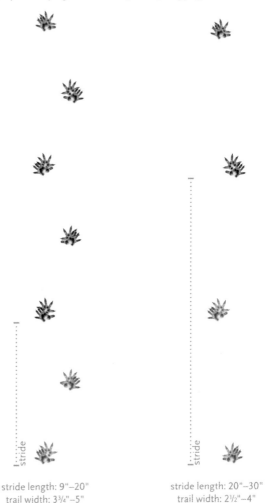

stride length: 9"–20"
trail width: 3¾"–5"

stride length: 20"–30"
trail width: 2½"–4"

walk   **trot**

FRONT FOOT • HIND FOOT
STRIDE: hind track to next hind track on same side

GAITS: Northern Raccoon (pg. 207)

These Northern Raccoon gaits are in proportion to each other.

Travels in a distinctive overstep walk, nearly unique to this species. Sometimes bounds. Flees in a gallop. May direct register walk in deep snow.

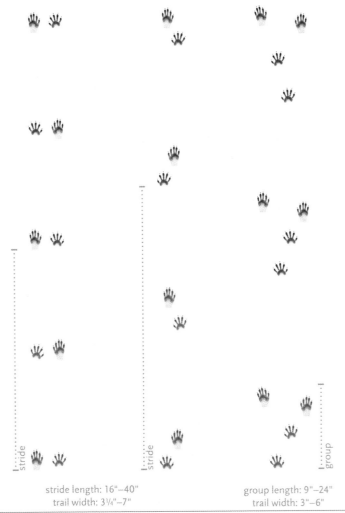

stride length: 16"–40"
trail width: 3¼"–7"

group length: 9"–24"
trail width: 3"–6"

walk   **extended walk**   **bound**

FRONT FOOT • HIND FOOT

STRIDE: hind track to next hind track on same side
GROUP: back edge of rearmost track to the front edge of the foremost track

Typically walks, using a direct register or an overstep walk, with feet slightly toed-in. Sometimes trots or lopes. May flee in a gallop. Usually direct register walks in deep snow.

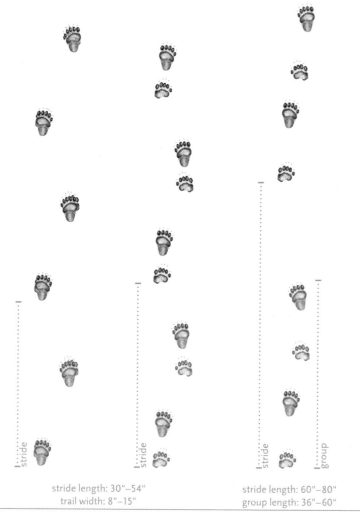

stride length: 30"–54"
trail width: 8"–15"

stride length: 60"–80"
group length: 36"–60"

walk   **overstep walk**   **lope**

FRONT FOOT • HIND FOOT

STRIDE: hind track to next hind track on same side
GROUP: back edge of rearmost track to the front edge of the foremost track

Commonly moves about in a lope or a trot, sometimes slowing to a walk. As with most other canines, uses both direct register and side trots regularly.

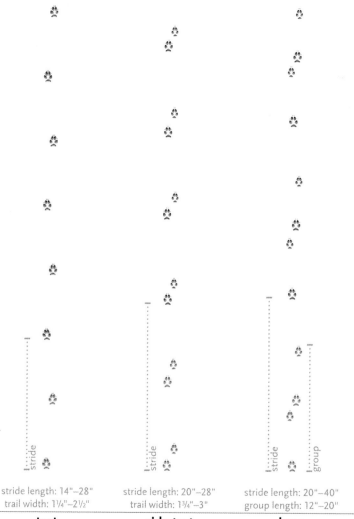

stride length: 14"–28"
trail width: 1¼"–2½"

trot

stride length: 20"–28"
trail width: 1¾"–3"

side trot

stride length: 20"–40"
group length: 12"–20"

lope

FRONT FOOT • HIND FOOT

STRIDE: hind track to next hind track on same side
GROUP: back edge of rearmost track to the front edge of the foremost track

Usually travels in a direct register trot. Commonly speeds up into a straddle trot, rather than the side trot typical of other canines. Sometimes walks. Lopes or gallops when chasing or fleeing. Avoids deep snow when possible.

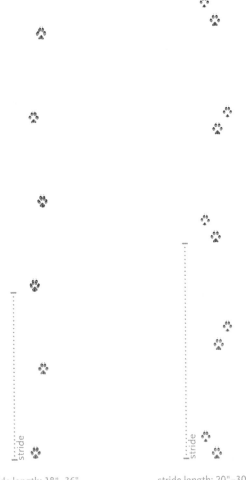

stride length: 18"–36"
trail width: 1½"–4"

trot

stride length: 20"–30"
trail width: 3½"–4½"

straddle trot

FRONT FOOT • HIND FOOT
STRIDE: hind track to next hind track on same side

324

Typically trots in a direct register or side trot. Direct register trots may leave an extremely narrow trail with all tracks in a single, nearly straight line. Lopes or gallops when chasing or fleeing. Often walks in deep snow, but may bound, leaving a series of whole-body imprints.

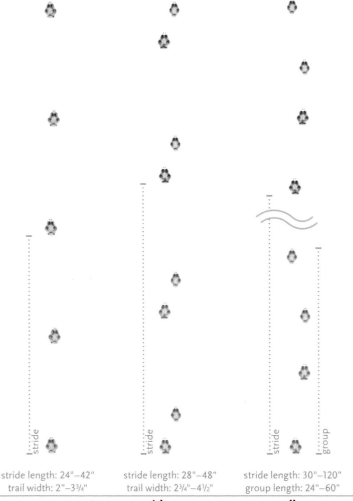

stride length: 24"–42"
trail width: 2"–3¾"

trot

stride length: 28"–48"
trail width: 2¾"–4½"

side trot

stride length: 30"–120"
group length: 24"–60"

gallop

FRONT FOOT • HIND FOOT

STRIDE: hind track to next hind track on same side
GROUP: back edge of rearmost track to the front edge of the foremost track

Typically trots (including side trot) when traveling, but walks frequently. Usually only lopes or gallops to pursue prey or flee. Exhibits an unusual variety of walks and trots, leaving more variants than other canids.

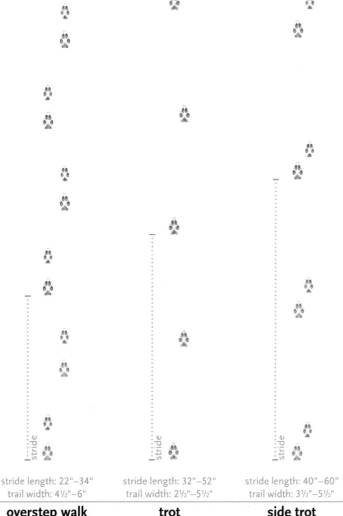

stride length: 22"–34"
trail width: 4½"–6"

overstep walk

stride length: 32"–52"
trail width: 2½"–5½"

trot

stride length: 40"–60"
trail width: 3½"–5½"

side trot

FRONT FOOT • HIND FOOT

STRIDE: hind track to next hind track on same side
GROUP: back edge of rearmost track to the front edge of the foremost track

Typically trots, but may lope or gallop without apparent need. Displays a wide variety of trots. Side trots are often irregular, with the hind foot sometimes landing directly in front of the front foot. Usually walks in deep snow, but may trot or bound at times.

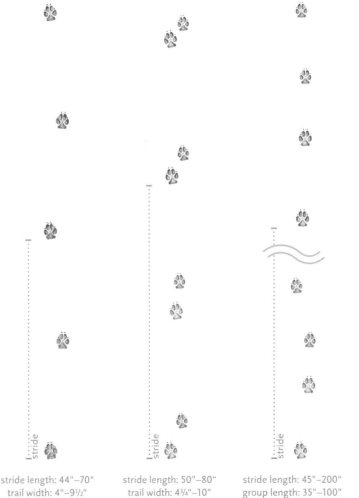

stride length: 44"–70"
trail width: 4"–9½"

stride length: 50"–80"
trail width: 4¾"–10"

stride length: 45"–200"
group length: 35"–100"

trot　　　　**side trot**　　　　**gallop**

FRONT FOOT • HIND FOOT
STRIDE: hind track to next hind track on same side
GROUP: back edge of rearmost track to the front edge of the foremost track

Usually walks, but may trot when feeling exposed or excited. Gallops when chasing prey or fleeing. Stalks prey in a slow, understep walk.

stride length: 10"–25"
trail width: 2"–4½"

walk

stride length: 20"–32"
trail width: 1¼"–3¼"

trot

FRONT FOOT • HIND FOOT
STRIDE: hind track to next hind track on same side
GROUP: back edge of rea most track to the front edge of the foremost track

Usually walks, often in an overstep. May trot when feeling exposed or excited. Gallops when chasing prey or playing. Stalks in a slow, understep walk. Direct register walks in deep snow, partially dragging its feet.

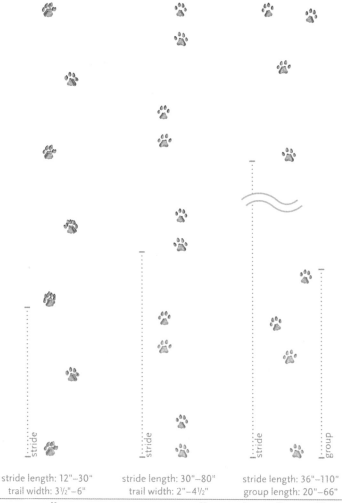

stride length: 12"–30"
trail width: 3½"–6"

walk

stride length: 30"–80"
trail width: 2"–4½"

overstep walk

stride length: 36"–110"
group length: 20"–66"

bounding gallop

FRONT FOOT • HIND FOOT

STRIDE: hind track to next hind track on same side
GROUP: back edge of rearmost track to the front edge of the foremost track

Walks in a direct register or overstep when hunting or moving in cover. Usually direct register walks in deep snow. May trot across exposed areas. Gallops when chasing prey or fleeing.

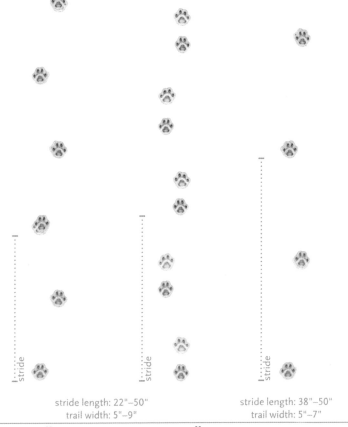

stride length: 22"–50"
trail width: 5"–9"

stride length: 38"–50"
trail width: 5"–7"

walk   **overstep walk**   **trot**

FRONT FOOT • HIND FOOT
STRIDE: hind track to next hind track on same side

Usually walks in a direct register or overstep, often leaving winding trails that snake across the landscape. May speed up to a trot when feeling exposed or excited. Gallops when chasing prey or fleeing.

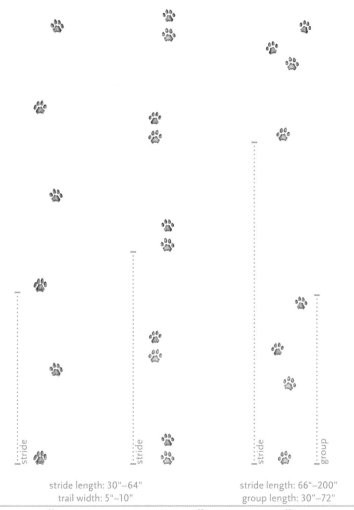

stride length: 30"–64"
trail width: 5"–10"

stride length: 66"–200"
group length: 30"–72"

walk   **overstep walk**   **gallop**

FRONT FOOT • HIND FOOT
STRIDE: hind track to next hind track on same side
GROUP: back edge of rearmost track to the front edge of the foremost track

Walks most of the time in either a direct register or an overstep. The overstep walk is unique among ungulates and diagnostic for the species. Be careful to correctly identify the front and hind feet, as understep walks are common in deer trails. Lopes or gallops when alarmed or threatened.

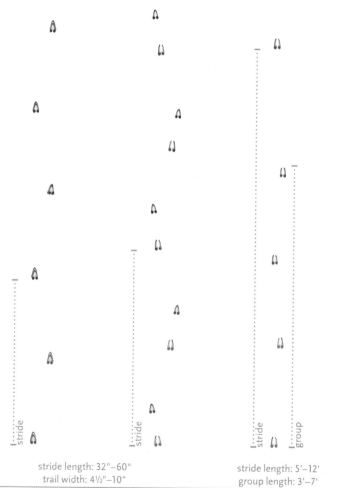

stride length: 32"–60"
trail width: 4½"–10"

stride length: 5'–12'
group length: 3'–7'

walk   **overstep walk**   **gallop**

FRONT FOOT • HIND FOOT

STRIDE: hind track to next hind track on same side
GROUP: back edge of rearmost track to the front edge of the foremost track

Walks most of the time. Occasionally trots, usually when mildly alarmed or agitated. Flees in a gallop. Walks in deep snow, dragging its feet as it steps, creating two parallel troughs.

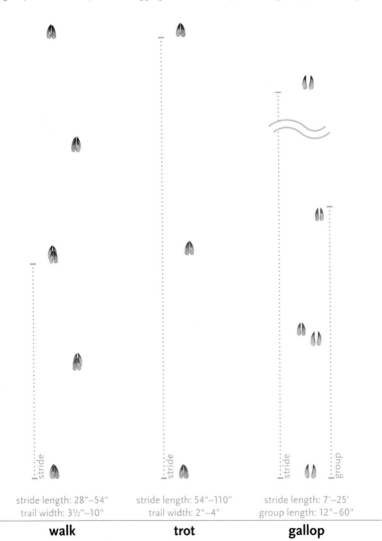

stride length: 28"–54"
trail width: 3½"–10"

stride length: 54"–110"
trail width: 2"–4"

stride length: 7'–25'
group length: 12"–60"

walk   **trot**   **gallop**

FRONT FOOT • HIND FOOT
STRIDE: hind track to next hind track on same side
GROUP: back edge of rearmost track to the front edge of the foremost track

Walks most of the time. Lopes, gallops or pronks when alarmed or threatened. Pronking is an unusual gait in which the deer leaps and lands with all four feet simultaneously. Trots when mildly agitated. Walks in deep snow, usually dragging its feet as it steps.

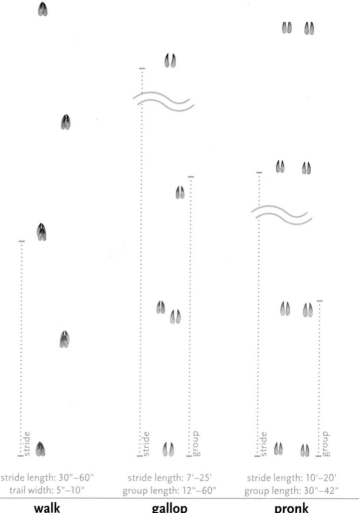

walk	gallop	pronk
stride length: 30"–60"	stride length: 7'–25'	stride length: 10'–20'
trail width: 5"–10"	group length: 12"–60"	group length: 30"–42"

FRONT FOOT • HIND FOOT

STRIDE: hind track to next hind track on same side
GROUP: back edge of rearmost track to the front edge of the foremost track

Walks most of the time. Lopes or gallops when alarmed or threatened. Trots when mildly alarmed or agitated, often using an overstep "straddle trot" with outer feet spread wider than inner feet. This straddle trot is unusual among ungulates and diagnostic for the species. Direct register walks in deep snow, leaving two parallel troughs.

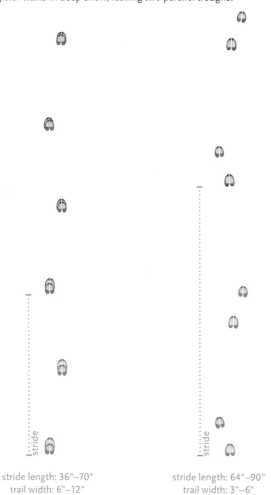

stride length: 36"–70"
trail width: 6"–12"

stride length: 64"–90"
trail width: 3"–6"

walk　　　　　　**straddle trot**

FRONT FOOT • HIND FOOT
STRIDE: hind track to next hind track on same side

335

Walks most of the time. Lopes or gallops when alarmed or threatened. Occasionally trots, usually when mildly alarmed or agitated. Direct register walks in deep snow, dragging its feet much less than smaller members of the deer family.

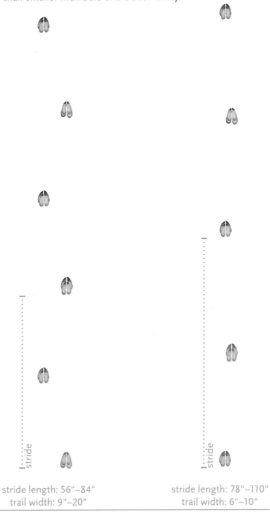

stride length: 56"–84"
trail width: 9"–20"

stride length: 78"–110"
trail width: 6"–10"

walk   **trot**

FRONT FOOT • HIND FOOT
STRIDE: hind track to next hind track on same side

Usually walks, often in an understep. May trot or lope for short distances when alarmed or when playing. Stampedes in a full gallop. Walks in deep snow, dragging its feet, sometimes plowing snow aside with its body or head.

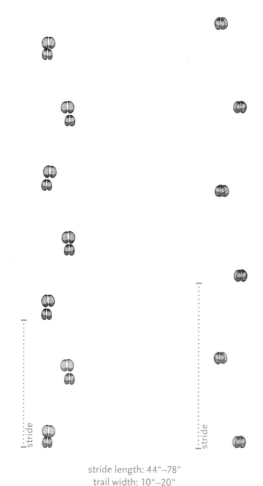

stride length: 44"–78"
trail width: 10"–20"

understep walk   **walk**

FRONT FOOT • HIND FOOT
STRIDE: hind track to next hind track on same side

337

Glossary

2x2 Lope: A loping gait common in members of the weasel family in which both hind feet land exactly in the tracks of the front feet leaving two side-by-side compressions. Many animals use a variation of this gait in deep snow.

3x4 Lope: A loping gait common in members of the weasel family in which one hind foot sometimes lands in the track made by one of the front feet producing what looks like a group of three, rather than four prints.

Arboreal: Tree-dwelling

Bound: A whole-body gait in which the hind feet move together as a pair and land in front of the front feet. In this gait, there are two moments in each cycle when the animal has all four feet off the ground.

Burrow: An excavation in the earth used by an animal for shelter or storage.

Cache: A store of food, built up by an individual animal for future consumption. Also, the act of storing food for later use.

Claws: The nails on an animal's foot used for such activities as digging, climbing and catching prey. In many animals, claws can show in tracks as round holes or narrow triangles in front of the toes.

Clear Print: A single footprint that shows the major features of the foot, including all of the toe, palm and heel pads that typically register.

Crepuscular: Active primarily during twilight, usually both dawn and dusk.

Direct Register: A gait in which the hind foot lands directly on top of the front track. When an animal direct registers, only the hind track is clearly visible.

Diurnal: Active primarily during the daytime.

Fossorial: Living underground.

Gait: The particular way in which an animal uses its body to move, including how it coordinates its limbs and the order of its foot placement. Examples of gaits include walking, trotting, loping and bounding. Each gait leaves a distinctive pattern of tracks.

Gallop: A whole-body gait in which the hind feet move independently of each other and land in front of the front feet. In this gait, there are two moments in each cycle when the animal has all four feet off the ground.

Habitat: The type of environment where an animal is typically found.

Heel: The rearmost portion of the foot. In some animals, the heel is held off the ground and rarely, if ever, registers in the track.

Hibernate: A dormant state that some mammals enter into in the winter. It is characterized by a sharp reduction in metabolic activity to conserve energy.

Hoof: The horny sheath covering the tips of the toes of deer, cattle, horses, swine and their relatives.

Hop: A whole-body gait in which the hind feet move together as a pair and land behind or even with the front feet. In this gait, there is only one moment in each cycle when the animal has all four feet off the ground.

Indirect Register: A gait in which the hind foot lands partially on top of the front track, leaving the front track partially visible.

Lope: A whole-body gait in which the hind feet move independently of each other and land behind or even with the front feet. In this gait, there is only one moment in each cycle when the animal has all four feet off the ground.

Masting: A forest tree dropping nuts to the ground.

Midden: A pile of material discarded by a feeding animal, especially the inedible portions of nuts, seeds and pine cones.

Nest: A structure made from leaves, grasses and similar soft materials used by an animal for shelter, especially for giving birth and nursing young.

Nocturnal: Active primarily at night.

Overstep: A stepping gait (walk or trot) in which the hind foot lands in front of (oversteps) the front foot on the same side of the body.

Pad: A patch of thick, calloused skin found on the bottom of an animal's foot that creates a distinct impression in a track.

Palm: The area of the foot located at the base of the toes.

Raccoon Walk: A distinctive gait used by raccoons in which the hind foot lands close to the front foot on the opposite side of the body, creating side-by-side pairs of front and hind tracks.

Range: The territory an animal covers in the course of its normal activities. Also, the geographic area where a particular species is known to live.

Run: A bipedal (two-legged) gait in which the animal has both feet off the ground mid-stride. While it is most similar to a quadrupedal (four-legged) trot, the word "run" is too ambiguous to be useful for describing quadrupedal gaits.

Scat: Poop. An animal's excrement, which can both aid in identification of the animal and also give clues about the animal's diet and behavior.

Sign: Any indication left behind by an animal that gives a clue about its past activity. Sometimes the word is used to mean every indication left behind that isn't a track. Such indications include scat, scent posts, nests, burrows, digs, scratch marks and feeding remains.

Step: The distance from one hind track to the next hind track on the opposite side of the body for an animal moving in a walk or a trot. Roughly equal to one-half of the animal's stride.

Stepping Gait: Any gait in which an animal keeps its body relatively still and moves its legs in an even rhythm. The resulting pattern is a continuous line of tracks with each front-hind pair spaced evenly apart.

Stride: The distance from any one track to the next track made by the same foot.

Substrate: The material or substance on which tracks are made. Substrates include soil, sand, mud and snow. Different substrates record tracks somewhat differently, and understanding how different substrates behave can help in interpreting tracks and trails, as well as predicting where to find clear tracks to study.

Subunguis: The soft material on the underside of an animal's nail. In ungulates (deer, cattle, horses, swine and their relatives), this forms part of the walking surface of the foot, in between the hard hoof and the soft pad.

Toes: The digits on the foot of an animal, and the impressions left by those digits in the animal's tracks.

Torpid/Torpor: Any extended period of dormancy or inactivity, including hibernation.

Track: A footprint left by an animal

Track Group: A set of four tracks that identifies an animal's gait pattern. Usually applied only to whole-body gaits, a group is the set of four tracks made by one complete cycle of the animal's body movement. Although a group always refers to a set of four tracks, some tracks may land on top of others creating the appearance of only 2 or 3 distinct footprints.

Trail: The path an animal followed when it left a set of tracks. Also a well-worn path used repeatedly by an animal or group of animals.

Trail Width: The total width of an animal's track pattern or gait. The distance from the outermost edge of an animal's left tracks to the outermost edge of the animal's right tracks, measured perpendicular to the animal's line of travel.

Trot: A stepping gait in which diagonally opposite legs move together and there is a moment when the animal has all four feet off the ground.

Understep: A stepping gait (walk or trot) in which the hind foot lands behind the front foot on the same side of the body.

Walk: A stepping gait in which each leg moves independently and the animal has at least one feet on the ground at all times.

Whole-body gait: Any gait produced by an animal flexing and extending its body, using the body and legs together for locomotion. These gaits have a cycling, rather than continuous rhythm and produce a similar-looking group of four tracks each cycle.

Index

Recommended Resources

Books

Tracking

Elbroch, M. (2003). *Mammal Tracks & Sign: A Guide to North American Species*. Stackpole Books.

Elbroch, M., Liebenberg, L., & Louw, A. (2010). *Practical Tracking: A Guide to Following Footprints and Finding Animals*. Stackpole Books.

Murie, O. J. & Elbroch, M. (2005). *Peterson Field Guide to Animal Tracks, Third Edition*. Houghton Mifflin Harcourt.

Rezendes, P. (1999). *Tracking & the Art of Seeing: How to Read Animal Tracks and Sign*. Collins Reference.

Yong, J. & Morgan, T. (2007). *Animal Tracking Basics*. Stackpole Books.

Tracker's Stories

Brown, T. J. (1978). *The Tracker*. Berkley Books.

Corbett, J. (1953). *Jungle Lore*. Oxford University Press.

Powell, M. N. (2001). *Ingwe*. Owl Link Media.

Nature Photography

Miotke, J. (2006). *The BetterPhoto Guide to Digital Nature Photography*. Amphoto Books.

Shaw, J. (2001). *John Shaw's Nature Photography Field Guide*. Amphoto Books.

Sullivan, T. J. & Platner, M. W. (2001). *The Keeping Track Guide to Photographing Animal Tracks and Sign*. Keeping Track, Inc.

Tracking Gear & Supplies

Wilderness Awareness School
26425 Northeast Allen Street
Duvall, WA 98019
(425) 788-1301
www.wildernessawareness.org

This wonderful organization offers classes, books, resources and correspondence courses in tracking and nature awareness. They offer free newsletters with inspiring stories and a monthly "Natural Mystery" contest.

Lightning Powder
13386 International Parkway
Jacksonville, FL 32218
800-852-0300
www.armorforensics.com

Manufacturers and distributors of equipment for crime scene investigation, including forensic rulers and snowprint wax—a product used for making casts of tracks in the snow.

Keeping Track®, Inc.
PO Box 444, Huntington, VT 05462
Phone: (802) 434-7000
Fax: (802) 434-5383
www.keepingtrack.org

Products include tracking rulers, reference cards, and The Keeping Track Guide to Photographing Animal Tracks and Sign.

Useful Websites

International Society of Professional Trackers
www.ispt.org

Wildlife Tracking in North America
www.wildlifetrackers.com

Beartracker's Animal Tracks Den
www.bear-tracker.com

Nature Tracking
www.naturetracking.com

CyberTracker International
www.cybertracker.org

Volunteer Opportunities

Wisconsin Volunteer Carnivore Tracking Program
Volunteers conduct winter snow track surveys to monitor wolves and other carnivores in northern and central Wisconsin. For information on volunteer training opportunities, visit the project website.

http://dnr.wi.gov/org/land/er/mammals/volunteer/

Minnesota Wildlife Tracking Project
A pilot program based on the Wisconsin model and focused on the perimeter of wolf range. To learn more or get involved, contact Jonathan Poppele or visit the project website.
www.mntracking.org

Additional References

Brown, T. (1986). *Tom Brown's Field Guide to Nature Observation and Tracking*. Berkley Trade.

Brown, T. (1999). *Tom Brown's Science and Art of Tracking*. Berkley Trade.

Charney, N., & Eiseman, C. (2010). *Tracks and Sign of Insects and Other Invertebrates: A Guide to North American Species*. Stackpole Books.

Elbroch, M., Marks, E., & Boretos, C. D. (2001). *Bird Tracks & Sign: A Guide to North American Species*. Stackpole Books.

Halfpenny, J. C. (1988). *A Field Guide to Mammal Tracking in North America*. Johnson Books.

Halfpenny, J. (2006). *Scats and Tracks of the Midwest: A Field Guide to the Signs of Seventy Wildlife Species*. FalconGuides.

Levine, L. (2008). *Mammal Tracks and Scat: Life-Size Tracking Guide*. Heartwood Press.

Lowery, J. C. (2006). *The Tracker's Field Guide: A Comprehensive Handbook for Animal Tracking in the United States* (1st ed.). Falcon.

Miller, D. S. (1981). *Track Finder: A Guide to Mammal Tracks of Eastern North America*. Nature Study Guild Publishers.

Reid, F. (2006). *A Field Guide to Mammals of North America North of Mexico* (4th ed.). Boston: Houghton Mifflin Co.

Sheldon, I., & Eder, T. (2000). *Animal Tracks of Minnesota & Wisconsin*. Lone Pine Publishing.

Tekiela, S. (2005). *Mammals of Minnesota Field Guide*. Adventure Publications.

Whitaker, J., & National Audubon Society. (1996). *National Audubon Society Field Guide to North American Mammals* (2nd ed.). New York: Knopf; Distributed by Random House.

About the Author

Jonathan Poppele is a naturalist, author and educator with wide-ranging interests. He earned a master's degree in Conservation Biology from the University of Minnesota studying citizen science, environmental education and how to cultivate a personal relationship with the natural world through animal tracking. He has taught ecology, environmental studies, biology and technical writing at the University of Minnesota. An avid outdoorsman and student of natural history, Jon is a member of the Minnesota Trackers Club and the International Society for Professional Trackers and is the founder of the Minnesota Wildlife Tracking Project. A Black Belt in the peaceful martial art of Ki-Aikido, Jon is also the founder and Director of the Center for Mind-Body Oneness in Saint Paul, MN. You can reach Jon through his website at www.jonathanpoppele.com, follow him on Twitter @jonathanpoppele or join him on Facebook.